MW00895593

CITIES UNDER AUSTERITY

Contents

Illustrations

Figures

Tables

Acknowledgments

Editing an academic book can at times be a thankless task. Careers are littered with those who have done it once and vowed never to do it again. That the tasks were shared between the two of us made it easier. That the two of us get on outside as much as inside of work made it more than easier. It made it enjoyable, the shared labor necessary to edit a book a means of catching up with what each other was up to both professional and personally.

The impetus for this book came out of a series of conversations between the two of us, the first outcome of which was our contribution to a 2014 special issue of the *Cambridge Journal of Regions, Economy and Society* on "Austerity and the city." In writing that article we became aware of how U.S. cities were restructuring themselves, although not under conditions of their own making. Austerity was reshaping all aspects of economic and social life and it was likely that the implications for urban futures were going to reveal themselves incrementally and unevenly over the next few decades. Given what we understood was at stake—intellectually and politically—we were surprised that there had been relatively few attempts to pull together and compare the experiences of U.S. cities. It is on that which this book is focused. How are cities seeking to chart a way through the financial challenges posed of them both by the Great Recession and the public sector cuts imposed under austerity? That is, different cities, with different industrial histories, political alliances, population characteristics and redevelopment trajectories but facing a common twofold challenge.

Mark would like to thank the friends and colleagues who have shared their thoughts on our emerging urban political landscape. During the tumult of the Great Recession, many aspects of urban governance became difficult to understand. In a quest to grapple with this troubling and exhilarating situation, many a conversation with Bill Kutz about the fate of bankrupt cities impacted Mark's thinking about where U.S. cities are now heading. Kurt Iveson has also been a constant source of inspiration, particularly when austerity made it into our joint reconsideration of critical urban scholarship. Rowland Atkinson, Lee Crookes, Chris Gibson, David Lukens, Deb Martin, Jim Murphy, and Elvin Wyly are also fellow travelers on the quest to understand these brutal times. Throughout the process of putting the collection together, Mark benefited immensely from the friendship and mentoring of Kevin Ward. Kevin's legacy to urban geography grows by the month, and Mark is grateful to be a small part of it. Most of all, Mark would like to thank Michelle, Sadie, and Sam for putting up with his absences, late nights, and weekend trips to the office. His eagerness to return to their company hastened the completion of this text and many other tasks.

Kevin would like to thank the various audiences for his work over the last few years, subject as they were to his many and varied attempts to make urban governance and finance sound interesting! A number of colleagues/friends have played their part in helping him understand the changing ways in which city governments are present in financial markets, and he would like to acknowledge this intellectual debt: Josh Akers, Allan Cochrane, Mark Davidson, Jason Hackworth, Andy Jonas, Sarah Knuth, Bill Kutz, Jamie Peck, Andy Pike, Nik Theodore, Rachel Weber, and Andy Wood.

Kevin gives special thanks for the love and support received from Colette and Jack, for whom the content of this book is a long way from what he should be doing if he were a "real geographer."

More formally, the editors would like to thank Michael Rinella at SUNY Press, and the anonymous reviewers whose constructive and supportive comments made this a better book.

Preface

Situating Austerity Urbanism

JAMIE PECK

"Most crisis analysis comes directly after crisis," Mark Gottdiener (1986b, p. 277) wrote more than three decades ago; "It catches a wave." Something broadly similar might be said about the working concept of austerity urbanism, which was developed in the aftermath of the Wall Street crash of 2008, tracking the global financial crisis and the onset of what proved to be a deep recession across the United States and across much of Europe, to be followed by a prolonged period of sluggish economic growth and restrictive government budgeting. This midlevel conceptual frame sought to capture, at least provisionally, some of the immediately evident urban dimensions of the crisis, which from its earliest stages seemed to be presenting as a conjuncturally significant and perhaps structural realignment, rather than a merely transitory or cyclical phenomenon. It should be recalled that the crash was initially read, quite widely in fact, not just as an indictment of the preceding period of financialized growth and neoliberal governance, but possibly as the death knell for this deeply embedded mode of market rule (see Hobsbawm, 2008; Rudd, 2009; Stiglitz, 2008; cf. Peck et al., 2010). However, even though the crisis evidently dealt a severe blow to the intellectual and political legitimacy of neoliberalism, this would prove to be a(nother) test case of the resilience and adaptability of this deeply entrenched mode of market-oriented and corporate-centric regulation. As the breakdown of the banking system was brazenly rescripted as another crisis of *and for* the social state, under the sign of austerity, so it would soon become clear that this did not mean a historic retreat of neoliberal hegemony but its *reconstitution*. After a brief period of open-ended legitimacy crisis and establishment-class disorientation, commitments to the antisocial credo of market fundamentalism were soon to be renewed and reinvigorated—in some cases in an even more doctrinaire fashion. "Austerity" became the watchword for another roiling phase of neoliberalization, based on the socially regressive redistribution of the long- and short-term costs of the crisis.

Notwithstanding the fact that the macroeconomic logic of austerity policies was questioned from the start (see Blyth, 2013; Crotty, 2012; Kitson et al., 2011), on grounds that would prove to be prescient, as a *political* strategy austerity apparently served the purpose of an unapologetic and often brutal restoration of elite and establishment interests. Here, the proven neoliberal tactics of deflection and displacement were once again mobilized to considerable effect. The blame for the crisis was discursively deflected away from the banks and financial (de)regulators and onto profligate (or corrupt) local politicians, onto public-sector workforces, retirees, and unions, and onto the vestiges of the social state and its "dependents." This audacious maneuver, which Mark Blyth (2013, p. 13) would describe as "the greatest bait and switch in human history," in turn enabled yet more audacious acts of displacement, as the costs of the crisis were dumped "downward" in both social and spatial terms. (The benefits of economic growth had for decades failed to trickle down, in the promised fashion, but now the pain caused by a neoliberal crisis definitely would.) As a result, it was no coincidence that cities, and especially *poor* cities, were to find themselves in the crosshairs, the implementation of austerity measures spurring new rounds of local-state downsizing, budget cuts, service retrenchment, and privatization (Peck, 2012). This was the (new) face of austerity urbanism.

But in what sense was austerity urbanism actually new, and *where* was it new? These questions of historicization and spatiality were in play right from the start. Austerity was hardly an entirely new condition for those cities that, for years or even decades, had been living under circumstances of normalized fiscal stress—invariably as a result of deindustrialization, suburbanization, white flight, and long-run economic decline, with its accompanying social and environmental fallout. In a more macro sense, various modalities of austere government have been around for centuries (see Blyth, 2013), while selective fiscal purging, systemic tax and expenditure restraint, and orientations toward lean administration have long been hallmarks of post-Keynesian neoliberalism, across its many phases, sites, scales, and stages. *Plus ça change, plus c'est la même chose,* perhaps? In a perverse but in some ways predictable echo of the elite-level groupthink that preceded the global financial crisis (which none of the leading agencies of macroeconomic governance had seen coming), post-crisis regulatory norms were rapidly recalibrated around the hoary axioms of austerity, even as the methods and discourses of crisis management continued to vary somewhat from country to country, as well as (apparently) between a European and an American pathway.

In this context, the concept of austerity urbanism—which had been formulated in order to understand the selective downdrafts of these policies, their sites of localized intensification, and the new forms of networking, contagion, and rescaling that were occurring in their wake—was in its original formulation a transatlantic one (see Peck, 2017a). It was transatlantic in the sense that Europe and the United States were early epicenters of the financial crisis as well as the principal incubators of the new generation of austerity measures, from Brussels to Washington, D.C., from Greece to Detroit, and lots of places in between. And it was transatlantic in a more methodological sense too, as it presented a remit, not for reductionism or "reading off" from macro trends, but to *theorize across* (geographical and political) difference, sifting recurrent features and repeating patterns from what would surely remain marked contextual differences and ingrained particularities, not least those deriving from the distinctive regulatory frameworks, budgetary cultures, and institutional structures.

Without suppressing important differences within and between these continental-scale sites of accelerated restructuring, as a midlevel conceptual formulation, austerity urbanism established a (provisional, partial, and always revisable) framework for exploring the metropolitan-level dynamics of austerity governance, recognizing that these dynamics were at the same time multiscalar *and* unevenly developed. In other words, while there was something distinctively *urban* about the political economy of austerity (including: the strategic use of devolved budgetary repression and disciplinary fiscal governance; tensions between localized responsibilities for revenue raising and service delivery, and the structural and cyclical diminution of intergovernmental transfer payments; the pronounced geographies of the recession across housing and labor markets; the spatial concentration of infrastructure deficits and social need; and not least, the strategic and symbolic role of cities as staging grounds for protests and social-movement mobilizing against austerity), none of this meant that the experience of cities would be anything like uniform—quite the contrary, in fact. Even though its effects were clearly far-reaching, austerity urbanism did not describe a totalizing or blanket condition; it was not an exhaustive social and institutional reality; and neither, for that matter, did it represent some permanent new stage or finishing state. Rather, it served as an analytical frame for conceptualizing and problematizing a rapidly shifting and spatially variegated (but at the same time apparently patterned) matrix of fiscally triggered, driven, or mandated programs of urban restructuring, which in turn was associated with new waves of policy making and modeling, as well as with a multidimensional array of political mobilizations, maneuvers, struggles, and protests, the local and combinatorial outcomes of which were inherently unpredictable (see della Porta, 2015; Donald et al., 2014; Schönig & Schipper, 2016; Warner & Clifton, 2014). Across this moving terrain, the governing logic of austerity urbanism was generically characterized by a marked intensification of the neoliberal rationality of socially regressive and market-validated redistribution (the actually existing form of trickle down, one might say), by the dumping of costs and risks on marginalized communities, and by the manufacture and application of a new generation of scapegoating and blame-shifting discourses.

The original sketches of austerity urbanism were not generalizations from supposedly paradigmatic cases, but instead were drawn in relation to operative conditions across a number of cities, states, and countries. On this context, the notion of austerity urbanism emerged as an intermediate formulation, keyed into a particular set of conjunctural conditions, and in theoretical terms positioned between more abstract accounts of post-crisis neoliberalization, the real-time patterning of political and institutional dynamics, and a quite wide array of metropolitan cases. Austerity urbanism, *U.S.-style,* took the immediate form of a cascading budget shock (only partly and temporarily ameliorated by Obama administration stimulus funds), entrenching conditions of fiscal restraint and imperative forms of public-service retrenchment and organizational rationalization, which in various ways would outlast the eventual recovery of (most) budgets in the years after the Great Recession. If the "Ford to City: Drop Dead" moment of the 1970s, coupled with the transformative effects of Reagan's "new federalism," had installed the ruling principle of "the city being asked to stand alone" (Gottddiener, 1986b, p. 285), the moment of austerity urbanism served as an unequivocal affirmation of this ongoing order, testing its limits. The severity of the post-2008 downturn revealed the extent to which city budgets and revenue flows had become cumulatively exposed to the whip of economic cycles and localized market conditions, circumstances compounded by long-term rollback of intergovernmental transfers, by the dismantling of automatic stabilizers, and by the fiscal gating of suburbs.

The U.S. model of austerity urbanism has been duly characterized by various combinations of the following, proximate features. First, "disciplining down," in accordance with the neoliberalized version of fiscal federalism: enforcing and institutionalizing an existential order of urban self-sufficiency, requiring cities to live increasingly on and within their local means (relying particularly on property taxes and user fees), which when structurally decoupled from Keynesian transfers and redistributive circuits actively undermines regimes of progressive sociospatial redistribution, and even transfers justified on a short-term basis ("bailouts," in the new parlance). Second, this further entrenches regulatory norms of lean municipal government: a predisposition to privatized, outsourced, and small(er)-state strategies, based on the embedded principles of tax aversion, restrained pubic spending, workforce trimming and deunionization, (barely) alleviated by episodic, project-based, and competitively selective models of federal- or state-financed programming. Third, a more deeply financialized operating environment is indicated by the tightening grip of bondholder value rationalities: increased dependency on municipal bond market in general and on the gatekeeping, surveillance, and monitoring roles of credit-rating agencies in particular (with consequences for governing borrowing costs, risk assessments, and access to finance), is reciprocated at the urban scale by a new emphasis on creative accounting, risk management, and coproduced financial "innovation," by the monetization and marketization of assets, infrastructure, and revenue streams, and by "debt-machine" models of technocratic governance that cater to the empowered "constituency" of Wall Street creditors. Fourth, a Calvinistic turn in urban discourse: based on reworked narratives of local- and social-state culpability-cum-failure, markedly pious and unforgiving in tone, this moralizing form of discursive responsibilization seeks to justify localized financial reliance *and culpability,* dictating that cities can only expect to "reap what they sow"; often racially coded and frequently targeted on working-class and Democratically controlled cities, this is part and parcel of a renewed, frontal attack on public-sector ideologies, institutions, and workforces, bolstered by narratives of dependency and dysfunction in which urban deficits are not just financial but political, sociocultural, entrepreneurial, and institutional. And fifth, financially challenged cities increasingly find themselves operating in an authoritarian, technocratic, and Caesarist political environment: compounding the well-established post-1970s trend toward the imposition of tax and expenditure limitations (TELs) on cities, now practiced by the majority of states, there has been a significant "hardening" of state laws and procedures concerning the declaration of localized fiscal emergencies and municipal takeover arrangements, including the assumption of draconian powers of "democratic dissolution" at the local scale, the empowerment of unelected financial technocrats and restructuring specialists, and unilateral governance by way of fiscal surveillance, strict audit measures, and budgetary fiat.

More concretely, while the cities (and the local government sector more generally) defined the sites where austerity measures were really "biting" across the United States, never was this uniformly the case. Austerity pressures were widespread, but by definition almost, they were not standardized in their form or their local effects. From the outset, state politics evidently made a significant difference. In Wisconsin and elsewhere, "standard-setting" fights were being picked with the public-sector unions, over wages, staffing levels, working conditions, pension rights, and more. In California and elsewhere, there were concerted moves to use local fiscal crises as a means to drive through structural changes to revenue-sharing arrangements and the design of pension programs. In Michigan and elsewhere, there was a legislative drive (backed up by new operational procedures) to extend and augment the capacities of states to impose emergency management at the local government level and to enact similar "takeover" provisions. In Colorado and elsewhere, budgetary struggles were being played out in the context of state-imposed restrictions on the tax-raising powers of local governments, some of them modeled on TABOR (or taxpayers' bill of rights) amendments. At the intrastate level, financial stress—and the character of responses to those stressed conditions—also varied markedly from city to city, albeit with some of the most intense problems persistently occurring among the bigger cities, among those with histories of economic dislocation and racialized exclusion, and among the hot spots of the subprime mortgage crisis. There have, in order words, been persistent and consequential *geographies* of austerity, from the outset of the 2008 crisis.

Meanwhile, *across* these checkerboard patterns at the state and local scales, there has been a plethora of connections, relays, and relational realignments—many of them either distinctively new or at least substantially modified, in comparison with previous practice—which have effectively stitched together more-than-local cultures, ecosystems, and dynamics of austerity urbanism. There has been much talk (and some solid indications) of credit-market contagion and ripple effects, both between neighboring jurisdictions and "upward," to the credit ratings of states containing "distressed" cities and across the increasingly restive municipal bond market more generally. In the legal domain, there has been a series of precedent-setting court rulings and norm-shaping legislative reforms, the consequences of which are likely to be relatively enduring. And in the realm of policy, politics, and practice, there has been an intensification of cross-jurisdictional policy advocacy, prescriptive model building, and shared forms of narrative (re)construction (often, but not always, following partisan lines, and frequently animated by think tanks, lobby groups, and advocacy organizations); political and administrative demonstration projects have been staged (and closely watched, many yielding clear demonstration *effects*); and a range of novel more-than-local communities of technocratic and operational practice have been constructed.

In these and other respects, austerity urbanism signaled a restructuring of the moving landscapes of intergovernmental budgeting and metropolitan governance, involving simultaneous forms of uneven financial development, financialized networking, and fiscal rescaling. Rather than foreclosing the longer-run outcomes of these developments, it offered a way to hold together, and in explanatory tension, what have proved to be particular (local) experiences and patterned (extralocal) responses to the unfolding financial crisis, recognizing that this is an open-ended process of restructuring. Furthermore, in this latter respect, these developments were understood all along to be both meaningfully urban and more than urban, in that they explicitly called attention to multiscalar and relational connections, across differentiated experiences at the local level and between these and what proved to be an unprecedented wave of political and fiscal maneuvering at the state and federal level.

The churn and change initiated by the crisis itself was considerable. But at this point it is useful to recall an observation that Alain Lipietz (1987, p. 15) made some time ago, that "the history of capitalism," and more particularly, the history of capitalist *crises,* has been "full of experiments which led nowhere . . . abandoned prototypes and all sorts of monstrosities." There was likewise a note of caution in contemporaneous remark from Mark Gottdiener concerning the perils of crisis theorizing—for all its necessity. Reflecting on two decades of urban crisis in the United States, from the riots of the 1960s through New York City's default of the mid-1970s to the retrenchments and devolved repurposing of local government during the Reagan years, Gottdiener concluded that these were institutional and regulatory inflection points more than they proved to be political turning points. They were inflection points on the path to a the kind of institutionalized normalcy that few would have anticipated at the time, but in retrospect resonates strongly with what today might be recognized as something quite similar to the restructuring present:

> The very nature of local politics has been altered. . . . [Municipal government] is currently constrained by accounting balance sheets, the nightmare of capital flight, and the specter of corporate bankers banging on the city's door for the past

payment of bills. [We] now possess a local urban government
far removed and insulated from its people. Technical managers administer cities running scared from default. Powerful
nonelective super-agencies raise tax exempt bond money to
pursue development without benefit of public participation.
Fiscal austerity itself beats back the plaints of the have-nots
and supplants other more negotiable goals of city administration. The reduction of the urban vision to instrumental capital
growth, it seems, gains hegemony everywhere. (Gottdiener,
1986b, p. 287)

The implications that were drawn at the time for political organizing
and progressive strategizing were rather sobering. Gottdiener (1986b, p.
287) concluded that it had been "a mistake for activists to have assumed
that organizing at the grass-roots level was sufficient for social change,"
the realm of urban politics having proved to be a "labyrinthine maze of
trenches and false tunnels that [had] dissipate[d] the collective energy of
grass-roots protest." His interpretation was that "local political activism
has been debilitated because the levels of politics at both the state and
nation have failed to produce the type of intermediary party structures
that could sustain grass-roots demands for change with overarching
extralocal auspices and a vision of social justice" (Gottdiener, 1986b, p.
287). These conditions of scalar disarticulation, on the progressive side
at least, have proved to be enduring.

History never repeats itself, of course, but if there is a lesson in these
historical experiences it may be that real-time conjunctural theorizing must
always be a reflexive process, subject to constant reevaluation and revision.
This certainly goes for working concepts, developed on the hoof, such as
austerity urbanism, which was very much about capturing the moment of
crisis itself. Hence, the timely remit of this collection, which is the first
systematically to explore, with the benefit of a degree of hindsight, some
of the longer-run effects of the moment of austerity urbanism—drawing
on a range of cases and examples, from coast to coast—while tracing
implications for financialized regimes of governance and for the political
economy of metropolitan restructuring more generally. As a prelude to
these investigations, this opening chapter concentrates on two contextual

themes that in a sense bracket the moment of austerity urbanism—one historical, the other concerning the emergent present—and looking back before looking forward. It next turns to the question of historical contextualization, positioning the most recent austerity moment in relation to its most conspicuous predecessor, the early-stage neoliberalism of the Reagan era. There follows a (necessarily somewhat speculative, at the time of writing) discussion of the future of urban governance in the age of Trump, which has prompted some to dust off, once again, obituaries to neoliberalism, but which seems more likely to entail yet another recalibration of the regime of market-centric rule, albeit in the context of a historically novel combination of federal and state-level authoritarianism, technocratic governance, and systemic financialization.

Austere Times/Remembering Reagan

"Austerity," even if it was to become one of the keywords for the global financial crisis, hardly had any currency at all in the United States at the start of what would become known as the Great Recession. True, a leading U.S. dictionary company, Merriam-Webster, had declared this to be its word of the year in 2010, albeit as a measure of the volume of user lookups, as public "attention was drawn to global economic conditions and the debt crises in Europe" (Merriam-Webster, 2010, p. 1). Indeed, in the United States, austerity was commonly seen as a "European word" (Gopnik, 2012; Wolff, 2013). Nevertheless, there was also a sense that austerity was capturing something about the zeitgeist, even if it was to remain a somewhat puzzling, offshore term. As Merriam-Webster's editor at large explained:

> *Austerity* clearly resonates with many people. . . . We often hear it used in the context of government measures, but we also apply it to our own personal finances and what is sometimes called the new normal. (Peter Sokolowski, quoted Merriam-Webster, 2010, p. 1)

Folk understandings of austerity, in fact, are almost always founded on an essentially metaphorical (and moralizing) commonsense analogy with personal or household finances: after running up debts and living beyond one's means, then a period of belt tightening must follow. This may have a certain everyday resonance, but it makes little or no sense in the aggregate, as a macroeconomic strategy, where the likely lock-in of deflationary effects threatens not only to impede economic recovery but to *worsen* problems of indebtedness (see Blyth, 2013; Krugman, 2012b). Economists at the International Monetary Fund (no less) would eventually come around to this view, but only after years of propounding austerity measures in accordance with the neoliberal orthodoxy that low taxes, deficit reduction, and public-sector restraint are surefire ways to build business confidence and economic growth (see Ostry et al., 2016). Instead, the macroeconomic evidence now strongly suggests that austerity policies have tended to impede economic growth while increasing unemployment, insecurity, and inequality—not to mention the regressively distributed social misery.

While the sums stubbornly refused to add up when it came to the economic rationale for austerity measures, the *political* calculation suggested otherwise. As Paul Krugman observed in the context of European austerity measures—which had been unilaterally imposed on Eurozone countries such as Greece by the so-called troika (comprising the European Commission, the European Central Bank, and the International Monetary Fund), but which was a policy of choice for the Conservative coalition government in the United Kingdom—"the drive for austerity was about *using the crisis, not solving it*" (Krugman, 2012b, p. A27; emphasis added). In this case, using the crisis meant using austerity, debt, and deficits as a pretext for the imposition, by imperative or "necessitarian" means, of a neoliberal agenda based on welfare cutbacks, public-expenditure reductions, privatization and public asset selloffs, corporate deregulation, and (even) tax cuts. Crucially, even though the a-word itself was less often heard in the United States, either on the streets or in the corridors of power, this neoliberal policy terrain was of course a profoundly familiar one. Here, there was an austerity policy installed *in all but name* (see Edsall, 2012; Peck, 2012; Polak & Schott, 2012). Somewhat bucking the trend, the incoming Obama administration had implemented a program of stimulus spending measures—widely seen as necessary to avert an even more far-reaching economic collapse, perhaps even a depression—but these were substantially diluted by congressional Republicans, such that the "stimulus" itself was reckoned by many analysts to have been no more than half-cooked, even as populist resentment *against* this spending program, stoked by negative coverage in the conservative media, played a part in fueling the Tea Party movement and the Republican resurgence at the local, state, and federal levels, beginning in 2010 (see Cassidy, 2014; *New York Times*, 2014; Skocpol and Williamson, 2012). Limited though it was overall, the stimulus program had provided a lifeline to state and local governments across the United States, many of which were struggling to cope with an unprecedented collapse in tax revenues. The American Recovery and Reinvestment Act of 2009 had directed $144 billion to the cause of "fiscal relief" at the state and local level, although perhaps more revealing was the fact that twice this sum was earmarked for tax cuts. Most of the provisions of the Act affecting state and local governments had expired by 2011, by which time the "new normal" had truly arrived.

While the United States had "never fully embraced the doctrine" of austerity in an explicit or officially sanctioned way, a "de facto austerity" policy had nevertheless been imposed across the country, albeit in a lagged and uneven fashion, "in the form of huge spending and employment cuts at the state and local level" (Krugman, 2012a, p. A27). For more than sixty years, local government employment in the United States had been "almost recession-proof," the one historical exception to the compensating pattern of Keynesian and quasi-Keynesian public sector job growth during recessions (which held for every cyclical downturn after 1955) being the Reagan cutbacks of the early 1980s; that is, until the Great Recession, post-2008, when the implementation of what Yale economists Ben Polak and Peter Schott (2012, pp. 1–2) dubbed a "hidden austerity program" involved a downward budgetary shock and large-scale job losses across the state and local government sector, an outcome that they described in the *New York Times* as a self-imposed state of "unprecedented austerity," which would only serve to slow the wider economic recovery.

Placing this recent period in its historical context, Figure P.1 reveals that the local government retrenchments of the early Reagan years were prelude to a pronounced *and sustained* localization of government employment, combining modest shrinkage at the federal scale with a moderate expansion across the state government sector and significant growth in

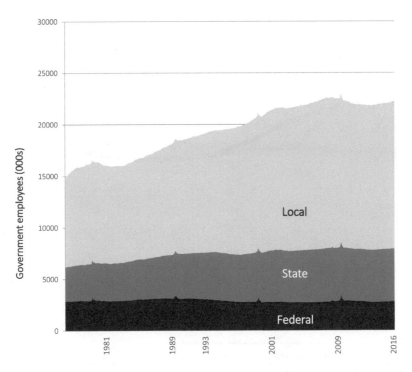

Figure P.1. The localization of U.S. government employment, 1977–2016. *Source*: author's calculation from Bureau of Labor Statistics Current Employment Statistics survey.

local government employment (see comparison to Obama presidency in Figure P.2 on page xxiv). Through a combination of political choice and (usually less than fully funded) state and federal government mandates, cities in particular have assumed a wide variety of new roles and responsibilities over the period since the mid-1980s, notably in social welfare, economic development, and more recently, in environmental policy. The revenue implications of these developments across the federal, state, and local government sectors have been complex, but as Figure P.3 on page xxiv reveals (with the reference to the most up-to-date standardized data) there has been a fairly consistent trend away from direct federal financing, apart from the uptick in stimulus funding between 2009 and 2011, coupled with a major expansion in the size of the municipal debt

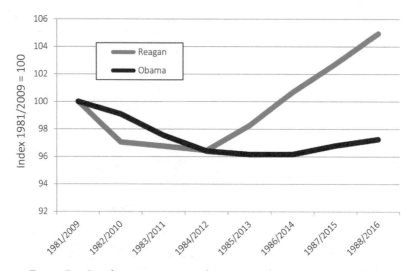

Figure P.2. Local government employment under Reagan and Obama.

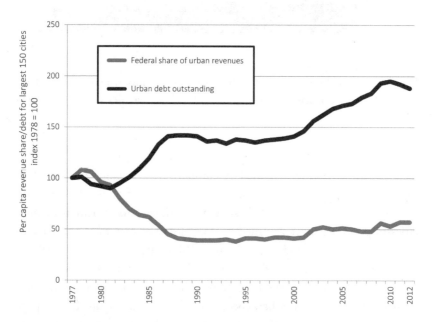

Figure P.3. Federal support versus debt load for U.S. cities, 1977–2012. *Source*: author's calculation from Fiscally Standardized Cities database of the 150 largest metro areas, Lincoln Institute of Land Policy; http://www.lincolninst.edu/subcenters/fiscally-standardized-cities/.

load. As recently as fiscal year 2013, total local government spending remained below the prerecession level of 2007, in part due to a generalized clawback in state aid, with the most severe cutbacks having occurred in the public education system (Reschovsky, 2016).

Overall, the model of decentralized neoliberal governance that has been installed since the 1980s has been associated with patterns of uneven growth and restructuring—and an "over-responsibilized" configuration in which local revenue increases have lagged the acquisition of new remits and mandates—across a labyrinthine network of 3,000 county governments, 19,500 municipalities, 16,500 townships, and more than 51,000 "special purpose" units of local government (see Kirkpatrick & Smith, 2011; Lobao, 2016; Perlman & Benton, 2014; Warner & Clifton, 2014). The post-2008 moment of austerity urbanism was the first significant correction to this long-run pattern of neoliberal localization, with more than half a million local government jobs being shed in the period after February 2009, before employment in the sector stabilized, beginning to recover since August 2014—a shakeout that was both longer and deeper than the precedent-setting cutbacks of the early Reagan years (Figure P.1). The Great Recession caused the largest collapse in state revenues on record, driving hard-wired reductions in governmental capacity and public services, much of the effects (and pain) of which was immediately passed on to the cities (see Oliff et al., 2012; Peck, 2012, 2014; Pollin & Thompson, 2011).

Across the long arc of three decades or more of state rescaling, punctuated by localized crises and a gradual accretion of normalized institutional patterns, new rules of the game have been established, along with an array of reciprocating, tactical responses at the urban level. New York City's default of 1975 established the "playbook" for the management of fiscal crises at the urban scale, being a recurring point of reference for those in the municipal finance business to this day, even as cities and states have since "continually test[ed] new solutions" (Scorsone, 2014: 3; see also Harvey, 2005; Tabb, 1982). By the late 1970s, in fact, critical urbanists in the United States had begun to talk in terms of a de facto austerity policy, as a generalized condition rather than as an isolated (or emergency) state (see Alcaly & Mermelstein, 1977; Clark & Ferguson, 1983; Clavel et al., 1980). In the wake of the

Carter administration's failure to deliver on a federal urban policy (see Harrison et al., 1979), austerity had become a late-Keynesian signifier for the *absence* of adequate investment in the cities, in a way that, in retrospect, seems almost benign. After years of fitful or negative economic growth and depressed corporate profits during the 1970s, an argument had been gaining ground that the (only) path to economic revitalization was to reduce business taxes, to hold down wages to "competitive" levels, and to remove burdensome regulations, which "when coupled with a widespread attack on government spending, [became] an *austerity policy,*" justifying the imposition of "regressive measures [on urban residents] so that the economy may once again be 'healthy'" (Kelman et al., 1980, pp. 2–3; original emphasis). Derided at the time as a "pagan ritual," propagated by a newly "dominant" (but unnamed) "economic school," this was diagnosed as an ideologically motivated assault, pretty much by stealth, on cities, municipal services, the urban poor, and the principles of urban planning:

> Such an austerity policy may be more covert than explicit, taking its toll more by the omission of effective and progressive policies than by the commission of particular acts. . . . The misleading focus on austerity, or more euphemistically, "creating necessary incentives for private investment," threatens to distract our attention from demands we need to face—as planners and citizens—in the years ahead. (Kelman et al., 1980, pp. 8, 3)

What had seemed to some like paganism in the 1970s would become, in effect, the established religion of the 1980s, the "new economists" of the incoming Reagan administration adopting a much harder line on all aspects of monetary and fiscal policy, particularly concerning cities. The Keynesian time during which "the growth of subnational expenditures" had been realized, in significant measure, by "federal largesse" had clearly now passed: with "the federal government . . . viewed as increasingly strapped," it was anticipated that "[m]ost cities in the 1980s [would] be characterized by a continued diminishment of revenues relative to the costs of providing public services" (Burchell & Listokin, 1981, pp.

xix, xlii–xliii). In their contribution to the collection, *Cities under Stress*, George Sternlieb and James Hughes (1981, p. 51) argued that central cities were showing signs of becoming "wards of the state and federal governments [although not] the result merely of fiscal maladministration, but rather of basic demographic tides." As sites of increasingly concentrated social and economic disadvantage, the inner cities had become a "wasting resource," Sternlieb and Hughes (1981, pp. 52, 75) continued, closing with the observation that, far from being "over," the urban crisis might be entering its most "fearful" stage, which the "thin façade" of downtown office development and gentrification by "swinging singles" would do little to alleviate.

America's central cities were sites of malign neglect during the Reagan years, a time when federal assistance to local government sector as a whole was gutted, falling by 60 percent, while programmatic rollbacks in welfare support, in housing subsidies and social services for low-income groups, and in community development funding were all associated with amplified effects in urban areas. Reagan's indifference to the cities, and to urban problems, was the stuff of legend. His secretary of Housing and Urban Development (HUD), Samuel Pierce, the only African American member appointed to a senior position in the administration, became the public face of a distinctly antiurban policy program, dismantling civil rights provisions and slashing low-income housing subsidies by 70 percent, while opening up new fronts for privatized cronyism. Sufficiently estranged from the mission of his agency that he was often found at his desk watching television, Pierce is credited with turning HUD into a "patronage mill for inexperienced Republican hacks" (Sugrue, 2016, p. 2). For his part, Reagan could hardly have been more disengaged, either. Introduced to his only black cabinet appointee at a White House reception early in his presidency, Reagan reportedly said: "How are you, Mr. Mayor? I'm glad to meet you. How are things in your city?" (quoted in Dreier, 2011, p. 2).

Ever since Edward Banfield's (1974, p. 335) forecast that "there is likely to be more rioting for many years to come," there had been a widespread sense that the conditions in U.S. cities might at any time become explosive, but even after the Reagan-era rollbacks this did not come to pass on anything like a generalized basis. Some with the benefit of a more historical perspective went as far as to counter that "the urban crisis that began in the mid-seventies [was] to a large extent an imaginary event" (Monkkonen, 1987, p. 21). At the very least, the urban crisis had been reclassified, and politically reframed. An increasingly dominant conservative narrative had it that the cities had fallen prey not to the long-run effects of economic decline and fiscal retrenchment but instead to the dysfunctions of liberal welfare-statism. From this perspective, the inner cities had become both the sites and the symbols of (racialized) social pathology, welfare dependency, and systemic corruption, as municipal leaders catered to social-service constituencies and public sector unions, rather than attending to the imperative of facilitating a positive business climate (see Glaeser, 2011; Magnet, 1993; cf. O'Connor, 2008). Radical urbanists rejected this diagnosis, even as it began to define a new kind of (neoliberal) orthodoxy, although they too would come to read the financial dislocations of the 1970s and 1980s in terms of a longer-run process of regulatory normalization:

> A decade [after the riots of the 1960s] cities were menaced by the specter of default. In this "fiscal crisis" funding sources for deficit spending dried up [and] municipalities were faced with instituting painful austerity measures and/or restructuring public finance, or bankruptcy. Although the threat of crisis only concerned a few cities, it ferreted out a more general condition of "fiscal strain" that characterized a larger group of urban regimes. . . . Cities have privatized many of their services, cut back on municipal employment, controlled the masses of poor and unemployed, and, in general, *managed fiscal strain rather than surrender to it.* . . . [Shifts in the wider] political environment . . . have enabled crisis restructuring and austerity to proceed with rather remarkable quiescence and social control rather than effective organized protest. (Gottdiener, 1986a, pp. 7, 10–11; emphasis added)

This financially restrained model of "overtasked" municipal governance did not so much buckle under the strain of generalized "fiscal stress," but instead initiated its cumulative internalization, as a new kind of normal.

It can be considered to be one of the more significant inflection points in the evolution of neoliberal urbanism, setting the stage for the "third way" realignments of the 1990s, with their accommodations to competitive rationalities and financialized models of growth, augmented by the advocacy of renewed ideologies of local leadership and the confrontation of "hard choices" in welfare and social policy reform—another new normal. While infrastructure deficits and localized problems remained, a new generation of growth machines had begun to drive a market-assisted and financialized, but still highly uneven, metropolitan revival (see Jonas & Wilson, 1997; Kirkpatrick & Smith, 2011). The first real challenge to this "soft neoliberal" consensus came with the Wall Street crash of 2008, and the turn toward devolved austerity governance (Peck et al., 2013, 2017). It seems likely that the election of Donald Trump will mark a further inflection point in the wayward course of neoliberal urbanism, propelled as his administration promises to be by surging currents of populism, revanchism, cronyism, and Caesarism, although perhaps with a new mandate to "rebuild" the inner cities. The years of actually existing austerity urbanism may prove to be an interregnum of sorts, the Obama years being a period of crisis management and restabilization, to be followed by a shift in the direction of yet another new normal.

Renewing Normal/Anticipating Trump

Donald Trump's election as president of the United States coincided with the announcement that the State of New Jersey would take over the municipal operations of the City of Atlantic City, the depressed resort that had comprehensively lost its wager on casino-based development, saddling the municipality with a $100 million budget deficit and a debt load of five times that amount. Since the late 1980s, Trump's name had been synonymous with what had once been Las Vegas East, the entrepreneur and the city sharing a checkered past of speculative development and corporate bankruptcy (Peck, 2017b). In the month prior to the presidential election, the Trump Taj Mahal, which for some years had been under new management but held on to the name, had closed its doors after a protracted labor dispute, the fifth of Atlantic City's twelve casinos to close since the Wall Street crash and the Great Recession. By this time, the municipality too was functionally bankrupt. The editorial board of the *New York Times* was not alone in seeing Atlantic City's crisis-assisted takeover at the hands of a state struggling with its own fiscal problems (with a credit rating to prove it) as a sign of things to come:

> The city [of Atlantic City] will be subject to a state financial control board with broad authority over the mayor and the City Council. The board has absolute power to shrink the city payroll from its heyday of casino tax support. It can restructure debt, dictate austerity restraints and sell off such city assets as its water utility. . . . [F]iscal overseers are taking over a vast amount of the city government's power, armed with extra authority to break city union contracts, [and to] hire and fire workers. . . . Aggrieved union workers who saw their health and pension benefits flatline as casinos folded are warning that the city's fate is an omen for the new administration of President-elect Donald Trump, whose four Atlantic City casinos failed. Think promises of grandeur followed by hard reality. (*New York Times*, 2016, p. A24)

The city of Atlantic City had been on the brink of bankruptcy for several years, its once-pioneering growth machine—focused entirely on the casino, hotel, and hospitality industry—having broken down even before the Wall Street crash, the subprime mortgage crisis, and the Great Recession. New Jersey's governor, Chris Christie, had earlier appointed an emergency manager to take control of the city's financial affairs, as the city's credit rating went into free fall and as access to the municipal bond markets began to dry up. Meanwhile, Atlantic City's (Republican) mayor had been "looking under every stone to find ways to . . . either reduce costs or bring in income" (Donald Guardian, quoted in Rojas, 2016, p. A18), liquidating and monetizing assets, cutting payrolls and services, and making last-minute interest payments with bridging loans, while enduring jibes from the governor's office that the City was guilty of "wasteful spending and mismanagement," and indeed that the mayor "just [has] not had the guts to do his job" (Chris Christie, quoted in McGeehan, 2016a, p. A17, Rojas; 2016, p. A18).

The municipality had been structurally adjusting itself, fearful of an even worse fate, but this had not been enough. Historically speaking, having first tried to grow itself out of an entrenched pattern of postwar economic decline, by way of a state-authorized experiment in casino-based entrepreneurialism, initiated in the late 1970s, Atlantic City now finds itself on the wrong side of a saturated regional gaming market with little prospect of even medium-term recovery; apparently having run out of politically or fiscally feasible options, New Jersey is now embarking on a plan to shrink the local state down to something commensurate with the city's diminished local economy, offering its underemployed and underserved residents little more than funding cuts, triaged services, privatization, and asset stripping. While this idea of "shrinking [a city] back to greatness" has been afforded some measure of intellectual credibility lately (Glaeser, 2011, 2013; cf. Peck, 2016), the practical and indeed ethical limitations of such a strategy had been acknowledged by none other than Atlantic City's emergency manager himself, whose two reports had concluded, candidly, that the "City simply cannot stand on its own," and furthermore that "cost reductions are *not nearly enough* to align the City toward a 'new normal'" (Emergency Manager, 2015, 6; 2016, p. 20; emphasis added).

Evidently, this "new normal" is no naturally occurring state. If Atlantic City and other fiscally stressed municipalities across the country are to ever get there, it will likely be courtesy of another painful period of crisis-driven and strategically targeted urban restructuring—politically administered, fiscally enforced, and technocratically managed. While this may well echo earlier rounds of financially mandated retrenchment, testimony to the nonrepeating nature of these histories of the restructuring present can be found in the rapidly evolving array of techniques, practices, and operative norms that have been developed in the wake of the Wall Street crash, including a structurally founded "local squeeze" on city budgets and an outbreak of municipal defaults and bankruptcies, many of which are analyzed in subsequent chapters of this book (see also Davidson & Ward, 2014; Kirkpatrick & Smith, 2011; Peck, 2014;

Pew Charitable Trusts, 2012; Tabb, 2014). It is not too far-fetched to say that some kind of new normal is being established here. Recall that the municipal bond market was regarded (for decades in fact) as a safe haven with an incredibly low rate of default, while the machinery for municipal bankruptcy, under chapter 9 of the Federal Code, has been used only infrequently since the 1930s (see Hempel, 1971; KBRA, 2011; Knox & Levinson, 2009; Sbragia, 1996). While there is some evidence that municipal bankruptcy filings, and the precedents that have been set by them, are being used strategically by state governments and restructuring advocates, perhaps most notably in the Detroit case (see Bomey, 2016; Peck, 2015; Peck & Whiteside, 2016), yet more concerted institutional and political efforts have been dedicated to the ongoing governance challenges of managing municipal downsizing and plans for (structural) adjustment *outside* the bankruptcy courts (albeit still in their shadows), not least through the development of new (or reconstructed) provisions for emergency management and state oversight, and through the fast-policy circulation of novel rubrics, rationales, tactics, and tech-nologies for local-state restructuring (see Peck, 2014, 2017a). This has involved the experimental and sometimes improvised manufacture of quite new forms of neoliberal statecraft, much of which has been focused on the stressed nexus of state-local government relations, the roots of which can be traced back to the historic retreat of the federal government from urban funding and programming in the 1970s (see Burchell & Listokin, 1981; Eide, 2012, 2016).[1] As Stephen Eide of the conservative think tank the Manhattan Institute has written:

> Local governments are the legal creations of state govern-
> ment, and, inevitably, their problems become states' problems.
> For the age of austerity—which is certainly real—it is more
> important to reassess the state and local relationship than the
> federal and state relationship. (2012, p. 8)

Conservative legal scholars, free market think tanks, and a newly mobilized network of politically connected technocrats, policy advocates, and crisis managers, have been especially active on this front, developing not only a barrage of new legal, organizational, and technical devices, but working (often creatively) on a no-less-essential battery of ideological rationales, political formulae, and justificatory narratives. Indicative of these efforts, the Manhattan Institute's advice for some time has been that "states' primary focus should be on avoiding bankruptcy through effective state intervention policies. . . . [They should] develop oversight policies to identify distress early on, prevent it with technical assistance, and generally encourage best practices in local financial management" (Eide, 2012, p. 8).

In the ideal(ized) world of neoliberal governance, of course, local autonomy is sacrosanct, while interventionist impulses (particularly from the top down) should be restrained at all costs (see Peck, 2011). In the real world of post-crisis, "late" neoliberalism, on the other hand, new modes of panurban, extraurban, and indeed antiurban governance are being formulated, informed by the "operating theory" that the underlying causes of municipal fiscal crisis are not only endogenous but can be traced to (or at least pegged to) "local management failures," to corruption, and ultimately to culpability (see Scorsone, 2014: cf. Anderson, 2012).[2] Drawing on "models" such as Michigan and North Carolina, states are now being urged to set in place much more aggressive, "bad cop" intervention policies and emergency management provisions, unilaterally to dismantle union agreements and "pro-labor mandates," and to take steps to avoid the effects of "contagion" in credit markets, given that these are not going to be passing problems since "local governments face a long-term gap between revenues and expenditures" (Eide, 2012, pp. 9, 4, 3). This begins to look like a fiscally mandated and externally enforced new normal, one that is being imposed from outside and indeed from "above" by the increasingly synchronized actions of credit-market gatekeepers and upstate politicians. Recognizing that the threats associated with municipal indebtedness, depressed tax revenues, and localized fiscal crisis "are not going away anytime soon," the Manhattan Institute has taken to calling, quite unapologetically, for a new Caesarism: "[I]f we want stronger cities, we should support more state-imposed constraints on them. . . . [S]tates need to step in, Caesar-like, earlier and more vigorously than they've been doing" (Eide, 2016, pp. 70, 75).

A new era of Caesarism certainly threatens at the federal level, too. On the campaign trail, Donald Trump periodically returned to the theme

of what he called his "urban renewal agenda," in fact "talk[ing] more
about cities than any major candidate for decades" (Sugrue, 2016, p.
1). This was a presidential candidate who frequently compares the inner
cities to "hellholes" and "war zones" (quoted in Fausset et al., 2016, p.
A25; Sugrue, 2016, p. 1), and whose pitch to African American and
Hispanic voters was to ask, "What do you have to lose?" Trump would
allude to a new era of free-enterprise job creation in urban America,
thanks mostly to an infrastructure-building initiative and to a hazy plan
to repatriate offshored factories, but also to the imposition of yet more
punitive and privatized modes of governance, evidently targeted on racialized minorities, including an intensification of aggressive policing tactics
("The problem is not the presence of police but the absence of police,"
he said), coupled with an entrepreneurial adaptation of workfare that
would convert welfare payments into "forgivable micro-loans" (Trump,
2016a, p. 3). His language, revealingly, was that of "fixing" the inner
cities, which may turn out to be the tenor as well as the method of the
Trump administration, which promises broadly to align with a Manhattan
Institute understanding of the "basics" for late-neoliberal urban development: a new law and order offensive, choice and charter-based education
reform, and new rounds of business deregulation, supplemented by a
$1 trillion program of slum clearance and infrastructure investment, to
be financed by scheme for "revenue-neutral" tax credits. Trump pledged
to retake the cities as sites for Republican policymaking, outlining an
agenda based on a combination of bold promises and a narrow package
of (mostly conventional) interventions:

> The conditions in our inner cities today are unacceptable. The
> Democrats have run our inner cities for fifty, sixty, seventy
> years or more. They've run the school boards, the city councils,
> the mayor's offices, and the congressional seats. Their policies
> have failed, and they've failed miserably. . . . The Clintons gave
> us NAFTA and China's entry into the World Trade Orga-
> nization, two deals that de-industrialized America, uprooted
> our industry, and stripped bare towns like Detroit and Balti-
> more. . . . Massive taxes, massive regulation of small business,
> and radical restrictions on American energy, have driven jobs

and opportunities out of our inner cities. . . . I . . . propose tax holidays for inner-city investment, and new tax incentives to get foreign companies to relocate in blighted American neighborhoods. I will further empower cities and states to seek a federal disaster designation for blighted communities in order to initiate the rebuilding of vital infrastructure, the demolition of abandoned properties, and the increased presence of law enforcement. (Trump, 2016a, pp. 2–3)

The cities have been pretty much enemy territory for Republicans since the Reagan years, being "full of Democrats, minorities, and poor people," prompting some skeptics to suggest that under the Trump administration, "there's not going to be much urban policy, period" (Mallach, 2016, p. 1; cf. Flint, 2016). Others have debated whether the reappropriation of the tainted language of "urban renewal" was merely a byproduct of Trump's off-the-cuff campaign style, or if it might signal a new era of bulldozer renewal—what the civil rights activists of the 1960s came to call, tellingly, "negro removal." Writing in the "upshot" column of the *New York Times*, Emily Badger (2016, p. 1) reads the tea leaves as potentially "scary for cities." More moderate voices have been urging mayors to "strike the right balance between confrontation and collaboration with the new administration," seeing some opportunities for pragmatic collaboration in fields such as infrastructure development (Katz, 2016, p. 1).

Should it be fully enacted, the promised infrastructure program will surely "help some cities, but if it predictably favors projects that can support private financing, a lot more money will end up in fast-growing urban areas like Houston or Denver than in the Midwest or Northeast" (Flint, 2016; Mallach, 2016, p. 2). Exacerbating established social and interurban inequalities built into the spatial divisions of credit availability and risk assessment, wherein cities are already subject to the judgments of credit-rating agencies, to Wall Street discipline, and to bondholder-value rationalities (Peck, 2017a; Peck & Whiteside, 2016), the Trump infrastructure program seems set to accelerate and intensify the ongoing financialization of urban governance, and indeed of the state more generally. Furthermore, the historically unprecedented levels of political control that the Republican Party now enjoys at the local, state, and federal levels means that many of the remaining obstacles to municipal privatization and the outsourcing of services, to conservative initiatives in schooling, crime control, and social welfare, and to cronyism in contracting and infrastructure deals, will have been all but removed, while further rollbacks can be anticipated in labor standards, in environmental protections, in gender and minority rights, and in affirmative action programs.

Some of Trump's allies have been urging the president to "stay on offense" with respect to his urban agenda, establishing new mandates for conservative urban governance and "dismantling" what Republican partisans continue to read as the "hyper-centralization" of the Obama years (Borrell, 2016, pp. 1, 3).[3] From these quarters at least, Trump's choice of retired neurosurgeon and failed presidential candidate Ben Carson as HUD secretary has been welcomed. A neophyte when it comes to urban policy, indeed to management itself, Carson's ideologically polarizing appointment soon drew unflattering comparisons with Samuel Pierce's term of office under Reagan (Sugrue, 2016). Carson's campaign-trail rants against "social engineering" and "welfare dependency," where he aligned the generally modest, rule-based policy measures introduced by the Obama administration with "the history of failed socialist experiments in this country" (see Carson, 2015, p. 1), imply significant tensions with HUD mandates in the areas of affirmative action and affordable housing. (This was consistent with the pattern of Trump's cabinet appointments, however, for which the qualifications of successful candidates were moderate to extreme levels of ideological disagreement with the departmental missions in question.) As Tom Sugrue has pointed out:

> We don't know much yet about how Carson will run HUD, but his lack of experience with urban policy, his bromides about socialist planning, his indifference to fair housing and his calls for individual boot-strapping don't bode well for the future of metropolitan America. And in a climate of privatization and deregulation, championed by the country's new real estate developer in chief, Carson's inexperience could be a serious liability. (2016, p. 4)

Most in the field of urban policy and metropolitan governance professed to knowing next to nothing or "absolutely nothing" about the new HUD secretary's plans for the cities; when Carson was asked if he intended to follow through on his campaign rhetoric to gut Great Society housing and affirmative action programs, however, he breezily dismissed the notion as "a bunch of crap" (quoted in Fritze, 2016, p. 2). In one way or another, it seems likely that there will be some continuation of the neoliberalized mode of urban governance, running from Reagan to Obama, under which the policymaking lexicon has been progressively reorganized around ideas like "promise" and "hope" for "enterprising" communities, where selectively targeted and competitively awarded initiatives are delivered by task forces and project managers, invariably larded with the language of "partnership" (as a euphemism not only for shared responsibilities, but for state and local government copays), and where major investments are predicated on market tests of different kinds—albeit perhaps with a harder edge.

If history is any guide, Carson will be tempted selectively to follow the policy advice from the Manhattan Institute, one of the few organizations publicly to enthuse about his offbeat appointment ("just the man for the job"), sharing as it does the incoming secretary's view that the public housing system is little but a "modern poorhouse" (Husock, 2016, pp. 3, 1). Quite probably signs of things to come, Manhattan's agenda has been predictably concerned with the termination of positive discrimination mandates in community development spending and in fair housing programs, with the termination of affordable housing mandates at Fannie Mae and Freddie Mac, with the privatization of what remains of public-sector estate management, and with the introduction of time limits for public and voucher housing. If nothing else, these proposals for "laying a new foundation at HUD," when read alongside the tough talk and big promises made by President Trump and by Secretary Carson on the campaign trail, confirm that the terrains of metropolitan governance and urban programming are always moving—as the conjunctural moment of austerity urbanism gives way to an emerging era of leveraged infrastructure development, redoubled policies for social control, market-based school reform, and entrepreneurial zoning. Those that are equating these developments with previous realignments in metropolitan modes of regulation, from the Great Society to the Reagan years (see Badger, 2016; Sugrue, 2016), surely have a point. No doubt some metro areas will thrive and grow, the beneficiaries of bond market–approved investments and Trumpian largesse, while others slip farther behind or find themselves confronted by new forms of neoliberal structural adjustment and conservative social engineering. This could indeed mean "scary times" for cities.

Notes

1. By the late 1970s, there was a "recognition on the part of locals that: (a) there will be a general slow-down of direct federal-to-local funds; and (b) the state will become an increasingly-frequent intergovernmental transfer partner" (Burchell & Listokin, 1981, p. xlii). Both the level of, and the degree of reliance on, state-to-local funding did indeed rise over subsequent decades, at least until 2008, since which time there have been sharp reductions in state aid to cities, once again unevenly restored (Peck, 2014; Reschovsky, 2016).

2. "Cities' problems are often of their own making," is the oft-repeated Manhattan Institute line, "mismanagement and corruption [being] ever-present dangers in political life," especially in the Democratically controlled cities, "[m]ost local governments becom[ing] insolvent from a lack of political will" (Eide, 2012, pp. 4, 3, 5).

3. It is difficult to square the accusation of hypercentralization with many of Obama's actual policy initiatives, even in health care or in stimulus programming. In the field of urban policy itself, generous assessments have concluded that the Obama legacy got little beyond "small innovations," tokenistic initiatives, modest accomplishments, and feel-good sentiments (see Graff, 2016; cf. DeFilippis, 2016). A concrete manifestation of the highest stage achieved by Obama-era urban policy is the plan for a "safer, stronger Baltimore," published as the final report of a post-riot task force in the final weeks of the administration (see Executive Office of the President, 2016).

Introduction

MARK DAVIDSON AND KEVIN WARD

The European debt crisis, and the ensuing austerity-fuelled chaos, can seem to Americans like a distant battle that portends a dark future. Yet a closer look reveals that the future is already here. American austerity has largely taken the form of municipal budget crises precipitated by predatory Wall Street lending practices. The debt financing of U.S. cities and towns, a neoliberal economic model that long precedes the current recession, has inflicted deep and growing suffering on communities across the country.

—Ann Larson, Cities in the Red: Austerity Hits America

Cities have played an important role in the crisis. They have embodied what the crisis and its aftermath meant in the spatially condensed form.

—K. Fujita, *Cities and Crisis: New Critical Urban Theory*

The spectral marauding of urban austerity draws the lifeblood from communities.

—W. K. Tabb, "The Wider Context of Austerity Urbanism"

Introduction

Rewind just over five years. It is the summer of 2011. Jefferson County, Alabama, was hitting the national headlines. This unlikely candidate for national media attention had become the latest victim of municipal fiscal crisis. The county suddenly faced a massive budget shortfall due to a Supreme Court decision that rendered Jefferson's $70 million occupational tax unconstitutional. In addition, the county was facing burgeoning repayments on a $3.14 billion sewer works project. This infrastructure program had been financed by Wall Street firm JP Morgan, one of a number of investment banks that had been eager to sell complex debt vehicles to cash-hungry municipalities. Unfortunately, the financial "solutions" sold by the investment bankers turned out to carry huge risks. And this was not an isolated incident. Across urban America city and county governments were going to be left counting the cost both figuratively and literally of experimenting with a range of financial vehicles (Davidson & Ward, 2014).

As Jefferson's recessionary budget crunch, which had begun in 2008, came to a climax in Summer 2011, so the county started to implement the types of cutbacks that have become a defining feature of U.S. austerity, characterized by "fiscal-discipline, local-government downsizing and privatization" (Peck, 2014, p. 18). In June 2011, the county started a process of cutting its workforce, sacking seven hundred employees, approximately one-third of those who had worked for it. By November 2011, the city government's efforts to balance its budget had failed to such an extent that it filed for Chapter 9 bankruptcy. It was not the first city government to make this move, of course. Thirteen municipalities filed between 2008 and early 2013, of which five were dismissed. That is, though, less than 1% of all those eligible according to their particular state's legislation (http://www.governing.com/blogs/by-the-numbers/municipal-bankruptcy-rate-and-state-law-limitations.html).

In the case of Jefferson County, the bankruptcy filing totaled $4.2 billion for the county of 658,000 residents. That is nearly $6,400 per person! This was the biggest bankruptcy by a U.S. city or country until two years later—June 2013—in Detroit's $18 billion case. In the course of bankruptcy proceedings, the apparent predatory and opaque lending practices of JP Morgan resulted in the Securities and Exchanges Commission fining the firm $75 million and denying it $647 million in future fees. The bankruptcy court also approved a settlement that included writing off $1.4 billion in debt associated with the sewer financing deal.

In the midst of Jefferson County's attempt to resolve its fiscal crisis, County Commissioner Jimmie Stephens commented that "[t]hese steps are the beginning of a new era . . . a reduced level of services for the citizens of Jefferson County" (Wyler, 2011, np). Cutbacks within the county have slashed the city's payroll. Further rollbacks continue as the state government continues on its own austerity drive. In addition to losing public services such as fire, libraries, and police, Jefferson's residents also now face possible school closures. Since 2008, the county has run a $10 million deficit within its school budget. As Alabama withdraws educational funding, there is no capacity within the county's budget to address the financing shortfall. What is emerging is a much-reduced state, with few in the county immune to the consequences of austerity. When Jefferson emerged from bankruptcy just before the end of 2013, the county was a financial and political mess. The repercussions of this economic and political meltdown were felt immediately in the form of rises in the sewage rates paid by residents. The county is also faced with a hugely uncertain financial future (http://www.al.com/news/birmingham/index.ssf/2014/12/one_year_later_jefferson_count.html). And it was not alone.

Jefferson County's story of fiscal collapse places it at the forefront of the most recent wave of U.S. urban restructuring. Precarious infrastructure financing, inadequate local fiscal tools, bankruptcy, unprecedented cutbacks: the county contained a nightmarish combination of factors that have, in varying degrees, played out across the whole country. With hindsight, it is almost as if those in charge had a death wish, or perhaps more aptly, a debt wish (Sbragia, 1996). While exceptional with regard to its levels of debt and leveraged financing—the only comparative civic entity being Detroit—Jefferson County's budgetary collapse represents a fate that many U.S. cities are still actively trying to avoid.

Since 2007, U.S. cities have been implementing austerity policies. The most extreme forms of austerity have been witnessed in cities such as Detroit, Michigan, and Vallejo, California, where employees and retirees have seen their incomes slashed and health care cut. However, a less dramatic and more insidious process of austerity reform has been undertaken across most U.S. cities. At the height of the fiscal crisis, the National League of Cities described the fiscal situation across the United States in the following way:

> The nation's city finance officers report that the fiscal condition of the nation's cities continues to weaken in 2010 as cities confront the effects of the economic downturn. Local and regional economies characterized by struggling housing markets, slow consumer spending, and high levels of unemployment are driving declines in city revenues. In response, cities are cutting personnel, infrastructure investments and key services. (NLOC, 2010, p. 1)

In 2010, 90 percent of U.S. municipal finance officers reported the implementation of spending cuts to counter falling revenues (ibid). U.S. urban austerity has therefore involved budget balancing processes whereby many "nonessential" items have been taken out of city budgets. However, in already lean neoliberal governments, this has often involved the redefinition of what is "essential." The most common austerity reforms have been personnel cuts that have stripped staffing levels down to a minimum and the cancellation or delay of infrastructure projects (ibid.). Alongside these reforms, many cities have instituted hiring freezes and/or wage reductions. The last eight years of austerity have therefore reshaped the composition of most city governments and redefined what types of projects a city may undertake.

Only now—in 2016—are some cities seeing their reconfigured budgets return their fiscal status to prerecession levels, and even then for most cities the recovery remains weak and inconsistent (NLOC, 2014). A similar trend has occurred at the state level, with fiscal rebuilding slow and painful for many (NASBO, 2014). At the federal level, the policies and the discourse are different. President Obama has persistently urged European leaders to follow the United States's example by increasing public expenditure to support slumping private sector growth (Bull & Bohan, 2012). However powerful this rhetoric is, it disguises the fact that the United States has been undergoing a major austerity drive of its own (Dolan, 2015). For example:

> [U.S. federal] Government spending at all levels is far below the level of any other recent recovery. Sixteen quarters after the end of the recession, spending during past recoveries has been 7–15% *higher* than it was at the start. This time it's 7% *lower,* despite the fact that the 2008–09 recession was the deepest of the bunch. Reagan, Clinton, and Bush all benefited from rising spending during the economic recoveries on their watches. Only Obama has been forced to manage a recovery while government spending has plummeted. (http://www.motherjones.com/kevin-drum/2013/09/obama-austerity-wrecked-american-economy)

The logic underpinning this approach is that "strategies of fiscal constraint can, counter-intuitively, produce expansionary effects in national economies" (Clarke & J. Newman, 2012, p. 301; see also Krugman, 2011). Yet, due in large part to the nature of its fiscal system (Oates, 1999; Peck, 2014), the federal government has been able to leave the dirty work and the heavy lifting of the "doing" of austerity to state and local governments. In the United States, then, austerity has been very much concerned "with social, spatial and scalar strategies of *redistribution*; it is about making 'others' pay" (Peck, 2014, p. 20). In many senses this has not marked much of a departure from past practices and strategies of the federal government. Recent years have seen nation-states restructuring themselves from within regardless of their organizational point of departure. This has involved functions and responsibilities being taken on by others, such as community organizations and private sector firms. It has also seen the emergence of what Brenner (2004) termed "new state spaces," whereby subnational branches of the state have been conscripted to do the work required of them under neoliberalization (Brenner et al., 2010). Under the U.S. variant of austerity urbanism this pattern has continued with the fiscal disciplining of municipalities and state authorities.

Of course, austerity was not always *the* response to the latest structural economic crisis. As the global economy threatened to unravel between 2007 and 2009, many policymakers and commentators (re) embraced Keynesianism (Krugman, 2014; Rudd, 2009). For some this was an opportunity to (re)assert the analytical superiority of an alternative economic doctrine (Galbraith, 2008). Yet in the context of what has been labeled "the Great Recession," the embrace of anti-austerity policies was also supported by others. As national governments found themselves the necessary saviors of corrupted and broken banking systems, state investment in the economy was championed, albeit momentarily (see Greenspan, 2013), by some of the most ardent supporters of neoliberal capitalism. Some of the key conductors of global capitalism, such as former Goldman Sachs CEO and then secretary of the treasury Hank Paulson, found themselves instigating unprecedented state interventions into the national economy. No straight route from structural economic crisis to austerity therefore existed. Initial responses varied across national contexts, and in places such as the United States, expansionary fiscal policies—such as the *Emergency Economic Stabilization Act of 2008*— were implemented.

There are many ways to interpret the subsequent transition toward austerity. For some, it should be explained as the reassertion of political and economic power by elites (Callinicos, 2012). Others have claimed that it resulted from a change in political strategies on the political Right (Williamson, 2013). The analysis of global institutions such as the International Monetary Fund argue that austerity emerged—where properly rolled out—as the correct response to economic restructuring (Batini et al., 2012). For Peck (2014, p. 20; original emphasis), what has been witnessed is "a concerted *renarration* of the financial crisis in the form of new homilies of (local) state failure." Whatever the best explanation, there is little doubt that a concerted process of state and social restructuring has been underway across many countries of the Global North. After a brief period of state intervention in the economy, we have therefore witnessed efforts to get the state out of the way of processes of capital restructuring. Ironically, in order for that to happen *more not less* state activity has been required. Furthermore, we have seen the state actively pursuing reforms to create greater opportunities for economic restructuring, for the business of austerity has the potential to be a profitable one (Davidson & Kutz, 2015).

Within this context, the American version of austerity deserves particular attention. In the immediate post-crisis period, the Obama administration injected billions of dollars into the U.S. economy. This stimulus package became very much the counterpoint to the European context, where many governments resisted similar deficit spending. This period was to end with the curtailment of federal stimulus funds. What has followed has returned federal fiscal structures to what has been the norm since the 1980s (Harvey, 1989; Peck, 2012). Municipal and state governments have therefore again found it necessary to provide public services without federal support. However, they must now do this in an even more uncertain economic situation and in the wake of decades of neoliberalization which has left them much "leaner" that they were in the 1980s. With fewer levers to pull and with many of its traditional functions and services no longer under their control, branches of the state have found themselves with relatively few budgets over which they can make the cuts demanded of them. It is perhaps not a surprise, then, that many U.S. cities have adopted relatively similar strategies (Ross et al., 2014); they are, after all, being forced to choose from a relatively limited menu. "What is striking about local strategies is just how un-local they are" wrote Peck and Tickell (1994, p. 281) more than two decades ago. This continues to characterize much of the "local" policy landscape in austerity urban America.

Austerity Defined

It is important to acknowledge the complicated, contested, and long history to austerity. In many ways, there are a variety of national-specific types of austerity, each with its own histories and meanings, reflecting the work that has been done by the term over the years. So, it is a notion that has a sense of geography embodied in its very DNA. That makes statements about a general type of austerity only partially useful. Nevertheless, there are some shared characteristics and features that are worth noting, not least because what in recent years has emerged in geographically discrete nations around the world is a variegated and relationally constituted austerity, one that is in part made through connections between nations and cities.

So, in general terms, austerity can be characterized as an economic and social reform agenda premised upon fiscal constraint and deficit reduction, reduced state expenditure, shrinking government achieved via privatization, and significant cuts to social welfare. All of these reforms are intended to restore an economy to a competitive position. As Mark Blyth (2012, p. 2) explains:

> Austerity is a form of voluntary deflation in which the economy adjusts through the reduction of wages, prices and public spending to restore competitiveness which is (supposedly) best achieved by cutting the state's budget, debts, and deficits. Doing so, its advocates believe, will inspire "business confidence" since the government will neither be "crowding-out" the market for investment by sucking up all the available capital through the issuance of debt, nor adding to the nation's already "too big" debt.

If a state amasses fiscally burdensome debt or social welfare functions, austerity therefore becomes a perceived route within which relative competiveness can be restored. Indeed, proponents of austerity reforms often point toward the largesse of the state (e.g., excessive social welfare and public employee spending) as the cause of economic stagnation and the consequent need for state restructuring (Edsall, 2012).

Economic austerity has its origins in liberal economic theory, in the works of people such as John Locke, David Hume, and Adam Smith. Liberal theorists, Blyth (2012) argues, were consistently concerned with the state, with some arguing against its necessity (i.e., Hume and Locke) and others arguing about who should pay for the state (i.e., Smith). In liberal formulations of state theory, the market becomes a mechanism to achieve social order, and the state introduces problems into the market-based social system. When an economic crisis occurs, the solution is often a reassertion of market forces (i.e., deregulation) and a withdrawal of the state as a significant market actor (i.e., public spending cuts). As liberal theory has waxed and waned in popularity in different nations, so has an embrace of antistate (including austerity) reform. In the 1920s, austerity became a widely adopted reform model. In the United States, Herbert Hoover's treasury secretary, Andrew Mellon, argued the response to the crisis of the late 1920s and early 1930s should be to "liquidate labor, liquidate stocks, liquidate the farmers, liquidate real estate," so that the "rottenness [will be purged] out of the system. . . . People will . . . live a more moral life . . . and enterprising people will pick up the wrecks from less competent people" (cited in Blyth, 2013, p. 84). As the implications of such thought and associated reform became evident in 1930s Europe, the legitimacy of austerity—and the liberal thought that inspired it—receded. Blyth (2013) argues the only places you could actually find austerity proponents through the mid-twentieth century were in Germany and within the small cabal of Austrian School economists. Austerity only reemerged as a legitimate reform option as part of the resurgence of (neo)liberal doctrine in the 1980s (Harvey, 2005; Peck, 2010).

New York City's fiscal crisis of 1975 is often identified as a trigger point in the rise of U.S. neoliberal governance (Harvey, 2005; Tabb, 1982). From the 1960s onward, New York City had run significant deficits as it relied on federal aid to counter recessionary decline. In 1975, the city finally ran out of cash, as financiers refused to renew loans. Estimates of the city's total deficit run from $600 million to $2.2 billion. The "remedy" imposed on New York City involved deferring fiscal revenues to bondholders, curbing union power, implementing wage freezes, cutting back public employment, slashing public services, and imposing user fees (Lichten, 1986; Tabb, 1982). This combination of fiscal disciplining techniques subsequently became a blueprint for the 1980s neoliberal reinvention of a restructured government:

> This amounted to a coup by the financial institutions against the democratically elected government of New York City. . . . The New York crisis was, Zevin argues, symptomatic of "an emerging strategy of disinflation coupled with a regressive redistribution of income, wealth and power" . . . the purpose of which was "to show others that what is happening

to New York could and in some cases will happen to them."
(Harvey, 2005, pp. 45–46)

In the years that followed, cities across the U.S. and in many other nations were to undergo a similar disciplining process (Brenner & Theodore, 2002; Peck & Tickell, 2002). In the United States, gone were the political culture and institutions of "New Deal Democrats" and in its place was generated a new regime of fiscal retrenchment, competition, and discipline. As Clark and Ferguson (1983, p. 5) found: "The New Deal coalitions have broken down and New Fiscal Populist leaders have devised new modes of governance and specific policies consistent with more limited resources and current citizen preferences." This resource-scarce environment appeared to demand austerity, and in retrospect the neoliberalized rounds of restructuring over the course of the 1980s and 1990s in urban America were simply the warmup for the main event, as advocates of free-market restructuring have made hay in the political slipstream of the Great Recession.

U.S. austerity initially came in the form of the federal government withdrawing redistributive funding and the emergence of an entrepreneurial urban system that demanded cities take more fiscal responsibility and, consequentially, operate services with fewer resources (Harvey, 1989). This occurred at the same time as the federal government was divesting itself of social welfare responsibilities and, thus, placing greater burdens on state and local governments (Peck, 2012). The transformation of urban governance in North America and much of Europe over the past four decades has therefore involved a certain type of austerity, one premised on ideological commitments to state downsizing, the insertion of market forces into many aspects of government leading to the production of a particular neoliberalized form of statecraft (Peck, 2001; Peck & Tickell, 2002).

In the United States, the decades preceding the 2007–08 financial crisis and Great Recession were dominated by this neoliberal reform agenda. From the 1980s onward, the hegemonic political ideology had demanded that state spending (with the possible exception of military spending) be reduced (Harvey, 2005). Across both North America and Western Europe, entire social systems became privatized. The current bout of austerity reform has therefore been implemented on an already austere governmental landscape:

> One way or another, fiscal conservatism is established as a bipartisan condition. This is reflected, in turn, in a pattern of fiscal revanchism that is quite unprecedented in its reach and intensity, even in comparison with the Reagan and Gingrich revolutions of the 1980s and 1990s. (Peck, 2012, p. 639)

Today's U.S. austerity reforms must therefore go farther, reach great depths, in order to find in the state retrenchment a commitment to austerity demands. It is in this extreme or severe context that health care, pensions, and social services have been cut and withdrawn across many cities (Davidson & Kutz, 2015; Davidson & Ward, 2014; Peck, 2012).

The 2008 financial crisis, which was subsequently engineered into a sovereign debt crisis (Blyth, 2013), and the austerity that has been implemented to remedy it, therefore involves a strange paradox. In the immediate fallout of the financial crisis, it appeared evident that the self-regulating and wealth-generating promises of neoliberal doctrine had been false. Indeed, this doctrine was identified as the cause of the economic calamity. In a now infamous piece written by then Australian prime minister Kevin Rudd (2009, np), it was claimed that neoliberalism was finished:

> The global financial crisis has demonstrated already that it is no respecter of persons, nor of particular industries, nor of national boundaries. It is a crisis which is simultaneously individual, national and global. It is a crisis of both the developed and the developing world. It is a crisis which is at once institutional, intellectual and ideological. It has called into question the prevailing neo-liberal economic orthodoxy of the past 30 years—the orthodoxy that has underpinned the national and global regulatory frameworks that have so spectacularly failed to prevent the economic mayhem which has now been visited upon us.

Given that these criticisms were coming from political elites, it is not immediately apparent how more austerity became the fix for already austere neoliberal nations and cities.

Part of the answer is ideological. Blyth (2013), for example, has claimed that part of the appeal of austerity is moral. In many European countries austerity has connotations to postwar reconstruction efforts and the collective project of national rebuilding. For example, in the UK, the notion of austerity draws partially and selectively on "a collective memory of rationing, making do and mending, and a culture of constraint" (Clarke & J. Newman, 2012, p. 307; see Kynaston, 2007, 2010). It is not a signifier of wholly negative resonance. Despite being an undeniably painful experience, austerity can therefore be regarded as virtuous and self-sacrificing.

In the United States the ideological landscape is dramatically different. The war-tinted appeal of austerity does not resonate to the same extent. In addition, the idea of deficit spending has become a difficult political sell:

> Pitched battles between haves and have-nots over health care, taxes, union rights and unemployment benefits—as well as, at the local level, cuts in police protection, garbage collection, and the numbers of teachers—have dominated public debate. A stagnant economy, ballooning deficits, and the mushrooming strength of antigovernment forces are producing a set of wedge issues centered on fiscal conflict and budget shortages to create a new politics of scarcity. (Edsall, 2012, p. 13)

While American austerity is being shaped by the particularities of its ideological and governmental structure (Peck, 2014), austerity itself has become a global creed. As Fontana and Sawyer (2011, pp. 57–58) note: "No policymaker around the world seems immune." From global institutions such as the International Monetary Fund down to thousands of local governments, reforms have been undertaken that have the effect of making government more austere. After decades of neoliberal reforms, governments across the Global North faced the 2008 Great Recession with very few resources to withstand a generational economic crash

(Peck, 2010, 2012). Many national governments had already reduced social welfare spending, run down surpluses, sold off state assets, and divested themselves of economic decision making (Plant, 2012). All of which meant that when the financial sector found itself bankrupt in 2007–08, many national governments struggled to find easy solutions to the fiscal crisis.

The poster child of austerity is, of course, Greece. Following the dramatic, but relatively swift, economic restructurings that took place in Iceland (Boyes, 2009) and Ireland (Kinsella, 2012), Greece has found itself in a protracted and politically charged bankruptcy (Varoufakis, 2014). The battle that has taken place over Greece's debt repayments is indicative of broader struggles over austerity reform. Burdened with unpayable debts—Greek debt is 175 percent of GDP—the Greek electorate put the left-wing party Syriza in government early in 2015. Following their election success, Syriza has pursued an anti-austerity program and, in doing so, has found itself pitched against the "troika" of creditors: the International Monetary Fund, European Central Bank, and European Union. The troika has only been willing to fund otherwise bankrupt Greece with the condition that further austerity reforms are implemented. These include privatization of state assets, reductions in state payments and benefits, reduced social services, and the production of budget surpluses. While its immediate place in the European Union seems secure for now, its longer-term future (and, inter alia, that of the EU) remains unclear. There certainly remains no appetite among national and international public and private sector elites for any changes in the current governmental system (Callinicos, 2012; Crotty, 2012).

Austerity Urbanism Produced, U.S.-Style

In recent years, several cities . . . have recognized that their fiscal position is no longer tenable and have filed for bankruptcy. Bankruptcy is a painful measure of last resort and one that they understandably seek to avoid. Unfortunately, the radical cuts in services that troubled cities have made to avoid bankruptcy are counterproductive. Such measures may or may not stave off a formal declaration of bankruptcy, but they cause more damage to the financial health of the city, and bring about more hardship for its residents, than bankruptcy itself. (Kiewiet & McCubbins, 2014, p. 106)

While austerity has been pursued in much of the Global North, it has taken a different form across national contexts. In the United States, it is often necessary to describe austerity reforms as efficiency programs: removing government waste, stopping overpaying unionized labor, privatizing in order to develop more productive modes of management, and so on (Peck, 2014). The U.S. version of austerity, therefore, tends to be surrounded by a different discourse than that witnessed elsewhere, albeit echoing the technocratic, nonpolitical, and "commonsense" emphasis that characterizes the parallel reforms.

What is clear, particularly in the U.S. context, is that austerity involves a continuation and extension of preceding neoliberal reforms (Tabb, 2014). Given that these neoliberal reforms were themselves, in part at least, responsible for the Great Recession, some have described this context as "zombie neoliberalism" (Peck, 2010). Peck (2010) argues that this involves neoliberalism recreating itself through more authoritarian statecraft, implementing defensive and socially corrosive measures to recreate a failed ideological program. Colin Crouch (2011) has made a similar argument, but Crouch emphasizes how actually existing neoliberalism is recreated not by ideological commitments, but rather by economic (i.e., corporate) interests. A dead but reassertive neoliberalism is therefore not about market solutions, but the defense of economic power.

It is therefore important to place the current U.S. austerity moment in its longer historical context. Understanding this process will clarify how previous rounds of neoliberalization were achieved, and where potential areas for even further austerity reform might reside.

The variegated U.S. municipal financial landscape is a consequence of more than thirty years of neoliberal restructuring (Davidson & Ward, 2014; Tabb, 2015). Current austerity programs are being overlaid upon a governmental landscape that differs radically from that which was subject to reform in the 1970s. The neoliberalization of U.S. cities has been a highly uneven and diverse process (Brenner et al., 2010). Although general ideological tenets are present across the political landscapes where neoliberalism has become creed, the ways in which city governance was transformed from the 1980s onward varies according to location. This stated, it is possible to identify general tendencies of governmental change across difference. The DNA-like characteristics of the neoliberal urban governance landscape are as follows (Davidson & Ward, 2014):

1. *Restructuring of intergovernmental relations*: This has involved the federal government downloading responsibilities to lower levels (i.e., state and municipal) of government. While it downloads responsibility it does not increase levels of funding. Indeed, oftentimes the opposite is true. The federal government does, however, maintain considerable political control through the establishment of various indicators and metrics, reporting procedures, and competitive funding arrangements that incentivize cooperation/partnership with private sector actors (Leitner et al., 2007).

2. *Restructuring of the logics of governmental decision making*: The reduction in guaranteed redistributive allocations from the federal (and state) government has necessitated the growth of speculative financing with municipal governments. Current governmental expenditures are therefore calculated in relation to predicted (i.e., speculative) future incomes. The operation of the municipal government must therefore prioritize its speculative activities in order to ensure the continued operation of its discretionary and required services (Weber, 2010).

3. *Restructuring of public finance*: As federal support for local services has been dismantled as a critical part of wider state restructuring, localities have transformed the structure of their financial and fiscal system. New funding sources have had to be developed, usually through the interaction of the city with various financial and development intermediaries

(see Byrne, 2005). As a consequence, the income streams identified in city budget documents look totally different to those you might have seen in the late 1970s.

4. *Restructuring of risk allocation*: As a consequence of restructuring and the city's need to develop its own income streams, the exposure of the city to financial risk has increased greatly. Federal and state government neither provides guaranteed redistributed funds nor allocations to buffer the municipality against economic change. The municipal government must therefore manage and respond to local and global economic changes (see Epple & Spatt, 1986; Liu, 2012).

These general tendencies meant most U.S. cities were in fiscal distress by 2010. For cities in a weak fiscal state, the recession and end of federal aid proved catastrophic (Davidson & Ward, 2014; Hall & Jonas, 2014; Peck, 2014; Ross et al., 2014; Skidmore & Scorsone, 2011). The uneven fiscal capacity of the United States was therefore laid bare by the financial crisis.

As cities such as Detroit, Michigan, and San Bernardino, California, filed for Chapter 9 bankruptcy protections, the disciplinary structure of neoliberal urbanism became conspicuous. Due to the changes already outlined, cities have become financial entities; they have been given the responsibility to manage their own financial fate. In the absence of higher levels of government controlling city budgets and funding, cities have come to look like businesses themselves. As such, they are responsible for balancing their budgets and, consequently, acting in fiscally conservative ways. A significance consequence of this financialization (Krippner, 2005; Tabb, 2105) process has been the necessity for cities to fund their activities through financial instruments such as loans and bonds (Davidson & Ward, 2014; Weber, 2002, 2010). When cities need funding for new services, infrastructure, or development projects they must engage with financial markets (Hackworth, 2006). Commonly, this has involved cities borrowing in the capital markets. Since the 1980s, cities across the United States have therefore sourced funding in the form of municipal bonds. It speaks volumes that in 1980 the municipal bond market was worth approximately $400 billion and by 2014 it was worth approximately $3.5 trillion, an almost eightfold increase in the amount of market-sourced debt held by municipalities.

The operation and development of cities has therefore become tied to financial markets. Municipal bonds have become a popular investment, offering modest returns with little or no (presumed) risk. Cities must therefore balance their books and repay their debts on time in order to maintain favorable credit ratings, in just the same way that individuals have been regulated by their credit scores. It has also meant that municipal services and infrastructures have been reworked into fee-generating mechanisms. For example, in order for a city to finance a sewer upgrade, it will institute a user fee (O'Neill, 2013). This creates a monthly income stream, which can be used as a financial tool in the same way that a mortgage payment is securitized.

The neoliberal rollback and transformation of the state therefore necessitated a change in the ways that cities pay for their activities. Alongside basic taxation (e.g., property taxes and sales taxes) now stand a host of financial arrangements that are, and can be made, subject to many kinds of volatility: bond repayments subject to both interest rate fluctuations and credit rating–related adjustments; debt instruments leveraged against interest rates; user fees subject to market and political changes. In addition, cities can simply be sold the wrong or poorly constructed financial instruments, usually by banks eager to collect origination fees and sell on a city's debt.

Neoliberalization and financialization are therefore intricately intertwined. However, it is a relationship not free from contradiction. The growth of the municipal debt market is an indicator of the growing debt burden of cities, and the citizens who fund cities (Sbragia, 1996). In order to keep up with debt payments, alongside other growing expenditures (e.g., public sector employee salaries and benefits), cities must maintain and/or grow their revenues. Usually, the latter is assumed in any organization of debt: the presumption is that a city's economy and related tax base will grow, and therefore more debt can be taken on over the long term. Indeed, because of the speculative basis of the competitive urban system (Davidson & Ward, 2014; Kirkpatrick & Smith, 2011), this has to be the assumption: one must spend (someone's) money, in order to accumulate it.

This arrangement becomes contradictory when entrepreneurial promises fail to materialize. As we see at the macro level, when compound economic growth does not materialize, the repayment of debts and liabilities becomes very difficult. It was within this context that the 2008 financial crisis hit. Cities had already been neoliberalized: they had become lean in terms of service delivery and highly integrated into the financial economy. Recession meant that neoliberalism required supplementing with austerity in the absence of much greater political and economic reform. Most U.S. cities therefore did not have a set of funding arrangements that were insulated from cyclical trends in the economy. Rather, they had to negotiate economic turbulence through a combination of protecting revenues, drawing down reserves, and adjusting service provisions.

The major revenue sources generated in U.S. cities are tied to the cyclical economy. As recession hit, the housing bubble burst. Declining house values meant declining property taxes. As house prices slumped, so cities found a primary source of their revenues in decline. In addition, local sales taxes fell as people started to cut back on spending. Capital markets also began to freeze up, since banks were reluctant to lend given they were unsure of counterparty risk. In short, the fiscal basis of most cities in the United States was plunged into crisis. This was made more severe since the main expenditures of cities—public sector salaries and benefits—did not adjust according to economic conditions. Falling revenues and static and/or growing expenditure demands create an almost unprecedented fiscal squeeze, to which cities have very few ways of responding.

In this context, it is unsurprising that the cities who were the first to experience financial trouble were those in previously buoyant property markets. The first city to declare bankruptcy was Vallejo, California. Situated just north of San Francisco, the city had experienced significant suburban development in the pre-crisis period. This had generated substantial revenue growth that was channeled into fire and police employee salaries. When the crisis hit, property values fell by 40 percent in Vallejo, and the city's entire revenues could then not cover the police and fire collective bargaining commitments (see Davidson & Kutz, 2015). Similar stories of fiscal calamity quickly emerged as the Great Recession revealed the precarious fiscal condition of many U.S. cities. While some have lauded Vallejo's rightsizing of its government, making the more general point that "California [is] a laboratory for how to run cities in an age of austerity" (Cha, 2012, p. A1), the evidence is a little less clear cut. What is more certain is that the residents of Vallejo have been conscripted into the restructuring of their government in a form of what Peck (2014, p. 37) rather cutely refers to as "a post-crisis variant of participatory budgeting."

A number of commentators have argued that the United States has not pursued austerity to the same extent that it has been pursued across Europe. The United States may therefore appear to be an example of a country that has rejected austerity in favor of deficit spending to stimulate economic recovery. At the federal level, this may have been true up until 2010 (Williamson, 2012). However, when recent elections and the fiscal federal system of the United States is factored into our analysis, the picture is quite different. As Peck (2014, p. 18) put it: "Even if it has never been the dominant narrative in any explicit way, localized austerity has deep roots in the American model of fiscal federalism."

When President Obama signed the American Recovery and Reinvestment Act, it was described as an economic stimulus that would "create or save three and a half million jobs over the next two years" (White House 2009, np). Such an intervention created a significant countermovement in Washington. Central to this was the economically and culturally conservative Tea Party. Williamson (2012) has claimed that what mobilized this suddenly powerful movement was austerity. Austerity, a form of "free market extremism," brought together an economic elite and a grassroots movement that wanted to reshape the U.S. government along radical libertarian lines. Although this coalition lacked the power to implement this agenda, Williamson (2012, p. 16) claims the strategic political gridlock they constructed has enabled this movement to implement austerity in the absence of lawmaking: "Despite a limited appeal among the general public, this energetic minority's policy of obstructionism has reversed the policy response to economic downturn, turning the agenda from stimulating government spending to deficit-cutting."

The right-wing political strategies carried out in Washington have been paired with austerity implemented at the lower rungs of the American federal system. In the 2008 fiscal year, General Fund spending across state governments was $687 billion. This dropped to $623 billion in 2010, before rising to pre-2008 levels in 2013 (NASBO, 2014). After sharp declines between 2007 and 2010, state governments have seen small year on year increases in spending from 2010 onward. However, these budget increases are smaller than prerecession levels and are not large enough to match rising health care (Medicaid) and (higher) education costs (ibid.). The National Association of State Budget Offices (ibid, p. 5) summarizes the current situation in the following way: "Since the end of the recession, states have successfully transitioned to a sustained period of fiscal rebuilding, but progress remains slow."

The fiscal situation has been more strained at the local level. In 2012, the National League of Cities (2012) reported that U.S. cities had experienced their sixth year of declining revenues. As a corollary, they had implemented six years of personnel cuts, service withdrawals, and infrastructure delays. These fiscal pressures came from "declining local tax bases, infrastructure costs, employee-related costs for health care, pensions, and wages and cuts in state and federal aid" (ibid, p. 1). Thanks in large part to federal stimulus funds, city revenues have only significantly declined since 2010, falling on average 3.6 percent; the largest yearly decline in decades. In 2011, revenues again shrunk, this time by 2.3 percent. Expenditures were being cut from by 4.2 percent in 2010 and 4 percent in 2011. The National League of Cities (ibid, p. 9) concluded their fiscal report with the following forecast: "Facing revenue and spending pressures, cities are likely to continue to operate with reduced workforces, cut services and infrastructure investment, and draw down ending balances in order to balance budgets."

American austerity has therefore been constructed at the federal level, through inaction and gridlock, and at the state and local level through enforced budget balancing and an absence of federal support. Due to this particular combination of political responses to the Great Recession, austerity in the United States has been highly variegated and somewhat uncoordinated (Ross et al., 2014). This should not come as a surprise. Nor should it raise an eyebrow that there has been no single, top-down budget restructuring solution to aid those cities most adversely affected. In a country characterized by a highly decentralized and uncoordinated financial and governmental system in which cities have increasingly had to rely on debt-based financing models, the response at the federal level has been to manufacture a context in which municipalities are required to be self-financing.

The Chapters

The contributions illustrate and explain the particular form of austerity that has been implemented across the United States. The impacts and social costs are dramatic and are set to become even greater as the magnitude and compounding effects of state withdrawal become evident. In order to trace out the particularities of U.S. austerity, the collection is organized about three themes: austerity-led statecraft, austerity-led public service reform, and austerity-led subject remaking. Placed alongside one another, these themes demonstrate that what is happening in U.S. cities is more than just austere fiscal management. Rather, we are witnessing a general assault on the public sector (and by invocation, notions of "the public" in the U.S.) and an attempt to erase the remaining vestiges of collective consumption in U.S. cities. Economic crisis in the form of the Great Recession has therefore been used as a strategic opportunity, with austerity being an excuse and cover to implement radically antistate programs of the sort that those on the right of the political spectrum could only dream a decade ago.

The collection turns first to what we might think of as *austerity-statecraft*. That is, the myriad of ways in which different levels and functions of the U.S. state have gone about restructuring what they do. The origins of this tendency are often hard to isolate and to name. They are always multiple and nonlinear, however. Sometimes the impulse or the requirement to "restructure" appears to stem from without, such as thorough federal budget cuts or through the work done by right-wing think tanks, such as the American Legislative Exchange Council (ALEC) and the Manhattan Institute. In other cases, the origins appear to be closer to home, from within, perhaps as a result of a change in elected officials. Most common, however, is that any "restructuring" occurs through a combination of internal and external changes that are mutually constitutive and reinforcing, leading to the emergence of a both a quantitatively and a qualitatively different type of state. This is one that Peck (2014, p. 18) rather playfully has labeled a "night watch-man state." In this a growing proportion of functions and services are either no longer delivered or are delivered by community or private sector providers while the state manages at a distance through a variety of performance indicators, in a form of contractual capitalism. The restructuring also involves changes in the way the internal architecture of the state is organized, with new departments and units formed through the dismantling and reconfiguration of structures. Markets for new products and services are manufactured through the restructuring, of course.

Nowhere is this tendency clearer than in the way the state has both been remade and remade itself in Detroit. One example of this is its role in speculating on sports-led redevelopment as a means of kickstarting the city's economy. L. Owen Kirkpatrick and Chalem Bolton (chapter 2) document the historic role the physical infrastructure around "sport" has played in Detroit. They highlight the ways in which even under the most extreme forms of austerity the state has found new ways to work with others to speculate on growth. Through both the Detroit Economic Growth Corporation (DEGC) and the Downtown Development Authority (DDA), and the use of financial vehicles such as Tax Increment Financing (TIF) to generate and capture "value," the city government has been indulging in financial experimentation. While the use of debt-based financial models is not entirely without precedent in Detroit, and across the United States more general (Johnson & Mann, 2001; Sbragia, 1996; Weber, 2002), the impetus for the more recent examples stems from more conventional municipal financing structures being rendered untenable due to the city's bankruptcy. Using the proposed Red Wings arena development, Kirkpatrick and Bolton detail the various ways in which the state has recrafted its involvement with a variety of representatives of local, national, and international capital in the name of redeveloping the center of Detroit.

Similar processes are at work in San Jose. Sara Hinkley (chapter 3) notes that the city was one of a number whose financial position was worsened by the California-wide abolition of Redevelopment Agencies (RDAs), and the associated inability to use Tax Increment Financing (TIF). These examples of how city governments around the state reworked their internal structures to involve themselves in debt-based financing models allowed the bypassing of Proposition 13 and the requirement for a two-thirds vote majority in local elections for special taxes to be increased. Institutionally, RDAs involved the establishing of arms-length agencies that oversaw the establishment of Tax Increment Financing (TIF) districts or projects. This resonates with the work of Caroline Sage Ponder (chapter 4). She draws out the way in which the construction and regulation of the environment has involved a dangerous intersection of austerity and local state environmental responsibility. With the latter ramping up, sometimes dramatically, municipal governments have been forced to choose between risky financial deals and the health of citizens.

Second, the collection turns what we refer to as *austerity-led public service reform*, which is evident across a range of policy areas, from crime to employment, housing to transport. This aspect of U.S. urban austerity has been driven by a prioritization of budget balancing over welfare provisioning. As such, this element of austerity has often been a focus of right-wing proponents, whereby the remaining "excesses" of city government have become the subject of reform agendas (e.g., Greenhut, 2012). For most U.S. cities, police and fire services make up the major public service expenditure items, and in austere times unprecedented cutbacks and reforms have been made to these staple services. In bankrupt Vallejo, California, reductions in police and fire services left parts of the city without services (York, 2009). Elsewhere in financially strained cities such as Foley, Minnesota (Fitzgerald, 2011), and Sharpstown, Texas (Lomax, 2015), governing councils have adopted privatized, contracted police forces as a cheaper public safety option. Austerity is therefore transforming the ways in which public services are delivered and the relationships that public servants have with the citizenry.

In Kathe Newman's (chapter 6) contribution, she explores how affordable housing provisioning is being undertaken in New York City under conditions of austerity. By tracing out the history of inclusionary zoning within prosperous New York City, Newman is able to demonstrate the contemporary particularities of housing provisioning. Under

Mayor di Blasio, ambitious affordable housing targets have been set, but the predominant mechanism of provisioning—inclusionary zoning—has remained. In this case study, the limits of the neoliberal state to supply public services under conditions of austerity are clearly illustrated.

A further exploration of housing-related public services is offered by Dan Hammel and Xueying Chen. Their chapter examines mortgage lending and homeownership in Toledo, Ohio, and explains how public service reform has itself been privatized. They point toward the ways in which social welfare spending has been withdrawn from neighborhoods of disadvantage and color through a pervasive set of austerity-inducing government regulations. Hammel and Chen therefore demonstrate a core tension within current public service reform, where the enactment of government regulation is creating behavior in the private market that creates austerity. Direct public service reform (i.e., the withdrawal of public services) is therefore being accompanied by more opaque forms of reform, both of which appear to have socially regressive impacts across the urban landscape.

Third, and finally, the collection highlights what we term *austerity-led subject making*. Alongside changing state forms and practices, austerity reforms have also been responsible for changing the ways in which the state is relating to its citizens. Here we are situating austerity reforms within a long-standing reconfiguration of governance practices. Over the past eight years, it is clear that austerity has demanded that many city residents take a different role within their municipality. For example, the withdrawal of state services, such as library services, community drop-ins, and welfare support, has demanded that citizens act individually and collectively in the ways necessary to recreate their urban community.

In his chapter Aaron Niznik examines changing patterns of residential mobility in recessionary Providence, Rhode Island. As a city hit particularly hard by economic downturn, Providence has suffered significant economic and political restructuring. As a part of this, residential neighborhoods have been reorganized as a concomitant effect of financial crisis being pushed down to the urban level. Niznik finds that in Providence, it has been certain parts of the urban populace who have paid the most significant price in terms of austerity reforms. With high rates of residential mobility brought on by economic necessity, Providence's

Hispanic community has seen their neighborhood-based relations dramatically changed. In the context of social welfare reductions, Niznik points toward the deepening poverty that disadvantaged groups now experience in the state capital of Rhode Island.

We end this introduction by returning to where we started: Jefferson County, Alabama. For families struggling in Jefferson, they now face years of steep rate increases which will threaten their livelihoods. Between 2014 and 2018, sewer rates will increase 7.9 percent every year, and by 3.5 percent until 2053. This is in addition to a 329 percent 1997–2008 increase in rates that was instigated by the capital program required to comply with an EPA decree to clean up the Cahaba River (Braun, 2013). Jefferson therefore provides a warning sign of the pernicious feedback loop that may emerge from U.S. urban austerity. It is now some ten years since the first home foreclosures started to spook mortgage investors. As the resulting economic downturn pushed many people in marginal forms of employment into Social Security offices, putting food on the table became more important than making monthly mortgage payments. Houses were then repossessed by banks. At the same time the process of shrinking the social state began. As austerity pushes more and more of the costs of economic crisis onto the most vulnerable populations in places like Jefferson and Providence, the likelihood of people choosing between rent payments and grocery bills becomes ever greater.

The stories of decline in Jefferson and Providence have been repeated across the United States. Many cities have seen whole neighborhoods slip into decline as local tax bases have shrunk. Credit ratings were consequently reassessed, increasing the cost of borrowing in the bond market. Meanwhile, city governments saw federal and state budgets cut as the federal government reinterpreted the financial crisis as a crisis of the state. Yet since this national program of austerity has been rolled out within a federalist system and across a highly uneven landscape, it cannot be characterized as a national program. Rather it was a program that was geographically uneven in its design, delivery, and impact. Cities were on the front line. Yet within cities this geography was the mirror image of the geography of who had done best out of the economic growth of the 2000s.

Austerity and the Spectacle

*Urban Triage and Post-Political
Development in Detroit*

L. OWEN KIRKPATRICK AND CHALEM BOLTON

On July 18, 2013, the city of Detroit entered Chapter 9 bankruptcy, the largest municipal filing in U.S. history. Struggles over the city's assets and liabilities were formally adjudicated by way of a state-appointed emergency manager (EM) and the U.S. Bankruptcy Court of the Eastern District of Michigan, but the "grand bargain" struck between the city, its creditors, and private foundations was shaped as much by the logic of urban austerity as by judicial precedent or legal statute. Even in the financial and political confusion of large-scale municipal bankruptcy, one thing was always clear: there would be no fiscal lifeline extended to the "Motor City" from higher scales of government. While federal officials had proven quite willing to bail out financial and corporate entities deemed "too big to fail," the city of Detroit received a firmer, less forgiving hand.

Such is the nature of fiscal austerity: a low-expenditure, "lean" model of governance that prioritizes a good business climate and financial confidence. The austerity measures adopted by federal and state governments generate social and fiscal pressures that filter down to the scale of the urban. U.S. cities exist at the low end of the fiscal totem pole—"the scale at which the neoliberal buck-passing ultimately has to stop" (Peck, 2012, p. 630). Hemmed in by state constitutional debt limitations and lacking the ability to run year-over-year deficits, hard-hit cities, in turn, seem to have little choice but to offload the costs of austerity onto the backs of urban communities via public sector rollbacks and retrenchment. Taken together, these measures and the narratives and ideologies that undergird them constitute "austerity urbanism" (ibid.; Davidson & Ward, 2014; Tonkiss, 2013).

In Detroit, austerity has asserted itself in often clear and nonnegotiable terms. In an effort to run the city in the manner of a business enterprise, the emergency manager and his allies undertook the painful process of municipal "right-sizing": public assets were privatized, public services slashed, and public infrastructure networks dismantled and partially decommissioned. But austerity has not been consistently enforced across the city. As Detroit residents wrestled with the effects of municipal bankruptcy it was publicly revealed that city officials were in negotiations with the local professional hockey team, the Detroit Red Wings. Those talks would result in plans for a new $450 million arena for the privately owned team, with the city paying nearly 60 percent of the upfront construction costs ($262 million). The public pricetag for the project climbs to roughly a half-billion dollars when including interest and fees paid on the bonds used to finance the subsidy, as well as the various infrastructure improvements and service amenities included as "deal sweeteners."

On the surface, Detroit's recovery strategy seems puzzling. On one hand, agents of austerity decry profligate spending and jealously guard the public purse, as in the case of pension and health care retrenchment and the dismantling of social services and public infrastructures. On the other hand, however, those same agents are also likely to support extravagant stadium-based redevelopment schemes that hinge on massive public subsidies for the billionaire owners of professional sports teams. In Detroit, the development of spectacular—and spectacularly expensive—downtown spaces has proven immune to even the most extreme socioeconomic and fiscal crises. Nor has public stadium funding been circumscribed by the austerity measures otherwise being enforced in and by the city.

The Red Wings deal begins to look less puzzling when we explicitly acknowledge that austerity must adapt to local conditions of development. The austerity agenda must find a way to coexist with the development agenda at the scale of the urban. Ultimately, austerity seeks to increase economic competitiveness, which for cities is largely achieved via development. Even under conditions of extreme and vigorously enforced austerity, cities are compelled to compete with other cities for mobile capital—whether in the form of the locational decisions of firms and employees or the tourism and entertainment decisions of families. Over the past twenty years, Detroit has tended to emphasize the latter, crafting a redevelopment strategy largely centered on the spectacle of professional sports; the new Red Wings arena will join a heavily subsidized football stadium (opened in 2002) and a heavily subsidized baseball stadium (opened in 2000) in downtown Detroit. The city is not anomalous in this regard. In the context of industrial decline, cities have embraced the promotion of leisure, entertainment, and tourism in their pursuit of growth. This is a strategy that hinges on the mobilization of the spectacle (Harvey, 1989b, pp. 88–92), the "controlled visual production" of fully commercialized, image-mediated spaces and experiences: cultural events, visitor attractions, retail exhibitions, and various "public events, [and] high-profile extravaganzas" (Gotham, 2005, p. 227).

Considered in the abstract, the extravagant municipal (and state) subsidies needed to prop up spectacle-based development projects should run afoul of the market discipline preached by the advocates of austerity. As a practical matter, however, urban austerity and the spectacle can coexist if certain conditions are met. Two such conditions appear to be especially important in the Detroit case. First, in the context of urban austerity, decisions regarding public subsidies for spectacle-based development must be able to circumvent traditional democratic channels. Over the years, as city budgets tightened and voters grew more skeptical of publicly funding private megaprojects, urban growth coalitions became more adept at de-democratizing the development process. Today, large-scale development in U.S. cities is largely governed and financed through an array of pseudo-public agencies and extrabudgetary mechanisms. In Detroit, spectacle-based development is governed through the city's Downtown Development Authority and funded by way of tax increment financing—a pair of quasi-public development tools used to avoid both the possibility of electoral defeat and the additional costs and constraints posed by democratic oversight. The ability to evade formal democratic checks is especially important in the context of austerity, when municipal budgets are at their tightest and public appetite for debt is at its lowest.

Second, city officials must be willing to sacrifice vulnerable populations and neighborhoods so that scarce municipal resources can be diverted to downtown development efforts. In the context of fiscal austerity, the social opportunity costs associated with megaproject development are heightened. This process has a spatial component that is most clearly observed in shrinking and distressed cities, where neighborhoods outside of the central business district are often starved of development capital. In Detroit, the sociospatial price of austerity is exacted via urban triage—a model of urban planning and (de)development based on the targeted withdrawal of public infrastructure networks and service systems from the poorest, least "viable" neighborhoods of the city (Kirkpatrick, 2015). Municipal resources pulled from neighborhoods deemed nonviable are subsequently redirected into the downtown and other areas still deemed worthy of public investment. Finally, due to low property demand in Detroit, large stakeholders have been able to amass the "empty" and abandoned downtown properties that will comprise the physical footprint of the massive project—further concentrating the social, spatial, and economic benefits of the city's targeted development strategy.

The following analysis of the Red Wings project explores the tensions between the urban austerity agenda and the urban development agenda, and highlights the ways in which these tensions can be overcome. On one hand, organizations not subject to traditional forms of democratic oversight and control now spearhead downtown development. Unconstrained by the rhetoric or reality of urban austerity, this "shadow government"—and the off-budget funding streams it controls—is free to pursue an entertainment- and tourism-based strategy that culminates in spectacular and monumental spaces of consumption. On the other hand, formal municipal agencies *are* constrained by austerity. It is precisely these constraints that have led local officials to adopt the triage tactics whereby scarce municipal resources are directed away from the city's most needy neighborhoods, and toward more promising areas. Before turning to the Red Wings case, however, we begin with an overview of the relevant literatures.

Urban Austerity, Publicly Financed Stadiums, and the Spectacle

Three bodies of research orient our analysis. The first is a burgeoning literature that critically interrogates austerity urbanism in the context of advanced neoliberalism (Peck, 2012). A second body of research, concerned with the public (fiscal) costs of private stadium construction, is nearly unanimous in its criticism of stadium subsidies (Long, 2013).[1] Considered in tandem, these literatures highlight the puzzle with which we began: agents of austerity demand fiscal restraint, and research unanimously warns against public subsidies for megaprojects, yet cities continue to provide generous supply-side subsidies for downtown development. A third literature on "the spectacle" begins to shed light on the situation. Apart from obvious fiscal tensions, urban austerity has certain structural affinities with spectacle-based development. These affinities help explain the persistence of lavish downtown spectacles in austere cities.

Urban Austerity

The term *austerity* reentered the public consciousness in the aftermath of the global financial crisis of 2008. The immediate reaction of most national governments to global recession was a combination of bailouts, massive stimulus spending, tax cuts, and ambitious new plans for regulatory intervention. But talk of a Keynesian revival was short-lived (Callinicos, 2012). With profit rates and financial markets stabilizing in the latter half of 2009, and "[w]ith the sense of having avoided the worst," political attention was redirected "from the reform of the financial system to the adjustment of public accounts" (Calcagno, 2012 p. 25). By 2010, from the perspective of deficit hawks, stimulus spending had pushed public debt to unacceptable levels and central governments needed to radically change course. Loss of competitiveness, capital flight, hyperinflation, and insolvency were frequently cited as likely outcomes of stimulus spending. For such commentators, the prescription was and remains fiscal austerity: a "voluntary deflation" achieved via the aggressive contraction of public "budgets, debts, and deficits" that will increase competitiveness and buoy "business confidence" (Blyth, 2013a). Advocates of austerity prefer low-tax, low-expenditure strategies due to their emphasis on achieving a (more) favorable business climate. From this perspective, growth can only properly be achieved through retrenchment. Others argue that contractionary policies (expenditure cuts, deficit reduction, and other forms of "fiscal consolidation") have direct expansionary effects over both short- and long-term time horizons (Alesina & Ardagna, 2009; Reinhart & Rogoff, 2010).

Despite the popularity of such claims, austerity policies have come under increased scrutiny. The International Monetary Fund (IMF), for instance, long a purveyor of antigovernment "structural adjustments," is now openly questioning the short-term wisdom of austerity (Baker, 2010; Piscatory et al., 2011). Others have identified methodological flaws in research supporting its long-term expansionary benefits (Krugman, 2013). At the same time, austerity has become a matter of widespread public concern, and social movements across the world have called on central governments to abandon austerity policies (Mayer, 2013; Walton, 1998). The simple, self-contained logic of fiscal austerity (i.e., spend less than you make) has a certain intuitive political appeal, but only in the highly idealized abstract (Blyth, 2013b, p. 42). In reality, austerity generates all manner of sociopolitical conflicts and contradictions, is unevenly enforced, and is regularly contested, appropriated, and mutated. This is especially true on the urban scale.

To begin, austerity entails the devolution of the risks and respon-sibilities associated with local economic competitiveness. Whereas, under conditions of Keynesianism, cities could rely on intergovernmental aid to assist in their development efforts (and could turn to state and federal agencies if such efforts failed), they must now bear all of the risks and responsibilities associated with local growth strategies. There are several important implications of this shift. First, a pivotal tension derives from the fact that austerity-enforced fiscal discipline does not, in or by itself, generate economic growth or lead to the "reinvigoration of private enterprise." This observation triggers the "awkward" realization "that the state and the market do not exist in a zero-sum relationship" (Peck, 2012, p. 629). Ultimately, therefore, urban austerity is never a purely negative, detractive force, focused exclusively on retrenchment and contraction; it is also a positive, fecund force that creates new development opportunities and produces new urban spaces. As Peck notes, " 'rollback' moments of deregulation, dismantling, deconstruction, and downsizing yield market failures and a host of negative externalities, prompting ostensibly corrective, 'rollout' responses in the form of experimental governance, pro-market reregulation, and all manner of short-term fixes, bandaids and bromides—complete with their own limits and contradictions" (ibid., p. 630).

Second, the devolution of risks and responsibilities to the local scale exacerbates patterns of uneven development on both inter- and intraurban levels. On one hand, cities must "develop or default" under conditions of austerity (ibid., p. 647), leading to a fierce interurban struggle for survival (framed in Darwinian terms by some austerity advocates; Peck, 2013, p. 37). Cities well positioned in the global economy become "the beneficiaries of selective public investment and regionalized economic growth" and thus largely escape the worst of austerity's bite, while declining and fiscally distressed cities must bear its brunt (Peck, 2012, p. 647). On the other hand, this form of "winner-takes-all urbanism" is also reflected within cities, as limited development resources tend to bypass marginalized populations and neighborhoods, concentrating instead in privileged urban spaces, where their "rollout" can take spectacular forms. As Peck argues, austerity subjects cities to a particularly intense form of creative destruction, in which "the destructive moment"—as well as the creative moment—is "amplif[ied]" (ibid., p. 631). In shrinking cities such as Detroit, the "destructive moment" is spatially expressed and enforced through (inter alia) the process of municipal "right-sizing," a strategy premised on the sociospatial elimination of poor and sparsely populated neighborhoods (Hackworth, 2015; Kirkpatrick, 2015).

Third, the downloading of risks and responsibilities to the level of the city is an imperative that cannot be effectively resisted through local democratic channels. Urban austerity and the substantial sacrifices it demands are presented as technical necessities, not political choices. "The grip of fiscal technopolitics appears to be tightening," observes Peck. "This is leading to the further 'automation' of restrictive fiscal regimes of governance, insulating local financial decision-making not only from protest politics but from the formal political arena itself" (Peck, 2013, p. 40). There are two types of mechanisms that can be used to evade the political resistance and discontent generated by the localized rollback and rollout of urban austerity measures. The first type of evasive mechanism consists of the many pseudo-public organizations and agencies that play a pivotal role in contemporary modes of urban governance and development, such as redevelopment authorities and special districts. Though they enjoy many of the powers of traditional municipal government (such as taxing authority), these hybrid entities exist largely outside the traditional system of local democratic control and oversight. This type of mechanism is broadly used and highly normalized across U.S. cities (Kirkpatrick & Smith, 2011). The second way in which austerity measures can be implemented in the face of democratic opposition involves methods of local emergency management. In this scenario, local democratic norms and processes are suspended while some extrademocratic entity (e.g., fiscal control board, emergency manager, etc.) steps in to make the "tough decisions" that elected officials may not be willing to make. This type of mechanism is relatively rare and is deployed in a highly targeted fashion (Anderson, 2012).

Localizing the causes of and responses to crisis is an important part of the rhetoric of austerity because it points to fiscal discipline and political dispossession as being the natural and necessary response to fiscal profligacy—the irresponsibility, corruption, and incompetence that bedevil large municipal bureaucracies, bloated unions, and inner city communities dependent on the state. This is not incidental, as a key objective of austerity is the sharp retrenchment of the social safety net, the beneficiaries of which tend to be concentrated in struggling central cities. "[Austerity] isn't really about debt and deficits at all," argues Krugman, "it's about using deficit panic as an excuse to dismantle social programs" (quoted in Peck, 2012, p. 628). Austerity has a disciplinary edge, as past sins and "perversities" are deemed offenses that require atonement (Peck, 2015; Somers & Block, 2005). By and large, however, those subject to austerity measures are not grateful for this redemptive opportunity. Because urban austerity entails the reduction of social services, the rollback of public benefits, and the targeted "rightsizing" of public infrastructure networks, it is invariably met with resistance and protest. But this is not the entire story. As the city exacts painful concessions from local residents, it also provides generous incentives to the likes of sports team owners—a process to which we now turn.

The Publicly Funded Stadium

If public stadium subsidies were a good municipal investment—if they spurred growth, or increased tax revenues, or otherwise contributed to the collective good—then we would not have to puzzle over their popularity; subsidizing megaprojects would be seen as sound fiscal strategy, even (or especially) under austere conditions. With respect to the fiscal impacts of public stadium financing, however, research overwhelmingly indicates the opposite: that public stadium subsidies are, to a greater or lesser extent, a fiscal boondoggle. We begin our overview of the literature with a brief history of stadium development in the United States (Long, 2013, pp. 32–38).

The first phase of stadium development in U.S. cities (1910s–30s) consisted of fledgling sports franchises playing in simple structures owned by the teams themselves (ibid., p. 32). In the second phase (1940s–70s), teams took advantage of the postwar boom by building larger facilities, but did so in the suburbs, as team owners "followed their audiences" away from the central city. Owners were undercapitalized, but suburban communities were eager to pick up the slack; through the 1960s–70s, "[suburban] voters consistently approved bond issues to pay for the full cost of new . . . facilities." The third stage (1980s–90s) saw the value of sports teams skyrocket, largely on the basis of television broadcasting revenues, but local governments were "less willing to foot the bill for new facilities" (ibid., p. 35). It is during this period that public-private partnerships (PPP) emerged as the preferred mechanism for stadium construction along with an explicit economic rationale (the shared benefits of growth) that justified the shared costs. By the turn of the century, however, a "plethora of cost-benefit analyses [had] convincingly concluded that sports facilities are in fact poor public investments." In the current phase (2000–present), and despite the fact that researchers remain virtually unanimous in their criticism of the practice, "cities continue to allocate substantial public funds toward [stadium] development, as if in ignorance of, or disagreement with, this collective wisdom" (ibid., p. 4.).

One reason for the persistence of this debunked tactic is that the promise of jobs and economic growth, no matter how tenuous or inflated, is a siren song in times of contraction and austerity (Baade & Dye, 1988, p. 266). Supporters point to the jobs that are generated as evidence of the intrinsic value of stadium development, but critics note that the well-paying jobs tend to be temporary (construction-related), while the permanent jobs tend to be low-paying, part-time, and seasonal (service-related). Industry boosters also claim that the presence of a professional sports franchise generates economic growth by way of positive externalities, whereby a new stadium "increase[s] an area's aggregate income by generating increased spending on lodging, meals, and other travel and entertainment" that accrues to the broader urban economy. But other studies have found that the construction of sports facilities "fail to increase income" in the area, while others "even find a negative impact on income" (Coates & Humphreys, 2000; Groothuis et al., 2004). Despite the preponderance of evidence, however, local officials continue to see new stadium construction as one of the best available tools for stimulating economic growth.

Just as the promised benefits of new stadium construction are commonly overestimated, so too are its costs commonly underestimated. Long's analysis of the 121 professional sports facilities in the United States demonstrates the point (2013, pp. 81–85). The average stadium in 2010 cost $353 million to build. As traditionally calculated, $170 million (48%) of the cost was paid by the public. But these figures exclude public costs related to land, infrastructure, net annual costs, and forgone property taxes. When these factors are included, the public's share soars to almost $260 million per facility. As Long notes, the adjusted figures "suggests that public-private partnerships for major league sports facilities are more accurately portrayed as uneven partnerships, with public partners paying 78% of total costs on average" (ibid). The revised figures allow us to better assess the opportunity costs associated with stadium-based development—the potentially higher returns on other types of public spending ("maintaining local infrastructure; increasing the quality or provision of public health, safety, or education; and attracting new businesses") that are displaced by stadium subsidies (Coates & Humphreys, 2000, p.19).

By the turn of the century, it appeared that the warnings and admonitions of "academics, public policy analysts, taxpayers, and some politicians" were finally slowing the onslaught of public stadium construction (Long, 2013, p. 37). And yet, while subsidies were becoming less likely to win voter approval, stadium construction remained strong in the 2000s.[2] Electoral repudiation proved ineffective in limiting the practice. As our case study demonstrates, this can be traced to the fact that stadium proponents were becoming more adept at evading traditional democratic channels. By the 1990s, scholars were noting an explosion of "hybrid, quasi-public mechanisms that could be used to bypass electoral controls, legislative hurdles, and constitutional debt limitations" for the purposes of large-scale development projects (Kirkpatrick & Smith, 2011, p. 481). These projects were increasingly designed according to the logic of the spectacle.

The Urban Spectacle

Several factors can help explain the persistent popularity of public stadium subsidies, despite the fact that their promised benefits have proven largely illusory and their public costs much higher than conventionally acknowledged. Some research points to supply-side factors, such as the monopoly power enjoyed by franchise owners due to the limited number of professional sports teams, which makes threats of relocation credible (Baade & Dye, 1988, p. 266; Long, 2013, p. 5). This both enhances the value of league properties and allows team owners to extract "sweetheart deals" from local officials (Coates & Humphreys, 2000). Such deals need also be understood in terms of the entrepreneurial functions of contemporary cities. Squeezed by economic contraction, interurban competition, and the cessation of federal and state aid, cities have become more enterprising, "focusing on investment and . . . the speculative development of place rather than the amelioration of conditions within a particular territory" (Harvey 1989a, p. 8). With cities adopting a more entrepreneurial stance in the 1970s, and with traditional manufacturing industries vacating central urban areas, officials trained their sights on the "popular culture" consumer economy, "broadly understood to include . . . sport, tourism, leisure, entertainment and retailing" (Roche & France, quoted in Bélanger, 2009, p. 51).

In their promotion of leisure and entertainment, cities have turned to the "mobilization of the spectacle": the precise orchestration of images, commodities, and consumers in monumental venues and phantasmagorical spaces of consumption. The spectacle leaves a particular imprint on the urban built environment. In the nineteenth-century city, spectacular spaces took the form of arcades, department stores, and exhibitions (Benjamin, 1969; Kohn, 2008, p. 476). Today, the urban spectacle takes the form of "multi-megaplexes of shopping and entertainment, theme parks, theme restaurants, arenas and stadiums" (Bélanger, 2009, p. 57), as well as tourist resorts, redeveloped waterfronts, trade expositions, festival markets, and the like (Gotham, 2005, p. 227). This type of spectacle-based development is highly compatible with urban entrepreneurialism. Cities seek to fuel growth and gain a competitive advantage via the speculative development of ever grander and more monumental megaprojects.

Counterintuitively, perhaps, spectacle-based development is also compatible with urban austerity. This is true in several key respects. To begin, there is a certain affinity between urban austerity and the spectacle at the level of circumstance. Cities subjected to an austerity regime are not suddenly rendered immune to the competitive pressures that fuel stadium construction. Neither does austerity necessarily force cities to adopt more cost-effective, fiscally conservative development strategies. Rather, austere cities may remain so deeply enmeshed in the system of interlocal competition and so entrenched in patterns of spectacle-based development that alternatives can be hard to imagine, let alone implement. Second, there also exists a deeper functional affinity between the two agendas. As Jamie Peck observes, the purveyors of urban austerity are proficient in "deficit politics," whereby long-term fiscal obligations serve to reinforce the necessity and unavoidability of current austerity measures. From their perspective, big-ticket stadiums and other spectacle-based development projects may provide an important latent function by creating fiscal scarcity (or the impression thereof), which in turn "set[s] the stage for 'starve the beast' tactics" in other parts of the city (Peck, 2012, p. 631).

Third, both urban austerity and spectacle-based development seek to maximize the economic competitiveness of cities. Maximizing a city's competitive advantage via the strategic deployment of the spectacle entails several steps. To begin, cities must re-engineer otherwise disparate social spaces for the optimal celebration of consumer goods and the maximal elevation of the act of consumption. As critics note, however, this tends to create aesthetically similar environments.[3] Spectacle-based development creates urban spaces that are similarly designed and commercially fungible, thus negating the historical, cultural, and geographical uniqueness of urban communities (Bélanger, 2009, p. 52). In addition to "visual coherence," the spectacle also "imposes a frame of meaning on the city" (Zukin, 1995, p. 53). By definition, the existing frame—unique, idiosyncratic, restive—is never suitable for complete commodification. Spectacular urban development "carefully selects a particular vision of the city's history and then imposes this vision as a unifying theme . . . [in] key city spaces" (Bélanger, 2009, p. 53). This new sense of place is "sanitized" and made safe for purposes of consumption: an "urban imaginary stripped of all references to any counter-narratives that might be told from the perspective of workers, residents and marginalized minorities" (ibid). The sanitized urban spectacle is prototypically embodied in the modern-day theme park, a total and totalizing sociocognitive form based on a profound "visual and spatial reorganization of public culture" (Zukin, 1995, p. 53).

Lastly, both urban austerity and the urban spectacle can have important depoliticizing effects. According to Guy Debord (1970), the spectacle gives the appearance of freedom by presenting a range of acceptable beliefs, products, and actions to choose from, while in reality producing profound political passivity. Collective action is impossible because the spectacle organizes individuals around a common object (commodity or experience) rather than authentic social interaction (Gotham & Krier, 2008). In the context of the spectacle, image and discourse are consumed rather than co-created; "Spectators are linked only by a one-way relationship to the very center that maintains their isolation from one another" (Debord, 1970, p. 22). More recently, analysts have emphasized the synergy between the spectacle and technologies of surveillance and control, such as those found in the "security complex" surrounding international mega-events (Boyle & Haggerty, 2009). A key characteristic of spectacular urban space, notes Sorkin, "is its obsession with 'security,' with rising levels of manipulation and surveillance over its citizenry and with a proliferation of new modes of segregation" (1992, p. xiii), all of which thwart subversion, disruption, and protest. But this is not to say that sociopolitical alternatives are impossible to conceive or pursue within the carefully commodified confines of the spectacle.[4] There exists a theoretical capacity for authentic communication and "meaningful social resistance" in the context of urban spectacle (Merrifield, 2013, p. 79), but the extent to which this capacity can be realized largely depends on local political economic variables. It is, thus, to the Detroit case that we now turn our attention.

The Red Wings Arena and Entertainment District

Ice hockey has deep roots in Detroit. The National Hockey League (NHL) was founded in 1917 and Detroit joined the league in 1926, becoming one of the "Original Six" teams that survived wartime contraction in 1942. Pizza magnate Mike Ilitch (1929–2017) bought the team in 1982 for $8 million, and thirty years later it was valued at $470 million (Bradley, 2014). In part, this appreciation can be traced to the stadium that came with the deal, Joe Louis Arena. In 1979, Detroit (aka Hockeytown) constructed the riverfront arena (and attendant parking garage) in a frantic effort to keep the team from moving to suburban Pontiac. Ilitch thus inherited a brand-new hockey arena, a team-friendly lease, and no stadium-related debt when he purchased the franchise. Nevertheless, team officials began publicly exploring new downtown stadium opportunities in the early 1990s (Felton, 2014a), efforts that would finally gain traction two decades later as Ilitch used the expiration of the arena lease and the city's growing post-crisis desperation as leverage for a new deal. Ground was broken for the project in late 2014 and the 18,000-seat arena and surrounding entertainment district opened for the 2017–18 season.

The following case study is organized around three key dimensions of the Detroit Red Wings project. To begin, we consider (1) the public costs of stadium construction, highlighting the fiscal tension between the exorbitant public price tag for the project and the rhetoric of fiscal discipline associated with urban austerity. We then turn our attention to two important ways this tension is mitigated, including (2) the de-democratization of urban development, and (3) the production of spectacular downtown spaces via a municipal system of triage.

Public Costs

Under conditions of fiscal crisis and austerity, the size and expense of the Red Wings project is especially notable. According to current projections, the new, cutting-edge arena will cost $450 million to construct. But the arena is merely the anchor for a much grander "plan to create a 45-acre district that includes retail, residential, office and restaurant space" (Shea, 2013a). The construction of the entertainment district will require an additional $200 million in upfront costs, putting the total price tag at $650 million. While the financial structure of the project is complex, its basic outline can be summarized as follows. In 2013, the State of Michigan approved the sale of $450 million in thirty-year, tax-exempt private activity bonds to be used to fund arena construction. Detroit's Downtown Development Authority (DDA) will repay $261.5 million of this amount (58%), by way of "captured" property taxes (discussed below). Olympia Development (the real estate development arm of the "Ilitch Empire") will repay the remaining $188.5 million (42%). For the DDA, debt payments will amount to $15.5 million annually, while Olympia Development's annual contribution is pegged at $11.5 million (Shea, 2014b), though repayment schedules will ultimately hinge on market conditions.[5] Of the additional $200 million price tag for the surrounding entertainment district, the DDA will pay $23 million (via additional property tax captures), while $177 million will be paid by private investors (Shea, 2013a). In total, according to current estimates, the new project will cost $650 million—$285 million of which will be paid via property taxes funneled through Detroit's DDA (Aguilar, 2013a).

Moreover, $285 million is more than likely a conservative estimate. First, official projections tend to grow over time, such that we would expect that the total cost of the project, and the public's official share of the total cost, will rise substantially by the time the development is completed and final tallies are taken. For example, when the city decided to build the Detroit Lions a new football stadium in the late 1990s, the initial budget for the project stood at $220 million. By the time of the stadium's completion in 2002, the project's official price tag was $430 million while the public's contribution was 300 percent more than originally estimated (Ankeny, 2003; Barkholz, 1997). Second, even postcompletion, retrospective calculations are systematically underestimated, as factors such as infrastructure costs and forgone property taxes are left out of the cost-benefit equation. For instance, Long's adjusted accounting puts the final, all-inclusive cost of Ford Field at $560 million (Long, 2013, p. 21). The public cost looms even larger when we include interest and fees paid on stadium bonds. In the case of the new Red Wings arena, this will ultimately swell the final public cost to a half-billion dollars.

While the public price tag for the new complex is substantial, the promised rewards are great. For instance, Olympia officials report that the new arena will create 1,100 permanent jobs and $210 million annually in economic activity, up from the six hundred jobs and $125 million generated by Joe Louis Arena (O'Connor, 2012). According to the Detroit Economic Growth Corporation, the arena and entertainment district combined will create a combined 8,300 jobs and have an "estimated economic impact" of $1.8 billion (Van Meek, 2012). Supporters argue that the project will draw sizable private investment to the area, creating jobs while keeping taxes low (O'Connor, 2012). Proponents also emphasize the extreme dereliction of the immediate neighborhood ("Cass Corridor"), reasoning that any development is better than none at all.

Many others are critical of the project and skeptical of the claims made to support it. Some argue, for instance, that the dereliction of Lower Cass Corridor is linked to Ilitch himself, who (at the time of the deal) had collected about half of the property in the area, having acquired the land largely without notice. Much of this land remained effectively abandoned for years (many parcels are used as gravel parking lots on game days), drawing criticism from individuals living and doing business in the area (Aguilar, 2013d). More fundamentally, critics have asked "why . . . the state [was] supplementing the cost of a billionaire's arena while its largest city was plunging into bankruptcy" (Felton, 2014a). While postbankruptcy austerity measures require many residents to make significant sacrifices, the new stadium will greatly increase the value of the Red Wings franchise and further enrich Ilitch—a devilish outcome that can be traced to the financial details of the deal.

In addition to the public funds pledged for arena construction, for instance, there is also the lease to consider.[6] The lease for Joe Louis Arena expired in 2010, at which point the team ceased paying the city for rent and concessions entirely, an amount equaling $6 million per year according to city officials. Ilitch also owed the city as much as $80 million due to a provision in the original lease that granted Detroit 25 percent of cable TV revenues for live events, which the city never received. In 2014, the city council voted 5–4 to approve a "bridge" lease (for 2010–15), which resolved all outstanding disputes, including the missing TV revenues (Nichols, 2014). According to a spokesperson for Detroit's emergency manager (EM), the amount owed would be difficult to determine precisely, thus rendering the claim " 'largely unenforceable.' " Furthermore, a quick settlement " 'clears the way for the construction of a new downtown arena' " (Nowling, quoted in Ferretti, 2014a). In the end, Detroit accepted just $5.17 million to resolve a debt estimated at $50–80 million by policy analysts.

While previous leases primed the franchise for value appreciation, they did not leave the city empty-handed. The new arena lease, by contrast, is remarkably generous. To begin, the city will allow the team to continue to avoid property taxes by retaining ownership of the new arena (Shea, 2013b).[7] Historically, the city could compensate for this revenue loss through rent payments made by the team. Under the terms of the "bridge" lease, for example, the city receives $1 million per year for rent. The lease for the new arena, by contrast, allows the team to "operate the facility rent free" (Felton, 2014a). Second, under the terms of the old Joe Louis lease, Detroit received a share of arena revenues: "10% share of ticket surcharges, 7% of suite sales, a 10% surcharge on concessions, and 5% on souvenir sales, generating anywhere from $2 million to $3 million annually." According to the terms of the lease for the new arena, by contrast, the team will receive "*all the revenues* generated at the arena," including 100 percent of naming rights revenues (Felton, 2014a; emphasis added). Curiously, the city has given the Red Wings its most generous package of subsidies at precisely the moment it can least afford to do so. As austerity urbanism flexes its grip on the municipal budget, squeezing painful concessions from a variety of stakeholders, stadium subsidies appear even more lavish. We can explain this tension via the politics of downtown development.

Stadium Politics

In Detroit, not only did pseudo-public development mechanisms exist, they were aggressively exploited and exacerbated by pro-development forces. To begin, because Detroit's bankruptcy rendered conventional municipal financing structures untenable, Ilitch turned to state lawmakers for help (Felton, 2014a). In 2012, state lawmakers responded by considering a bill that would specifically facilitate the construction of the arena by codifying the political and financial structure of the project (Galleherand & Egan, 2012). Much of the "convoluted" politics of the bill's evolution—nicknamed "Project Puck" by sympathetic lawmakers—took place behind closed doors, and when the state senate considered the bill in December 2012, the contours of the deal were publicly unveiled for the first time. Yet even then, "[n]o location, nor specs of the arena, nor intimate details of the project's funding were given" (Felton, 2014a). Remarkably, despite the fact that substantive details remained largely unknown, public deliberations lasted only thirty-five minutes, before the Senate passed the bill (Public Act 396) by a vote of 27–11 (ibid.). But while the legislative process that reshaped the law is opaque, several of its effects are clear.

Importantly, the bill carved out an enhanced role for Detroit's Downtown Development Authority (DDA). Detroit's share of construction costs is covered through tax increment financing (TIF), which is overseen by its DDA.[8] A TIF is triggered with the creation of a development authority, which establishes a baseline valuation for property tax revenues in the area. In subsequent years, revenues in excess of the baseline are diverted to the issuing authority, to be used for purposes of redevelopment (Pacewicz, 2012; Weber, 2010). The Detroit DDA thus "captures" taxes that would otherwise flow to the city, the local school district, the county, and the state. Detroit's DDA was established in 1978, which sets the area's baseline value at $249 million. In 2013, the taxable value of properties in the downtown district was valued at $587 million. The act of tax capture allows subsidy supporters to claim that revenues are not being diverted from the general fund of host cities. But this is true only in the most formal sense. In 2013, the DDA reduced the tax base by $338 million, while capturing a tax yield of $11 million, over half of which came from Detroit's general fund (CRC, 1996, p. 4; Felton, 2014c).

Public Act 396 enhanced the already sizable fiscal reach of Detroit's DDA by allowing it to capture state school taxes within the greater downtown area. After a long period in which the funds ($13 million in annual tax revenue) had been diverted for other purposes, they were on the brink of being restored to public school funding streams. "For the first time in nearly two decades," noted Senate Minority Leader Gretchen Whitmer, "the property taxes in Detroit were finally going to the right place, the schools" (quoted in O'Connor, 2012). PA 396 re-diverted these funds. Critics howled at the "particularly craven" maneuver (Bradley, 2014), but supporters argued that the capture would cause minimal disruption, as education budgets had grown accustomed to it. Further, state officials had assured the Detroit Public Schools that it would be reimbursed for any reduction in revenues caused by DDA diversions (Shea, 2014a). But in the end, the law's priorities were clear: stadiums and spectacles trump students and schools.

Traditional urban actors and agencies have also played an important role in the arena project. Consider the Detroit City Council. In February 2014, the body voted 6–3 to transfer thirty-seven publicly owned properties to Olympia Development for the price of $1 (Aguilar, 2013e; Aguilar & Ferretti, 2014a). Municipal estimates put the value of the donated land at $2.9 million (Devitt, 2014a), though this is no doubt conservative. By January 2014, a month before the city council would approve the land transfer, arena rumors had sparked a run on properties in and around the proposed district. Developers reported that even blighted and empty parcels were being purchased for millions of dollars (Aguilar, 2014a). The city council took another important step in support of the project when they expanded the DDA's tax-capture zone to include the entirety of the proposed arena and entertainment district. Until it did so, the development would not fall within the boundaries of the DDA and the project could not proceed as planned.

Ilitch proved adept at influencing the arena project through both traditional (city council) and nontraditional (DDA and TIF) channels. This is not to say that communities and their political representatives did not seek to influence the project. For example, retiree and pension-holder organizations fought to pull the DDA and its sizable budget into bankruptcy negotiations, but city and state officials adamantly rejected the notion. Similarly, small business owners have come out against the project, arguing that it gives Ilitch-related enterprises an unfair advantage (Aguilar, 2013b; Aguilar, 2013c). Neighborhood organizations and historical preservationists have also attempted to shape the form and functions of the project. By and large, however, Ilitch managed to evade these efforts.

The case of community benefits agreements (CBAs)—legally binding agreements between a private developer and local community organizations—is indicative of this pattern. In 2013, the Corridors Alliance (a neighborhood organization born in response to the new arena) developed "a list of community benefit requests—simple planning considerations like use of green space and preservation efforts" (Felton, 2014a), and presented it to Olympia Development. But the community's concerns were summarily rebuffed. "They have said they will not sign a Community Benefits Agreement," recounted an Alliance official. "And [they] have been reluctant to meet since we announced that is what we wanted" (Grunow, quoted in ibid.). While the Ilitch camp holds firm in its opposition to CBAs, it has also made certain modest concessions, such as agreeing to a Neighborhood Advisory Committee that would consult with developers on matters such as security, parking, and historic preservation. While supporters touted the measure for giving the community a "voice" (Aguilar & Ferretti, 2014c), its detractors portrayed the committee as a "glorified focus group" with "no oversight or . . . enforcement" capacity (Felton, 2014a).

To its credit, the city council kept pressing for concessions. In late 2014, a council committee made a proposal involving "public gathering spaces, parking limitations and the inclusion of the vacant Park Avenue Hotel in the planned district." According to a city planner, the proposal presented "a number of obstacles" that the developer could not or would not address. Doug Kuiper, a VP at Ilitch Holdings Inc., ominously warned that, " '[the] amendments would jeopardize a transformative project' " (Ferretti, 2014b). The council responded by passing an ordinance that would *require* developers of large projects to engage local communities in the CBA process—a potentially powerful tool for exerting local control over the development process. But state lawmakers responded forcefully, as a House committee quickly approved a proposal that would ban cities "from requiring community benefits agreements for real estate developments" (Livengood, 2014). As one lawmaker explained, the bill would establish a " 'consistent and predictable business environment where people can invest and hire without having to worry about, 'Am I complying with whatever some obscure local requirement might be?' " (Poleski, quoted in ibid.). These efforts culminated in the "Local Government Labor Regulatory Limitation Act" (MI HB 4052), signed into law by Governor Snyder (R) in the summer of 2015. The new law preempts localities on a range of issues related to wages, benefits, and other local requirements that would incur expenses for an employer—thereby nullifying Detroit's CBA ordinance.[9]

The struggle between the city and the state over CBAs demonstrates an important theme. Urban austerity entails the strict enforcement of market discipline, and local communities that buck this expectation are quickly pulled into line. Critics see this discipline as an attack on democratic self-determination. According to state representative Rashida Tlaib (D-Detroit), the law "sets up the state as a dictatorship telling local units of government that they cannot do what is best for their community, workers, and residents" (quoted in Cwiek, 2014b). Further conflicts arise because the agents of austerity do not consistently apply market discipline. Rather, austerity urbanism carves out broad exceptions to market rule in the pursuit of downtown stadium development. This may cause sociopolitical tensions, as when cities impose demand-side austerity measures while simultaneously providing extravagant supply-side subsidies to team owners and stadium developers. Where this occurs, extrademocratic methods of governance and development may be employed to bypass popular and electoral resistance.

Urban Triage and the Downtown Spectacle

The Red Wings' new downtown facility will be a state of the art arena, a phantasmagoria of consumption highlighted by "a soaring glass-covered concourse pulsating with nightclub electricity, where food vendors, restaurants and shops will cater to a high-energy crowd that comes together to celebrate."[10] But Ilitch had much grander ambitions than a mere hockey rink. His vision was of nothing less than a new city-within-a-city that he termed, "The District Detroit." According to promotional materials, "The District Detroit will be 50 blocks of thriving businesses, parks, restaurants, bars and event destinations. It will be . . . where the action is. The District will connect Downtown and Midtown into one contiguous, walkable area, where families, sports fans, entrepreneurs, job seekers, entertainment lovers and others . . . who want to live and work in a tight-knit community within the boundaries of an urban city."

"The District Detroit" will consist of five distinct neighborhoods, "each anchored by world-class venues" such as the Fox Theatre, Masonic Temple, MotorCity Casino Hotel, and Detroit Opera House. Olympia Development describes the five neighborhoods thusly:

1. *Woodward Square*: "[T]he soul of The District Detroit [and] new home [of] the Red Wings . . . this neighborhood will be . . . buzzing every day, all year long as tourists and fun-seekers come together for community, sports and entertainment events."

2. *Wildcat Corner*: Anchored by Comerica Park (Tigers) and Ford Field (Lions), this "neighborhood is home to an authentic experience like few other places in the nation. On game day, [it] morphs into party central. . . . Bars, shops and street vendors [offer] a variety of delights day or night."

3. *Columbia Street*: "Rich with architectural flare [*sic*] and downtown personality, this neighborhood already has . . . the heart of small town Main Street. By day[:] . . . unique shops, boutiques, galleries, and cafes. . . . [After dark:] wine bars, jazz clubs and speakeasies."

4. *Cass Park Village*: "Part entrepreneurial, part punk, this neighborhood . . . will build on the creative energy of nearby Wayne State University . . . to become a hotbed for artists [and] . . . a free-spirited attitude that is not pretentious or flashy."

5. *Columbia Park*: "This neighborhood, once an important industrial center, will become a place to relax and refresh. . . . New offices, retail specialty shops and loft-style condos will surround [a] tree-shaded respite . . . [and] manicured gardens."

If all goes as planned, the new neighborhoods of "The District Detroit" will establish tourism and the sale of themed retail commodities as the economic engines of the area (Gotham, 2002). However, this requires reformatting the localized past into a universal (fully commodifiable) present, scrubbed clean of dangerous and subversive content. As Bélanger observes (2000), in order to create a distinct image in and around new spaces of spectacular consumption, local traditions and histories are reinterpreted to envision business interests as culture bearers while obscuring past political conflicts. The spectacle thus tends to produce "a particular vision of the past, invoking particular nostalgia, not only to legitimate the new arena . . . but more importantly to convince the public to 'let go' of the old one" (2009, p. 55).

For example, the new entertainment district appropriates the term *wildcat* as a pun for the feline-themed sports teams anchoring "Wildcat Corner" (i.e., the Detroit Lions and Detroit Tigers), while the term's connotation as a radical labor strategy, and its importance in the social history of the area (Jennings, 1975), is deemphasized to the point of erasure. Here the spectacle is framed in the context of cultural memory, but apolitical interpretations are emphasized and made to appear "official"

(Bélanger, 2002). "The lively atmosphere of the street pays homage to times gone by," we are told, including the neighborhood's "industrial roots." The contradiction inherent in the proposition that a highly commercialized spectacle can act as "homage" to the city's radical labor history can be evaded, in part, because the intended audience for this sanitized imagery consists of outsiders and newcomers rather than those long-term residents personally affected by local history and culture. The "vapid rebranding" of the area as a sterilized entertainment district (Bradley, 2015) is a project undertaken for the benefit of consumers with the tastes and resources necessary to buy into the images of the spectacle.

The community erasure brought about by the urban spectacle extends beyond the symbolic and cultural; it is also physical and spatial. One dimension of this material erasure involves the displacement of people, activities, and infrastructures on or adjacent to the project site. Low property demand makes assembling the footprint for downtown megaprojects a much more manageable affair, but other things can get in the way of a spectacle of this size and scope. For example, the ability to create a contiguous, walkable commercial corridor (of the length and breadth envisioned) is currently limited by two freeways bisecting the area (I-75 and I-375). Historical monuments to the suburbanization of capital, the freeways now stand as concrete obstacles to spectacle-based profits in the urban core. Several solutions to the problem are being considered. One option is eliminating the I-375 spur and replacing it with a surface road, a tactic preferred by the Ilitch family. " 'The freeway created both a physical and emotional barrier,' " notes Christopher Ilitch. " 'It's essential to connect those neighborhoods again.' " Mayor Mike Duggan concurs: " '[F]reeways cut off and isolate neighbourhoods' " (Aguilar, 2014b). For many planners and urbanists this is a most welcome realization. But while the impacts of spectacle-based development on the infrastructural core of the city is being publicly debated, much less attention is being paid to its effects on communities located on the margins of the city.

In Detroit, urban triage has provided both the means and the justification for prioritizing downtown megaprojects at the expense of struggling neighborhoods. Rejecting the government's traditional role in lifting up a city's neediest communities, urban triage insists instead that such communities must be sacrificed for the fiscal good of the city as a whole (Kirkpatrick, 2015). The term *triage* is borrowed from the battlefield practice of concentrating medical attention on fallen soldiers who would most benefit from it. Some patients would survive regardless of intervention, others would not survive, and the lives of still others hung in the balance. It was this final group that would receive the medic's limited attention and resources (Kleniewski, 1986). The same logic can be applied by cities seeking to leverage scarce development resources. In times of austerity, officials may decide to target their development efforts in areas where they will get the biggest "bang for their buck." In its milder iterations, triage entails directing capital improvement funds to "in-between" neighborhoods deemed ripe for revitalization. In more extreme cases, most commonly associated with shrinking and fiscally distressed cities, local officials actively remove public resources, services, and infrastructures from the hardest hit areas of the city (Marcuse, Medoff, & Pereira, 1982). It is this more aggressive form of urban triage—also known as planned shrinkage—that we see in Detroit.

Detroit's strategy is most clearly articulated in the Detroit Future City (DFC) plan, a fifty-year strategic framework for planning and development in the city based on a long-term vision of a smaller, greener city (Detroit Works Project, 2012). This can be achieved if residents currently living in sparsely populated areas (neighborhoods with high rates of vacancy, blight, and abandonment) move to high density "clusters" interspersed with vast green spaces. Importantly, the plan hinges on fiscal and infrastructural "right-sizing" (Hackworth, 2015; Kirkpatrick, 2015, p. 264). After decades of population loss, it is reasoned, the administrative and physical framework of the city is grossly overbuilt and inefficient. Targeted municipal contraction promises to both align the city with current demographic realities, as well as to accelerate depopulation in high-vacancy areas through the incremental withdrawal of city systems. In this scenario, public amenities ranging from water and sewer systems to bus service are dismantled and incrementally withdrawn or decommissioned, pushing residents into areas of the city that still enjoy access to public goods. While advocates cite the significant fiscal and ecological benefits of the proposal, questions remain about the social costs of planned shrinkage.

According to the plan's own estimates, the city's high-vacancy zone—those areas slated for depopulation and "greening"—is home to more than 88,000 people (Detroit Works Project, 2012, pp. 107–109).[11] These people must be compelled to relocate if the plan's vision is to be realized, it is argued, and they can be so compelled by denying them access to crucial public networks and services. This strategy entails redirecting municipal revenues and resources away from high-vacancy neighborhoods and toward areas such as Downtown Detroit. Spectacular megaprojects are the most visible and celebrated manifestation of the triage system, of course, but the urban spectacle cannot be understood apart from the populations and neighborhoods sacrificed for its benefit. In this manner, the development of spectacular spaces in the downtown core of the city is intimately linked to the sociospatial erasure of poor communities living at the urban margins.

Austerity and the Spectacle of Sport: Two Sides of the Same Urban Coin

On the face of things, the Red Wings deal is perplexing. It is puzzling in the context of research on stadium subsidies, which stands as a collective indictment of the practice. The project is also somewhat bewildering when considered in light of the stated principles of austerity; ostensibly, the "rules" apply to everyone, as the market is a strict, but fair, taskmaster. But on closer inspection, market discipline proves to be unevenly enforced. For example, residential water shut-offs continue in struggling Detroit neighborhoods (as impacted residents are cast as consumers who cannot pay their bills, not citizens with rights), while team owners and downtown developers receive lavish subsidies—a generous dispensation in defiance of the same strict standard. This contradiction can be explained in terms of the economic, political, and sociospatial dimensions of the project.

While public stadium projects have questionable benefits for the city as a whole, they most certainly produce sizable *economic* rewards for a select number of privileged beneficiaries—including a new class of owners-*cum*-oligarchs. As the city gradually descended into fiscal crisis and socioeconomic despair, these billionaires flexed their political and economic muscle. As owner of the Detroit Red Wings (*and* the Detroit Tigers), Mike Ilitch certainly played this lucrative role. In 1998, before the construction of the Tigers' Comerica Park, Ilitch was worth $630 million. In 2013, before the construction of the new Red Wings arena, his net worth had increased to $3.2 billion (Felton, 2014a). The growth of the Ilitch empire inversely mirrors the decline of the city. And just as the municipal sector reached its lowest point—bankrupt and controlled by an emergency manager—Ilitch "managed to shake loose hundreds of millions of dollars" for a new stadium (ibid). In Detroit, the ability of billionaire owners "to persuade local government officials to open the public purse to their private ambitions" (Baade & Dye, 1988, p. 266) appears enhanced, not hindered, by fiscal decline and austerity.

There is a *political* calculus at work in the Red Wings case that goes beyond brute oligarchic force. Ilitch was patient, biding his time until the political environment was ripe for a subsidy-laden deal. A 1992 poll found 68 percent of Detroit residents were opposed to stadium subsidies, and plans for various downtown facilities stalled several times due to organized opposition in the 1990s (Felton, 2014a). But Ilitch found he no longer needed to worry about political contestation or electoral disruption—even in the context of strict municipal austerity. This was due, most dramatically, to the imposition of a powerful emergency manager (EM) sympathetic to the arena project. Detroit's EM, Kevyn Orr, influenced the project in two primary ways. First, he shaped parts of the project directly, such as having "final say over the ["bridge" lease] deal" (Cwiek, 2014a). Second, Orr exerted more subtle influence, as demonstrated in his impact on key city council actions (the land transfer and the DDA boundary expansion). At every turn, Orr hovered behind the scenes, exerting a palpable if implicit influence on the process. Ultimately, while council interventions were symbolically important, they were not technically necessary, because the EM "[had] the authority to . . . unilaterally usher [the deals] through," if need be (Felton, 2014a). The city council could have refused to play along, thus forcing the EM to become openly and directly involved, but in the end it would not have mattered. This is a key point. In Detroit, stadium construction has been so thoroughly routinized and de-democratized that emergency mechanisms of austere governance, in place and ready to be deployed, were largely unnecessary. This is because a political and fiscal architecture was utilized that largely exists outside the confines of traditional municipal democracy.

A cornerstone of this extrademocratic architecture was and remains Detroit's Downtown Development Authority (DDA), whose autonomous power derives from its exclusive control over tax increment financing (TIF) in the greater downtown area, a method of revenue extraction that bypasses traditional forms of political deliberation and fiscal oversight. The boundary separating DDA-controlled funds from Detroit's general fund is so well enforced that TIF revenues were even protected from the city's bankruptcy proceedings and from its underfunded public schools—safe from the claims of angry investors, panicked pensioners, and frustrated students and teachers alike. The strategy of strictly segregating certain revenue streams for the sole purpose of spectacular downtown development has also proven to be an effective rhetorical strategy. Most pervasively, it has spawned a familiar trope: that the city is not paying for any of the upfront public costs for the arena and is "only" subsidizing the project through the land transfer. This is a common refrain in local media reports and faithfully recited by local officials. "We obviously wanted more," an executive vice president of Detroit Economic Growth Corporation noted about the negotiations. But, "[g]iven the amount of money that the city's put into this—which is zero—it's a great deal for the city and its residents (Holdwick, quoted in Guillen & Reindle, 2014). The structural cleaving of TIF monies from the city's general fund allows and encourages the naturalization of this narrative, but the claim is a fiction. The taxes "captured" by the DDA originate in the city and if it were not for the structural segregation of TIF revenues—a thoroughly and unmistakably political artifice—those resources would be tallied with the city's general fund or directed to other agencies and actors subject to democratic oversight and control.

Urban analysts have noted the emergence of the postpolitical (Davidson & Iveson, 2015; Swyngedouw, 2009) or postdemocratic (MacLeod, 2011) city, a key dimension of which is the proliferation of pseudo-public agencies and partnerships that limit the capacity of urban communities to directly intervene in city planning, development, and governance. In Detroit, powerful quasi-public authorities and private nonprofit organizations have taken the lead in developing spectacular downtown megaprojects. The cumulative effect of these trends was the emergence of a postpolitical form of development. "All of that was back-door dealings," observed State Representative Rashida Tlaib (D-Detroit). "Every single thing that happened here in the legislature, as well as on the city level, all of that was agreed upon without consulting the community. Even if they had meetings with us, it was already green light, move forward. Even if the City Council says no, [they could] get the [emergency manager] to do it" (Tlaib, quoted in Felton, 2014a).

We point, lastly, to the extreme *sociospatial* differentiation that attends the marriage of urban austerity and the spectacle. The social costs of austerity in Detroit are exacted by way of municipal triage, whereby resources are concentrated in "viable" neighborhoods, while service systems and infrastructure networks are gradually defunded and decommissioned in struggling areas. In this context, the redevelopment strategy exemplified by the new Red Wings arena, and its city-within-a-city, promises to create concentrated areas of gentrification and spectacular spaces of consumption in favored areas (particularly the 7.2 square mile Greater Downtown Area) but it also creates vast "sacrifice zones" across the (140 square mile) city, wherein residents are deprived of the basic necessities of modern life. By and large, the social and physical costs of austerity are safely relegated "out there," to the margins of the city. It is there that we can most clearly observe "the politics of everyday austerity at the street level, where the effects of public-service cut-backs, job losses and increased exposure to economic risks are experienced in daily life" (Peck, 2012 p. 632).

With respect to the marriage of austerity and the spectacle—and the dramatically uneven sociospatial effects of such a pairing—Detroit is extreme but not anomalous. Cities are imbricated in a "winner-takes-all" urbanism (ibid., p. 650), the brutal implications of which are increasingly manifest both between *and within* cities. When private investment and public largesse dovetail in the pursuit of the spectacle, the result is glittering spaces of spectacular consumption and state-of-the-art venues for downtown mega-events. But behind and all around the spectacle lies the devastation wrought by private sector abandonment and public sector triage. As such, the Red Wings project stands as an island of spectacular extravagance in a stark sea of austerity.

Notes

1. Unless otherwise noted, we use the term *stadium* as shorthand for *professional sports facility*, which encompasses ballparks, arenas, and stadiums proper.

2. Between 2000 and 2010, fifty-one new facilities were constructed, compared to fifty-five in the previous decade, while the dollar value of public funding shot from $8 billion to $12 billion (Long, 2013, 37).

3. According to Harvey, the "architecture of spectacle," can be identified by "its sense of surface glitter and transitory participatory pleasure, of display and ephemerality, of *jouissance*" (1989b, p. 91).

4. As Harvey notes, " 'Bread and circuses' is [a form of] social control . . . frequently . . . deployed to pacify restless or discontented elements in a population. *But spectacle can also be an essential aspect of revolutionary movement*" (1989b, p. 88; emphasis added). Benjamin also appreciated the surreal spontaneity and "blissful confusion" attendant to the spectacle of the crowd, "veiling the real nature of the economy but nonetheless ensuring intense and enchanting human experience" (Merrifield, 2013, p. 59).

5. Bonds backed by the DDA will be sold at a variable rate, while the interest rate for the remainder of the bonds (backed by Olympia Development) will be determined via swap (Felton, 2014b; Shea, 2014b).

6. "Practically speaking," notes Long, "facility leases are . . . complex legal documents, whose inherent opacity gives decision-makers tremendous latitude to conceal or reveal . . . public obligations" (2013, p. 13).

7. As Long reports, "Teams have been very successful in gaining the cooperation of host cities on this issue, sometimes creating layers of public ownership, using leases and sub-leases, to spare teams from the [property] taxes that they might otherwise owe" (2013, p. 13).

8. Michigan authorized the creation of DDAs in 1974, and twenty years later there were 276 operating in cities, villages, and townships across the state (CRC, 1996, p. 4).

9. The bill prevents any "local government body" from passing any worker protections "exceeding those imposed by state or federal law" (HB

4052). Notably, the law would also override all local worker protections based on sexual orientation and gender identity. There are currently thirty-eight Michigan municipalities with LGBT protections that would be effectively nullified (Ford, 2015).

10. Unless otherwise indicated, quotes in this section come from the "The District Detroit," a website created by Olympia Development of Michigan (available at: http://www.districtdetroit.com/).

11. The distribution of the social costs of austerity via triage is also shaped by local race relations; for a brief introduction to the topic, see Reese, Sands, and Skidmore (2014). It is also shaped by regional political dynamics (see, for instance, Hall & Jonas, 2014).

3

Austerity as the New Normal

The Fiscal Politics of Retrenchment in San Jose, California

SARA HINKLEY

Introduction

The City of Detroit dominated headlines of the Great Recession's urban crisis, looming ominously over the persistent national discourse of urban scarcity and precarity. Detroit's bankruptcy emerged from a particularly toxic combination of financial risk, economic restructuring, and historic deep economic and demographic decline. While Detroit's woes share common elements with many other U.S. cities, it can rightly be framed as an extreme case. The restructuring of urban fiscal governance through austerity in the United States since 2007 must also be considered as reflected in a city such as San Jose, California. Throughout his tenure, San Jose's Mayor Chuck Reed repeatedly framed the city as "broke" and in dire, "structural" crisis, a narrative meticulously crafted to justify an ambitious restructuring of the social contract between San Jose's citizens, government, and workers. While Detroit's bankruptcy dominates headlines, I argue that San Jose presents a different kind of symbol of the "new normal."

The San Jose mayor's rhetoric of urban fiscal responsibility reflects a national discourse dominated by calls for "commonsense" balanced budgeting and belt tightening. This commonsense narrative has been used for decades to accomplish "rollback" neoliberalism through a relentless focus on government paying for itself, streamlining its operations, and improving efficiencies (see, e.g., Peck et al., 2009; Tabb, 2014). The post-2007 financial crisis, as it cut deep into cities' revenues, gave new purchase to the rolling back of city spending. As Davidson and Ward describe in the introduction to this volume, austerity has been pursued by cities across the board, with few alternatives gaining serious traction. But even in the presence of ideological momentum and the impetus of scarcity, austerity must be politically accomplished, and its local proponents must articulate and justify a specific vision of austerity that adjusts resident expectations from city government.

While urban service retrenchment, as in earlier recessions, has been significant—including cuts to the sacred cows of police and fire—the ideological and political fights over how to achieve urban fiscal health have centered on a particular target: public pensions and other legacy costs of public budgeting. Pushing austerity in the name of fiscal crisis has opened up legal, policy, and political avenues for focusing on public pensions—and other long-term obligations—as the central problem of urban fiscal health. This chapter traces the relationship between the framing and justification of austerity in San Jose and a nationwide shift that has reframed legacy obligations as debts.

Background

The Great Recession produced widespread fiscal stress in the United States. Although the recession officially ended in 2009, American cities experienced declining revenues for six straight years, with the worst effects of the recession beginning only in 2012 (see, e.g., Pagano et al., 2012). Persistent unemployment, stagnant wages, and lagging property values fueled budget shortages as struggling residents relied on government support in growing numbers. Even in the absence of recession, U.S. cities face significant obstacles to fiscal stability: most cities rely primarily on cyclical property and sales taxes revenues, are required to balance their budgets annually, and face strong statutory and political obstacles to raising revenues. These challenges are compounded by cities' existence "downstream," as it were, from other geographies also experiencing fiscal crisis. By 2009, the federal government had shifted its policy response from stimulus to retrenchment, and states (most of which are also required to balance their budget at the end of every fiscal year) devolved their own budget deficits onto local governments (Gonzalez & Oosterlynck, 2014; Peck, 2012). Governors and state legislatures have not only made significant reductions in fiscal aid to local governments and revenue sharing, they have cut funding for programs that are operated by cities, such as libraries, medical clinics, and mental health (Cooper, 2002; Kellogg, 2012).

My interest in San Jose emerged from a larger project, in which I constructed a national dataset from the Census Bureau's Annual Survey of State & Local Government Finance from 1997 through 2012,[1] for a group of 425 cities with more than 75,000 residents.[2] In San Jose, I also reviewed adopted budgets and Comprehensive Annual Financial Reports (CAFRs) from fiscal years 2006–07 to 2012–13. I also analyzed local and national media coverage of budget issues, public officials' speeches, and other venues for political claim making around the fiscal crisis.

According to Census data, city spending across the United States declined significantly from 2008 to 2012; particularly after 2010 (see Figure 3.1). Over that period, total general expenditures by cities in my

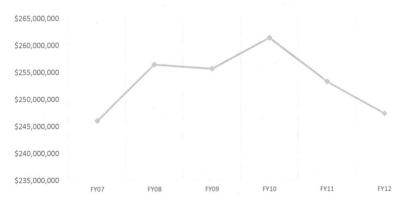

Figure 3.1. San Jose's Total General Direct Expenditures, FY2007–FY2012.

study declined by 4 percent in real dollars, while the population living in those cities grew by 1 percent. The most common targets of retrenchment from 2008–2012 were general government (down 16 percent) and quality of life (e.g., libraries and parks, down 15 percent) (Census Annual Survey of Local Government Finances). But within these categories there is significant variation: police spending grew by 4 percent, and fire by 1 percent, while the other aspects of public safety such as court services were cut significantly. This decline in general spending marks a significant reversal of the overall growth in those cities' spending during the country's climb out of the early 2000s recession. General spending grew 17 percent from 2002–08 (about 3 percent a year), keeping pace with population growth and the rising costs of everything from oil to health care.

Mapping out retrenchment in San Jose exemplifies the challenges in researching urban austerity. San Jose organizes its budget by "City Service Areas," which map only partially onto city departments. The city also has dozens of special funds (differentiated from the general fund) that raise and spend money separate from the general fund. The use of such funds has grown in recent years as a way to remove "self-sustaining" services from the general budget, items with specific revenue sources such as a fee/tax/charge or a state/federal grant (Chiang, 2011). In San Jose, these Special Purpose Funds make up 27 percent of the city's overall budget, the same proportion represented by the General Fund. Capital Funds account for the remaining 46 percent of the city's total budget. This shift away from general funds reflects both increasing use of municipal debt to fund infrastructure and the political mandate to make city services "self-funding" whenever possible (see Ashton et al., 2012).

San Jose's Fiscal Crisis

> The budget deficit is public enemy number one, an enemy that will steal our hopes and kill our dreams of becoming a great city if we ignore it. (San Jose mayor Chuck Reed, 2007)

San Jose's mayor from 2007–2015, Democrat Chuck Reed, promoted a narrative of structural fiscal crisis from the very beginning of his tenure.

He repeatedly argued that the city faced a serious structural crisis, assigned blame, and outlined the need for permanent fiscal restructuring. While San Jose's fiscal troubles have not approached the point of insolvency (indeed, it remained largely absent from lists of teetering California cities), the political conflict generated by the official narrative of crisis has been as intense as anywhere in the country, closely watched by the broader financial community and leaders of other U.S. cities.

San Jose—"Capital of Silicon Valley"—the tenth-largest city in the country, sits in the center of the nation's high-tech economy. This city of more than one million residents has doubled in size since 1970. Like most of California, its economy is more volatile than the U.S. economy as a whole, with unemployment fluctuating more widely (rising significantly in 2002–03 and 2009–11) but recovering more quickly (see Figure 3.2). The city's economy has recovered from the recession better than nearly any other U.S. city, with unemployment below the national average and well below California's (Friedhoff & Kulkami, 2013). In 2014, San Jose had the highest median household income in the nation, and its county, Santa Clara, was the nation's wealthiest (Avalos, 2014).

But, as for many U.S. cities, local economic prosperity has not brought the city itself fiscal stability. That paradox makes San Jose an interesting site for studying how the narrative of urban fiscal scarcity

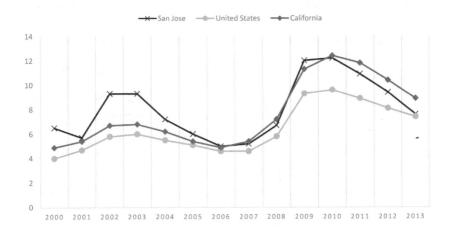

Figure 3.2. Unemployment in San Jose Area, 2000–2013.

persists in an environment of economic growth and entrepreneurialism. San Jose offers a counterpoint to the narrative emerging from Detroit (where fiscal decline can be attributed at least in part to economic stagnation) and also offers potential insight into the failure of many U.S. cities to fiscally recover from the recession despite signs of economic resilience. Private prosperity exists alongside public scarcity, as the global financial-economic crisis has been "socialized into a fiscal crisis of the state" (Oosterlynck & Gonzalez, 2013).

Before the 2007–09 recession began, San Jose's budget had just begun to recover from the downturn of the early 2000s, which hit San Jose's tech-centered economy especially hard. During the post-2001 recessionary period the city slashed 470 positions and cut its budget by $360 million (to less than $1.1 billion in 2008–09). The city's budget for 2006–07 added staff for the first time in five years, just regaining levels of 1999–2000. On the heels of this slow recovery, property values in San Jose dropped sharply in 2009, threatening one of the city's primary sources of revenue. Ultimately, property tax revenue fell by 9 percent from 2008–2013; sales taxes by 10 percent, and total general fund revenues by 7 percent (over the same period, San Jose's population grew by more than 5 percent).

California and its cities have been severely constrained in their revenue options since the passage of 1978's Proposition 13, which caps local property tax rates at $1/$100 valuation, requires two-thirds voter approval of any tax rate increase, and freezes assessment increases to the annual rate of inflation unless a property is sold (*People's Initiative to Limit Property Taxation*, 1978).[3] Many other states impose similar constraints on cities' ability to raise revenues, and such limitations have increased in recent years (Liner, 1989; Nelson, 2012). The state's own dire budget crisis has also been a source of considerable uncertainty and instability for California's cities. Vallejo's bankruptcy early in the recession (2008), followed by the bankruptcies of San Bernardino and Stockton (Lowenstein, 2011), drew policy and press attention to the prospect of widespread California urban fiscal crisis. In 2012, Moody's targeted thirty-two California cities for ratings review, and downgraded several municipal pension bonds ("Moody's targets California cities for downgrades," 2012).

San Jose's fiscal recovery was also hampered by California's elimination of Redevelopment Agency (RDA) funding in 2012, which effectively diverted millions in property tax revenues back to the state. Although the direct budget impacts are hard to quantify (because redevelopment agencies spent money on behalf of the city but were not part of the general fund budget), the mayor repeatedly highlighted the damage done to San Jose by the elimination of RDA funding (Reed, 2012a). Because of simultaneous state education funding cuts, most of those property tax revenues will instead be spent on local school districts, effectively allowing the state to balance its own budget and avoid catastrophic education cuts by removing a significant source of revenue from cities. Cuts in state aid have been common nationwide during the Great Recession; Detroit lost an estimated $700 million in state revenue-sharing (Bing, 2013), and most states with general aid funds to cities have reduced or eliminated that aid since 2007. State intergovernmental revenue directed to cities declined by 6 percent in real dollars from 2008 to 2012 (Census Annual Survey of Local Government Finances).

Unlike Detroit, San Jose's reliance on debt financing, and thus its exposure to financial risk, has been relatively limited for a city of its size. As of June 2008, the city was using only a fraction of its legal debt capacity; after the state eliminated redevelopment agencies, $2 billion in bonded debt was moved off the city's budget to the replacement agency designated to complete existing projects. San Jose's troubles are not, unlike Detroit and the large California bankruptcies, tied to complex financial instruments, although financialization has taken other forms: the proliferation of enterprise funds and Reed's own aggressive efforts to move "self-funding" budget items out of the general fund.

Shortly after taking office in 2007, Mayor Reed created a General Fund Structural Deficit Task Force, spearheaded by a consultant firm (Management Partners Incorporated, 2008). Following its first report, Reed announced that the city faced a structural fiscal crisis to a degree that "will require us to cut services that are vital to our residents and businesses" (Reed, 2008, p. 1). In November 2008, the task force issued a "structural deficit elimination plan" containing pages of narrative about reducing the cost of "service delivery" through efficiency, and an equal amount of spending cuts through cutting benefits ("reducing the rate of increase in personnel costs") (Office of the City Manager, 2008, p. 30).

The mayor continued to sound the fiscal alarm through 2010 and 2011, spending the better part of a year trying to get the city council to declare a fiscal emergency for the city, which under California law would have enabled the restructuring of city contracts, including union and pension commitments (Fong, 2011; Koehn, 2012). By 2012, the mayor's efforts to frame the city as facing structural crisis, although foundering at the city council, brought San Jose national media attention. In February 2012, the *New York Times* covered the fiscal impact of the recession on Silicon Valley, highlighting the new libraries that San Jose could not afford to open and the flashy city hall that had been built during "better times" (Cooper, 2012). The story also emphasized the reduction in fire and police staff and residents' frustration with climbing rates of homicide and prostitution. The business and nonprofit communities affirmed the message of crisis and the Mayor's focus on structural reform, particularly for pensions (see, e.g., Silicon Valley Community Foundation, 2012).

In March 2012, the city lost its top AAA credit rating from Moody's (it had lost the top rating from Fitch in 2011). The rating report referenced declining reserves and weakened revenues, but also emphasized the question of pensions: "The city's management is also being significantly challenged to manage retirement costs and faces arduous barriers to reduce the impact of those obligations" (Moody's Investors Service, 2012). Under "strengths," the rating report cited the city's "aggressive pursuit of opportunities to effectively manage retirement costs," presumably referencing the mayor's attempts at pension restructuring. In both national news coverage and Moody's analysis, the city's efforts to reform pensions are framed as the only "fixable" part of the city's fiscal troubles; revenue challenges merit only a brief mention (Lyman & Walsh, 2013). Moody's assessment gave the mayor's push for pension reform added weight, and rewarded his aggressive pursuit of service retrenchment.

Service Cuts

The city's initial response to falling revenues, beginning in 2008, was planned service reductions and eliminations. The Structural Deficit

Elimination Plan proposes eliminating services to save $70–80 million over five years, with $60 million in cuts the first year. The cuts are to be made utilizing an "Analytical Framework for Service Reductions/Eliminations," which sets forth the following criteria for program elimination:

> 1. Not typically provided by California cities; 2. The city is not the primary provider of the service; 3. Not all residents benefit from the service; 4. "Revenue neutral" program that could be covered by a user fee; 5. Funded above the level needed to achieve "minimally acceptable service;" 6. A candidate for "optimization." (Office of the City Manager, 2008, p. 71)

This set of criteria is a roadmap for reducing city spending to the bare essentials of city function; there is no suggestion in the plan that these cuts would be temporary. The plan lays out the gradual steps by which services that can be moved out of the general fund will be restructured to "revenue neutral" fee-funded services, and subjects the value of services provided to the metric of return on investment (Office of the City Manager, 2008, p. 72). This technocratic, apolitical, and economistic language of budgeting laid the groundwork for a process of service cuts that would unfold over the next several years (see also Merrifield, 2014). Early in the recession, the police union agreed to a 3.95 percent budget reduction, using the savings to avoid laying off seventy officers. In addition to these targeted reductions, departments were directed to target overall spending cuts of 3 percent (only 1 percent for police and fire) (Office of the City Manager, 2008, p. 20). In 2010–11, the city implemented a 10 percent reduction in pay and benefits for nonuniformed employees, allocating the savings to "preserve library hours, keep community centers open, and restore some funding for crossing guards, park rangers, and the anti-graffiti program" (Reed, 2010).

As the Great Recession wore on, San Jose gained notoriety for deeper public safety cuts. As Davidson and Ward write in the introductory chapter, this recession has been marked by cuts to the night-watchman state, which was once considered immune to cyclical spending purges: police and fire services and staff, "city services and operations once thought beyond the reach of neoliberalism" (Davidson & Ward, 2014,

p. 85). Public safety spending (police and fire, and, in some cities, corrections and the courts) has been protected better than any other category of operating expenditures through the past decades of austerity. While the current recession has indeed brought widespread cuts to public safety budgets, including San Jose's, the cuts are nearly always made with assurances that they are temporary, with positions remaining unfilled rather than eliminated (see, e.g., Office of the City Manager, 2008). The protections and assurances given to "uniformed" unions in obtaining security and benefits for their members diverge sharply from "civilian" unions representing other city employees. Uniformed workers have been given fewer furlough days, more frequent and higher pay raises, and better health benefits than non-uniformed workers. San Jose's commitment to public safety is embodied in its mission: "Remaining the Safest Big City in America." From fiscal year 2007–08 to 2012–13, real spending on police increased by 16 percent, and made up 30 percent of the FY2012–13 budget (compared to 27 percent in FY2007–08). Fire spending rose by 25 percent, to reach 16 percent of general fund spending in FY2012–13. Over the same period, total general fund spending rose by just 4 percent (San Jose Adopted Budgets in Brief, FY2007–FY2013). Combined, police and fire spending accounted for almost one-half of the city's general expenditures in 2012.

Despite the relative protection of police and fire from the drastic cuts affecting other programs, a narrative of public safety retrenchment has been central to the narrative of San Jose's crisis, and to the mayor's illustration of the damage pension obligations are doing to the city. In a presentation on the state of the city, Reed argued that the rising cost of pensions and health care were eating into public safety staffing (Office of Mayor Chuck Reed, 2014). One slide—"The Crushing Burden of Retirement Cost Increases"—shows a 45 percent budget increase for the police department from FY2001–02 to FY2011–12, and a 20 percent staff decrease over the same period (Office of Mayor Chuck Reed, 2014, p. 4). This direct juxtaposition of public safety cuts with pension increases (two trends that certainly occurred at the same time, but are of course not necessarily inextricably linked) has been central to Reed's framing of the city's budget cuts and the need for pension reform.

Revenue Options

And what of alternatives to cutting spending? Periodically throughout the recession, options for increasing revenue have been proposed in San Jose, with mixed results. The city's 2008 Structural Deficit Elimination Plan outlines a modest and vague revenue-raising plan: through "asset management" (monetizing property the city owns, by selling or leasing), added fees for public services (parking and parks, among others), and several economic development projects projected to increase various tax revenues (Office of the City Manager, 2008). These revenue strategies added up to only $22–48 million over five years, compared to the $70–80 million in spending cuts, and consisted primarily of estimates of additional economic activity generated by development programs (Office of the City Manager, 2008, p. 7). San Jose's strategy parallels the national trend of relying on temporary or permanent fee increases (the most regressive form of revenue raising, and also the one least likely to meet with voter protest), while holding steady or even reducing proportional taxes on businesses or residents.

In 2012, the mayor began discussions around raising business taxes in the city for the first time since 1986 (Segall, 2012). The private sector offered support for the small increase only as part of the pension restructuring push: "Chamber officials are pressing for pension and benefit reform to help City Hall 'regain financial stability,' and they would only support 'new revenue sources' if that reform takes place" (Segall, 2012). In 2014, the city council rejected a sales tax increase because of a split over whether the money should go to the general fund or be earmarked for public safety (Pickoff-White, 2014). Ultimately, aside from these abortive efforts and a series of small fee increases, revenue strategies were largely absent from the proposed solutions to San Jose's so-called structural crisis.

National Pension "Crisis"

Public pension liability has become central to the narrative of fiscal crisis in the United States, with more cities and states coming under scrutiny each year (Munnell et al., 2013). Many large U.S. cities manage their own pension plans to provide for public employees upon retirement, with defined benefits negotiated through labor contracts.[4] In the current crisis, such public pension funds have been described as "chronically underfunded," threatening to hobble governments if measures are not taken to cut benefits for current and future retirees (Cohen, 2013; Passantino & Summers, 2005). Some financial analysts have described the structural threat posed by pension and health care costs as "unsustainable" and "ridiculous" (Chappatta, 2012). The bankruptcies of Detroit and Stockton fueled reports of a widespread public pension crisis, and prompted much national handwringing and calls for reform (see, e.g., Cohen, 2013).

Of course, public workers have always taken significant hits during retrenchment, through wage freezes and layoffs, and pension cuts can be seen as an extension of previous patterns of retrenchment. But the narrative in the current recession has successfully framed obligations to public workers as unsustainable "legacy costs," equivalent to debt, necessitating new legal avenues for restructuring. This reframing has been made real through the technologies of financial rating and monitoring. In November 2009, Moody's commented that pension costs were "pressuring" state and local governments, and could affect municipal ratings. The funding trouble for pension plans, Moody's states, results from a combination of demographic pressure, investment losses, and "decisions by select governments to defer pension contributions during periods of budgetary stress" (Moody's Investors Service, 2009, p. 1). In 2009, Moody's announced that it would conduct a review of all large cities' pension liabilities and would also refine their method for incorporating pension information into a city's rating (Moody's Investors Service, 2009, p. 7).

In 2010, the Government Accounting Standards Board (GASB) incorporated unfunded pension liabilities into cities' required financial statements for the first time (Moody's Investors Service, 2010). In 2012, it increased the role played by pension liabilities in the calculation of municipal debt and credit ratings (Government Accounting Standards Board, 2012). In both 2011 and 2013, Moody's revised its ratings methodology first to classify pension liabilities as debt, and then to increase the weight of a city's debt in its overall rating calculation (Moody's Investors

Service, 2013). The ratings agencies themselves thus lend legitimacy and material consequence to the narrative that cities are buried by pension obligations. Within the span of a few short years the pension crisis has become a matter of fact, not opinion or politics, despite the complexity of evaluating pension liabilities in a volatile financial climate. Mayor Reed of San Jose has played a significant role in this simplified discourse of a national pension crisis facing U.S. cities.

San Jose's Pension Crisis

What can San Jose's politics of austerity reveal about how pension commitments became a central figure in the story of the Great Recession's urban fiscal crisis? In this atmosphere of crisis, both Detroit and San Jose became pivotal national sites for testing the possibilities of restructuring pension commitments to retirees and to current workers: Detroit through bankruptcy, and San Jose through the ballot box. Mayor Reed aggressively pursued pension restructuring during his entire tenure as mayor. The mayor's deficit elimination committee proposed in its early reports the possibility of moving public workers to defined contribution plans in order to conform to common practice in the private sector (Office of the City Manager, 2008, p. 122). Reed successfully framed pensions as responsible for decimating city services: "[Annual pension] costs have grown from $73 million to $245 million in the past decade and forced the city to shed some 2,000 jobs, leaving a workforce of about 5,200" (Woolfolk, 2012a). His efforts placed San Jose at the forefront of policy experimentation with restructuring union commitments and contributed to the national narrative of out-of-control pension costs (Dembosky & Bullock, 2012).

In 2012, the mayor successfully pushed to place a pension reform measure on the San Jose ballot that would reduce pension benefits for future employees, raise the retirement age, and require current employees to contribute an additional 16 percent of their salary in order to remain in the plan. The measure also allows the city to temporarily suspend cost-of-living pension increases for retirees in case of a fiscal emergency (Woolfolk, 2012b). On June 5, 2012, 69 percent of voters in San Jose approved the measure; the same day, San Diego voters also approved a measure that would reduce the pensions of both current and future workers (Carlson, 2012; Raphael, 2012). These measures represent an unprecedented attempt to circumvent constitutional protections for public employees (although San Jose's was ultimately struck down by the courts, it was replaced by a revised measure in late 2016).

San Jose's approach to retrenchment has not been uncontested. Unions representing city workers have launched legal challenges, arguing in part that officials have inflated the estimates of pension costs and their impact on future budgets. The actuarial estimation of pension liabilities is complex, as even Moody's has acknowledged; as the stock market recovered during the recession, pension plan health improved significantly. City council members have also countered the mayor's claims that the city faces structural crisis. A state audit of San Jose's finances in 2012, requested by a council member, found that the projections of future costs used by the mayor to declare the pension system in crisis were unsupported by actuarial methodologies, but also found that rising pension contributions from 2010 to 2012 had possibly cut into spending for non-public safety programs, such as parks and libraries (California State Auditor, 2012). Even in Detroit, where retirees now outnumber current workers two to one (suggesting a bona fide structural imbalance, also faced by the auto companies after radical downsizing), the fixation on pension liabilities as a cause of bankruptcy has been criticized, as several financial analysts pointed out that the city's pension payments conformed to accepted practice (Bomey & Gallagher, 2013; Devitt, 2013). In Detroit and other cities, it was risky investments taken on to manage pension obligations (and get around city budget limitations) that led to fiscal collapse, not the underlying pension obligations themselves (Farmer, 2013). The movement for tighter financial regulation successfully mediated, early in the recession, claims that cities were to blame for their own fates in the downturn. As the recession wore on, however, the initial public backlash against austerity began to fade.

The mayor's continued focus on the idea of San Jose as being in structural crisis is always accompanied by offering pension reform as the central—if not only—long-term strategy for increasing the city's fiscal stability. Once the question had been put to voters, and achieved significant news coverage, it would persist in the public imagination. Reed told a reporter after the vote: "The voters get it. They understand the connection between having to put huge amounts of money into retirement and cutting services to the people" (Vakshin & Nash, 2012). Broader solutions to pension risk have been foreclosed by the presumption that economic risk must be passed on to individual workers: national retirement security, or public centralization of pension programs that would broadly disperse risk and responsibility for retirement security, have never been seriously discussed, and the only state intervention proposed by Reed is legislative action to reduce pension benefits. When the response to stagnating revenues was framed as only two alternatives—cutting services or cutting pensions—San Jose's voters choose the latter.

The motivation for attacking public pensions is certainly in part ideological, but it is also a strategic move in an ongoing political effort to delegitimize worker protections and benefits and neutralize other political responses to inequality and increased precarity. Retrenchment accomplished by going after workers—in particular by divorcing public workers from the services they provide—makes the debate over how to respond to scarcity one of fairness between public and private workers (or public workers and "taxpayers," as if they are two distinct groups of people), rather than about the broader structure of urban finance that produces cyclical vulnerability. San Diego's mayor, campaigning for his own pension measure, said: "Public employees should have no better retirement benefits than the taxpayers they serve" (Dembosky & Bullock, 2012). Reed has explicitly framed the choice as one between pensions and residents: "Every dollar the city pays for retirement costs is a dollar we can't spend on services for our residents" (Reed, 2012b). The city as a site of collective consumption becomes reframed as a site of political conflict between the "haves" (public workers with their pensions and job security) and the "have nots" (private sector workers with their tax bills, insecure jobs, and dwindling real incomes).[5]

This framing is not hard to accomplish in a country in which mainstream political figures have proposed privatizing Social Security (the most popular public safety net program), and in which any non-private health care system faces intractable political resistance. The attack on public pensions has occurred simultaneously with a wave of state legislation seeking to limit labor rights and dismantle public employee unions, which now represent about one-half of all union members in the United States; 40 percent of local government workers are unionized (55 percent in California), compared to just over 6 percent of private workers (U.S. Bureau of Labor Statistics). Particularly during the recession, public employee unions have been one of the few constituency groups (and the best-resourced) to articulate a strong argument for public funding of services, government's role in stimulus spending, and other pro-public strategies.[6] The strategic implications of dismantling one of public employee unions' central member benefits, and of eroding popular support for public unions by blaming them directly for service declines, could cause significant long-term damage to a pro-public, anti-neoliberal urban policy agenda. Public workers and their unions face a complex public messaging challenge in defending their benefits within this discursive framework.

Conclusion: Studying the Post-Crisis City

In the wake of New York City's near-bankruptcy in 1975, researchers documented the forms of the "welfare state" that had disappeared: an ambitious urban project of free higher education, a safety net for the poor, and widely available public health care were successfully framed as an unsustainable experiment (see, e.g., Auletta, 1979). This legacy of service retrenchment certainly echoes throughout the recent recession, but the predominant political framing of the recent urban fiscal crisis has been less about government excess via ambitious service agendas, and instead about government excess embodied by its commitments as an employer. This shift is in part because scarcity and limited urban governance have been widely naturalized after several cycles of fiscal contraction. Since New York's crisis of the 1970s, we have seen the dismantling of federal revenue sharing, the devolution and evisceration of federal welfare programs, and the last vestiges of general income assistance eliminated during a time of prosperity (U.S. federal welfare reform was passed in 1996, during a period of robust economic growth).

In many states, and at the federal level, large cities face a landscape of dwindling political power and a push by some state policymakers for greater state intervention in local fiscal affairs. Mayor Reed's aggressive pursuit of both state intervention and pension reform marks a contrast from other Democratic mayors, such as in Philadelphia and Detroit, who struggled to prevent state takeover and sought to draw attention to alternative structural causes of their cities' troubles: revenue restraints, state funding cuts, and the lack of meaningful countercyclical economic policy. When we reach sufficient distance from this recession to assess its long-term effects on urban policy, which city's story will be placed alongside the tale of New York's 1975 urban social welfare state gone awry? Which of the "structural" failures of urban fiscal policy will have shaped the subsequent decade of urban finance?

Notes

1. The dataset for years 2007–2012 was built from raw data files, as the Census had ceased publishing local government finance data by city in 2006.

2. This group includes all cities with more than 75,000 residents that responded to the Census finance survey for all years in my dataset, to facilitate comparison of sums from year to year.

3. The passage of Proposition 13 caused California property tax revenue to plummet by 57 percent within a single year (see Yuan, Cordes, Brunori, & Bell, 2009, p. 153).

4. For many public workers, who are ineligible for federal social security, their pension will be their only source of retirement income.

5. Although San Jose, unlike private employers, does not pay into the federal social security system, meaning that its employees (like many public employees) will not collect social security when they retire.

6. See for example Public Works, a project of Demos, www.demos.org.

4

The Difference a Crisis Makes

Environmental Demands and Disciplinary
Governance in the Age of Austerity

C. S. PONDER

Introduction

While the flames of racial tension and social outrage run through
Ferguson, Missouri, over the nonindictment of police officer Darren
Wilson for the killing of Black teen Michael Brown, another fire burns
underground at a landfill just ten miles west of there, and has been for
the past five years. The long-lived fire at the Bridgeton Landfill in St.
Louis County, caused by chemical reactions occurring within the buried refuse, is producing a noxious mixture of gases containing known
carcinogens and neurotoxins that are affecting the health of residents
and their children. Locals describe the odor emitted from the gases in
terms ranging from "rotten eggs mixed with skunk and fertilizer" to
"dead bodies" (Rivas, 2014).

What's worse, the perimeter of the fire sits just 1,200 feet away
from an Environmental Protection Agency (EPA) Superfund site containing an estimated 8,700 tons of radioactive nuclear waste (Hseih,
2013). No one is actually sure how much is really down there, though,

as the site was used as nuclear dumping grounds multiple times—waste from the Manhattan Project is buried there (by private federal subcontractors), along with nuclear waste dumped by other private entities (Barker, 2015a; Barker 2015b; Schuessler, 2015). Meanwhile, a report compiled for the Missouri Department of Natural Resources stated that temperature readings from the nuclear waste suggest the underground fire is moving closer (Emshwiller, 2014). Both landfills are located in a floodplain, just 1.5 miles away from the Missouri River, and eight miles upstream from a water reservoir that serves approximately three hundred thousand St. Louis residents.

Various EPA reports have noted that the Superfund site may release even more radioactive radon into the air, and possibly contaminate groundwater as well if heated by the underground fire. A landfill fire expert has explained that if the chemical reaction fueling the fire grows too fast it could "cause the landfill surface to cave in," bringing flames above ground and giving it better (and quicker) access to the radioactive waste. And expert landfill consultant Peter Anderson has warned that the worst-case scenario facing the city is the ignition of a "dirty bomb" that would result in the "non-detonated mass release of floating radioactive particles in metro St. Louis," up to ten miles from the site of dispersal—thus bringing Ferguson into radiation fallout range (Emshwiller, 2014; Hsieh, 2013; Lacapra, 2014a). Astonishingly, the solution the EPA has decided upon to resolve the imminent threat to public health this situation poses is to pile "five feet of dirt and rocks" (Hseih, 2013) on top of 8,700+ tons of radioactive refuse sitting in a floodplain, and call it good—despite the potential presence of an oncoming chemical fire.

Meanwhile, in the same city, the EPA has served the St. Louis metropolitan sewer district with a $4.7 *billion* dollar Clean Water Act (CWA) consent decree, mandating unfunded upgrades to the city's sewage system (EPA, 2011). To put this figure into perspective, the entire national Community Development Block Grant program, one of the longest running national programs for local infrastructure development, was funded at $3.06 billion for the nation as a whole in 2016. All of the local governments throughout the entire nation collectively received a billion dollars *less* in funding than the projected needs of a single city for a single infrastructural issue. Similarly exorbitant unfunded infrastructural mandates have recently been handed down by the EPA to other cities as well, including Kansas City, Missouri (est. $2.5 billion), Chattanooga, Tennessee (est. +$250 million), Jackson, Mississippi (est. $400 million), and Baton Rouge, Louisiana (2002 est. $618 million, 2013 actual cost, $2.9 billion) (Allen, 2013; Anderson, 2013; EPA, enforcement, n.d.). And Birmingham, Alabama, has been caught up in the midst of an EPA consent decree–induced financial crisis since 2011, when its home county was forced into bankruptcy after borrowing $3.2 billion through municipal bonds and complex interest-rate swaps in an attempt to finance a 1996 Clean Water Act consent decree.

How can we reconcile an EPA that selects a $41 million dollar "in-situ cap" solution to a Superfund site with more than 8,700 tons of nuclear waste sitting less than one thousand feet away from an underground fire and less than two miles away from the Missouri River—over the alternative of a $400 million dollar excavation and complete removal of radioactive waste (Tomich, 2013a)—with an EPA that imposes multibillion dollar Clean Water Act consent decrees on struggling cities across the nation? This chapter works through this question in four sections, using two case studies. The first two sections think through the EPA's problematic calculus regarding the relationship between financial and environmental risk by placing the institution within the historic context of neoliberalization and, now, post-crisis urban austerity. In section one, following Bakker (2010), I make the case that while the same overarching neoliberal logic is at work among all the various branches of the EPA, the different socio-natures over which the Superfund and CWA are responsible have caused them to undergo the *process* of neoliberalization along materially different lines.

However, and as this book aims to make clear, contemporary urban governance landscapes have been ruptured by a nationally extensive financial-turned-fiscal crisis. In this new era of intensified social service asceticism, calculating the difference between pecuniary expenditure and environmental risk is now accomplished using a much higher benchmark. In the second section I explore the idea that under the austerity-driven state, bodies exposed to socioecological vulnerabilities have become (further) devalued in relation to the task of paying off newly acquired financial debt from the banking system. By extension, the effects of such vulnerabilities are exacerbated within exposed populations, and the resulting austerity-induced inequities produce their own undesirable path dependencies. I do this first by providing an initial overview of the market-driven funding context cities are currently faced with in the long-term absence of federal support. I then go on to present the first of the case studies—the ongoing water crisis happening in Detroit, Michigan. Here I show that the regulatory violence endemic to general processes of neoliberalization has qualitatively intensified during this period of fiscal austerity.

The third section pushes this line of reasoning farther, considering how austerity-induced regulatory violence produces and reproduces both new and historic sociospatial inequalities. Here I use the lens of "infrastructural downloading"—shifting the financial burden of replacing aging infrastructure away from the federal and state-level governments and onto cities—to present a comparative case study of two locales: pre-crisis Atlanta and post-crisis Birmingham/Jefferson County, Alabama. The story of these two municipalities highlights the changing positionality of consent decree cities within the American political landscape: whereas pre-crisis Atlanta was able to broker financial assistance and even a working partnership with the state of Georgia, Jefferson County, Alabama, is now considered anathema to its post-crisis state-level government—as are other American cities in the same position.

A fourth and final section puts a name to the face of those bodies and cities made most vulnerable in the crucible of austerity. While the era of austerity is indeed a new mode of social regulation, the violence it inflicts remains bound to historic circuits of abuse and oppression.

The Neoliberalization of the EPA in Two Acts

The EPA was established in 1970, and marked the eleventh-hour launch of what has been described (Purcell, 2012) as "environmental Keynesianism." This was perhaps the last significant wave of Keynesian "collectivist" legislation to see daylight in the United States, as the American state apparatus began transitioning to a neoliberal operational framework during those same years. In its broadest depiction (Peck &

Tickell, 2002), neoliberalism is characterized by an ideological adherence to market-based solutions to governing, and a similarly strong disavowal regarding the legitimacy and effectiveness of state-based collectivist logics (Keynesian or otherwise). More recently, the analytical depiction of the process of neoliberalization has been further refined to include the idea that neoliberalism is "variegated" (Bakker, 2010; Brenner et al., 2010)—in other words, that neoliberal processes unfold differently in different locales, according to specific institutional path dependencies, sociocultural inheritances, or even according to the different biophysical characteristics of the surrounding (or policy-relevant) environment. This section examines the variegated processes by which the neoliberal transition took place in the two legislative acts most relevant to our unfolding story: CERCLA, the act governing the Superfund program, and the Clean Water Act, which is responsible for regulating the pollution produced by municipal sewer systems.

CERCLA: Keynesianism's "Parting Shot" and Roll-Back/Roll-Out Neoliberalism

The Keynesian creation of the EPA was followed in short order by the passage of several more collectivist-type laws of major environmental significance, including the Clean Air Act (1970), the Clean Water Act (1972; 1977), the Safe Drinking Water Act (1974), the Toxic Substances Control Act (1976), and the Resource Conservation and Recovery Act (1976). Then, in December 1980, in the very last weeks before the inauguration of Ronald Reagan and the national metastasis of the neoliberal agenda, President Carter passed the Comprehensive Environmental Response, Compensation, and Liability Act, or CERCLA—a move Mark Purcell (2012) describes as a "parting shot from a dying Keynesian tradition."

The EPA's Superfund program was established under CERCLA and operates under its auspices. Both the legislation and the Superfund[1] were created in response to public outrage over the discovery in the 1970s of illegal toxic waste dumps in multiple locations around the country; Love Canal, New York, and the "Valley of the Drums" in Bullitt County, Kentucky, are two of the most famous cases. Now there are 1,322 Superfund sites in total, while an additional forty-seven have been proposed

(U.S. EPA, National Priorities List, n.d.). CERCLA is a "polluter pays" law, and the original intent of the Superfund program, as indicated by its name, was to create a type of endowment out of fees charged to polluting entities in order to finance the cleanup of these illegal dumping grounds. Yet by the end of the Reagan administration's two terms in office, while 799 sites had been given Superfund status, only sixteen had been cleaned up. And the federal agency had only managed to collect $40 million out of $700 million in potential cleanup fees from polluting companies (*New York Times*, 2/7/1994).

The underperformance of the Reagan administration in this context is best understood as an initial move in what Peck and Tickell (2002) describe as "roll-back" neoliberalism. The process of neoliberalization as it has so far unfolded in North America appears to have two broad brush moves: first, a "roll-back" period of state dismantlement, involving deregulation and devolution of responsibilities to state and local governments and other organizations; and then a second phase of "roll-out" neoliberalism, involving "active state [re-]building and regulatory reform" (p. 384).

The Reagan administration's deregulatory impulse, embodied by its deficient progress on Superfund cleanups and fee collection, was paired with additional "roll-back" tactics, including downloading decision-making authority over the cleanups from the federal-level U.S. EPA, to regional and state-level EPAs—with other local agencies at the municipal, state, and county scales eventually shouldering day-to-day oversight of cleanups (Purcell, 2012). The EPA itself is now largely left with the role of safeguarding only the letter of the law. This "strict constructionist" outlook of the federal agency is clearly seen in a 2013 response by a regional administrator of the EPA to concerned St. Louis County residents on the topic of why the Bridgeton Landfill fire's presence next to a radioactive, urban Superfund site is considered by the EPA to only warrant further groundwater testing rather than removal of the toxic waste: "We can't invent new procedures, we can't invent new rules. It [the process of finding an appropriate cleanup remedy] will be done with the evidence that we have with the law that we're obligated to follow" (Tomich, 2013b).

But new procedures and new rules *can,* in fact, be invented. The invention of a new stipulation in the budgetary process of procuring remedies for Superfund sites is precisely what happened in 1995, and is precisely why the EPA today considers further groundwater testing rather than removal of toxic waste the appropriate action to take in the St. Louis County situation. Neoliberal regulatory reforms "rolled-out" during the Clinton administration established the National Remedy Review Board (NRRB), a panel of scientists and policymakers tasked with automatically reviewing any Superfund project whose proposed remedy carries a price tag of $25 million or higher (EPA, review criteria, n.d.). According to the EPA, the establishment of the NRRB is "designed to make the Superfund program faster, fairer, and more efficient" (ibid.). In the context of the Bridgeton landfill fire, this has substantively translated into further groundwater testing and radiation scans—while an underground fire grows hotter, and likely inches closer to the toxic waste.

The life-risking implications of this lengthy debate over price during an environmental emergency are further magnified by the EPA's continued acceptance of studies commissioned by Republic Services, Inc. in their official position as potentially responsible party (PRP). Studies commissioned by Republic Services are in *direct* opposition to conclusions drawn from studies conducted by other vested parties, including the Missouri Department of Natural Resources, a separate EPA division of engineering risk management in Cincinnati, and a nuclear analyst who formerly served as a Department of Energy senior policy advisor under the Clinton administration (Lacapra, 2014a; Lacapra, 2014b; Lacapra & Skiöld-Hanlin, 2013). Unsurprisingly perhaps, the PRP insists that the report compiled for the state's Department of Natural Resources is simply wrong and that the "subsurface smoldering event" is actually moving away from the Superfund site. Further, they claim that even if the heat from the so-called smoldering event does somehow manage to reach the radioactive waste, "scientific data 'strongly indicates' it wouldn't present a public health threat" (Emshwiller, 2014).

Meanwhile, the underground chemical refuse grows hotter—temperatures of 300 degrees Fahrenheit have been recorded—and inches ever closer to the nuclear waste, at an estimated rate of one to two feet per day, according to the disregarded Missouri Department of Natural Resources. With approximately nine hundred feet remaining between the underground fire and the radioactive nuclear waste as of early March 2014, many members of the community initiated requests for EPA-sponsored relocation through the Superfund program (Lacapra, 2014a). In November 2014, the EPA denied all such requests, stating that their own (inferred as adequate) response to the issue—which has been to "cover the site with an earthen cap," monitor toxicity levels, and implement a no-trespassing ordinance marked by what residents have dubbed the "magical" chain-link fence—"makes temporary or permanent relocation inconsistent with EPA's authority and practice as well as with the scientific evidence" (EPA, 2014; Schuessler, 2015; Tomich, 2013).

The Neoliberalization of the Clean Water Act: Bait and Switch Neoliberalism

We turn now to a consideration of how neoliberalization progressed through the EPA under the Clean Water Act. Prior to 1972, water pollution was considered by the U.S. government to be a state and local problem (Copeland, 2002). The Federal Water Pollution Control Act of 1948 was the first legislation to federally regulate water pollution, but it did so only in terms of granting technical assistance and funding to help states and localities solve their own issues and set their own standards; federal enforcement of water pollution control was limited to interstate waters only (ibid.). The 1972 Amendments reversed that relationship, and designated the newly created EPA as the federal agency responsible for regulating water pollution nationwide, with states thereafter responsible only for the execution and enforcement of policies created by the federal agency (ibid.). Notably, with the introduction of this legislation the role of municipalities swung from that of (ostensible) regulators of local water standards, to being among the principal entities *subject to* CWA regulation.

The 1972 Amendments were extremely ambitious, declaring as primary goals, (1) that all water be "fishable" and "swimmable" by 1983, and (2) to attain "zero discharge" of pollutants into waterways by 1985. These goals have not yet been reached, but remain in effect. One of the most important institutional and operational ramifications of the ongoing pursuit of these goals is related to their "technology-forcing" nature. Those regulated by the Clean Water Act are required to meet ever higher and more technologically advanced levels of pollution control, thus compelling both regulated cities and firms to incur greater and greater costs over time to remain in compliance (Copeland, 2014). In order to give municipalities the wherewithal to attain these goals, the 1972 Amendments established Title II: "Grants for Construction of Treatment Works," a fund that provided 75 percent of the costs for the construction of municipal water treatment facilities across the country. This grant program remained in operation until 1989, when it was replaced by the Clean Water State Revolving Fund (Anderson, 2007; Copeland, 2014).

The 1987 Water Quality Act established the Clean Water State Revolving Fund (Title VI), replacing the Title II Grants for Construction of Treatment Works in the same move. More to the point, Title VI replaced a municipal *grant* program with a *loan* program. Municipalities thus retained the technology-forcing regulatory obligations of the CWA while becoming newly responsible for financing approximately 95 percent of the costs of such undertakings themselves (Anderson, 2007).

The implications of this "bait-and-switch" legislation were made clear five years later in 1994, when the EPA released an updated pollution control policy regarding "combined sewer overflow" (CSO) systems. CSOs transport both sewage and storm water in a single pipe system for delivery to a water treatment facility. While their valve system easily prevents sewage from coming back into buildings when pipes are backed up, their Achilles heel is that heavy storms can overwhelm CSO systems, causing both storm water and sewage to discharge into rivers and other waterways (Holeywell, 2012). After the updated policy was released, the EPA began applying an "aggressive legal framework" against the 772 municipalities around the country that use CSOs, in order to force them into compliance (ibid.). With the revocation of CWA grant funding, cities are shouldering the enormous burden of paying for these new CWA-compliant systems themselves, now under both economic and legal duress.

So, on the one hand both CERCLA and the CWA have been subject to structurally similar roll-back and roll-out dynamics of neoliberalization: by turn, CERCLA has been the victim of strategic underperformance, of devolution of responsibilities, and of newly invented accounting procedures designed to reduce the cost of cleanup, but which in reality serve to delay or reduce the effectiveness of actually implemented remedies. The CWA, meanwhile, has experienced a sped-up version of the roll-back/ roll-out process, as the section of the Act establishing a federally funded grant program for cities to maintain their water systems was legislatively supplanted by a loan program. On top of these structural similarities, though, important differences between the respective socio-natures of illegal toxic waste dumps and municipal water systems have produced important variegated differences between neoliberalized CERCLA and CWA; regarding not only the actual processes of neoliberalization (Bakker, 2010) just described, but also the changed relational positionalities of key actors in each area.

The original intent behind CERCLA, for example, was to create a Superfund financed by polluters, including the initial costs of paying for studies to identify the extent of pollution and implications for the surrounding population. These first-move duties are generally assigned to be carried out and paid for by the entity identified as the PRP (potentially responsible party). In the case of the Bridgeton Landfill fire in St. Louis County, Republic Services, Inc. has—perhaps logically; *definitely* strategically—used its position as PRP to indemnify itself via sublimation tactics. By bringing the battle over the Bridgeton Landfill fire and the West Lake Superfund site into the realm of science—whose science is correct, the PRP's or the Missouri Department of Natural Resources'? Is the fire moving closer or further away? Is it dangerous if heated, or not?—Republic Services, Inc. has successfully delayed, and possibly avoided paying out hundreds of millions of dollars in cleanup fees. The position of PRP here is no longer punitive, but powerful. It has the power to cast unfavorable findings by state departments and federal agencies into doubt, and to stymie the progress of cleanup efforts for years, all while the underlying population remains exposed to the life-threatening consequences of living next door to an irradiated, possibly burning toxic waste dump.

Conversely, the positionality of municipalities within EPA governance structures has steadily worsened over the years. Once seen as a regulated partner in the quest to clean the nation's waterway system, cities are now essentially criminalized by the litigation process employed by the EPA to ensure CWA compliance. The next section considers both the financial and social impacts of these litigation tactics on municipal governments as they search for ways to fund projects the federal agency has punitively fined and threatened to sue them for if not carried out—either at all, or, as is more typically the case, at a fast-enough pace.

EPA and Consent Decrees in the Age of Austerity

Since 1999, the EPA has finalized consent decrees for violations against the Clean Water Act with approximately sixty-six municipalities around the country, including their associated counties and sewer districts (EPA, civil cases and settlements by statute, n.d.).[2] Fully half of the nation's thirty largest metro areas have received CWA consent decrees since then; and in 2012 the EPA released estimates that the nation's cities will need to spend somewhere between $530 and $733 billion in wastewater infrastructure improvements over the next twenty years alone.[3] However, the current post-crisis milieu in which cities find themselves searching for funds to finance needed improvements is very different from the growth years of the 1990s, when the bulk of the original North American neoliberal "roll-out" reforms were disseminated. The political economy they go up against today is neoliberalism in crisis management mode—a fiscal environment produced by the successful grafting of the 2008 banking crisis onto the public sphere, where the costs have been absorbed and socialized.

This transfiguration of private debt into public debt is what Mark Blyth has termed *the* "greatest bait and switch in human history" (Blyth, 2013, p. 13). It has gone on to produce extreme budgetary and service provision cutbacks in the state apparatus. The bulk of these have been subsequently passed down to smaller scales of government in a second historical wave of state devolution and dismantlement (Peck, 2012, 2014). The post-crisis fiscal landscape today is, as Jamie Peck notes, "roll-out neoliberalism's very own roll-back moment."

With federal financial support now substantively withdrawn, the technological imperative of the Clean Water Act is experienced by municipalities in much the same way they experience the capitalist drive for economic growth: both must be accomplished in the short-to-medium term, and both must be obtained by whatever (increasingly speculative) means necessary (Davidson & Ward, 2014; Kirkpatrick & Smith, 2011). To that end, municipal service providers with unfunded mandates to meet are shunted toward the same false harbor that cities have been obliged to fund their economic growth strategies with for the past thirty-five years: the municipal bond market.

The spectacular growth of a private market for municipal debt coincides not only with the rise of neoliberalism and the "hollowing-out" of the Keynesian state apparatus, but it also maps onto the rise of financialization[4] (Krippner, 2011). A changing fiscal and financial regulatory environment at the state and federal levels of government from 1981 onward produced a thirty-year period in which the size of the municipal bond market increased by about $110 billion each year, on average.[5] The conditions of possibility that gave rise to this kind of enormous growth in municipal debt were themselves produced by legislative changes regarding the deteriorating positionality of cities vis-à-vis other levels of government. These changes, which are still ongoing—and even deepening in many instances, as we will shortly see—constrained federal sources of funding as well as the taxing powers of local governments (Davidson & Ward, 2014). In turn, cities have been forced to become increasingly entrepreneurial and speculative in their search for resources. The surge of leverage taken on by cities adopting these kinds of risk-taking positions in the years leading up to the financial collapse of 2008 is astounding: while the market grew by $110 billion each year on average from 1981–2011, for the years 2000–2008 that figure more than doubled, so that the debt and compound interest owed by municipal entities to private investors grew by $254.5 billion each year during that period alone.[6]

The money garnered from the bond market to finance the large majority of EPA consent decrees and other waterworks improvements (as well as the familiar litany of risky types of urban growth ventures), is typically secured not through the taxing authority of the cities, or loans from the states, but primarily via the promise to investors of future revenue streams earned from the projects themselves (Davidson & Ward, 2014, p. 82). These promised future revenue streams almost inevitably come in the form of increased user fees; in the case of CWA consent decrees and other water projects in particular, they are revenue streams that come by way of increased utility rates. Detroit provides an egregious, real-time example of what happens when an urban citizenry is unable to pay their water bills, as more than 27,000 city residents have had their water turned off in 2014 alone, and a further 300,000 face imminent water shutoff, at the time of writing (Detroit Water Project, 2015; Gottesdiener, 2014).

Austerity Water Wars

The Detroit Water and Sewerage Department (DWSD) emerged from thirty-seven years of federal oversight in March 2013, just two days after the city of Detroit was itself placed under the emergency management of Kevyn Orr. Federal Judge John Feikens was the overseer of the DWSD from 1977–2013, after the EPA sued the city for dumping toxic waste into the Detroit River. During its time under federal oversight, the DWSD entered into multiple "predatory interest rate swap agreements" and at least once used more than $500 million meant for system repairs to service debt instead (Bellant et al., 2014; Gottesdiener, 2014; The Michigan Citizen, 2015). At its untimely exit from federal oversight in 2013, the department was left approximately $5.4 billion in debt, and was immediately put under control of emergency manager (EM) Orr. One month later, Orr entered the DWSD into a $5.6 million contract with the demolition firm Homrich, with directions for the demo enterprise to enforce seventy thousand water shutoffs over a two-year period in an attempt to collect unpaid utility fees (Bellant et al., 2014; The Michigan Citizen, 2015). Interestingly, the firm was contracted for $600,000 more than was promised in 2006 to fund a Water Affordability Program that would have linked utility bills to users' income. Both the funding and structure of the affordability program were later revoked, however, and as of October 2014, up to three thousand shutoffs per week have been reported (ibid.; Center for the Human Rights of Children, Loyola University, 2015).

The context in which this austerity-induced mass shutoff is taking place is that of a city where 40 percent of the population lives below the poverty line and water bills have already risen 120 percent over the past decade. It is a context where commercial and industrial sectors do not appear to experience shutoffs, yet nevertheless owe $30 million in unpaid water bills: as of October 2014 the Detroit hockey arena owed $80,000 while the stadium owed $55,000. And it comes in the context of a water and sewage department that has a 2014 budget paying out $53 million more[7] in debt servicing payments than it expends to operate the actual water and sewage system (Bellant et al., 2014; Gottesdiener, 2014). A lawsuit was filed on behalf of affected residents, *Lyda vs. City of Detroit*, but the bankruptcy judge for the city determined that while "water is a necessary ingredient to sustaining life," city residents do not have an enforceable right to it. He determined that it is the city, rather, that has the enforceable right to shut off water in its attempt to recoup costs (Church and Raphael, 2014; Gottesdiener, 2014).

UN officials who investigated the situation in Detroit disagreed with the judge, calling the shutoffs a violation of human rights and a public health threat. At least one public high school began opening its doors at 5 a.m. so that students could have the opportunity to take showers and wash clothes before class (Gottesdiener, 2014). One elementary teacher admitted that she tells her students not to let her know if the water has been shut off at their homes, because otherwise she is compelled to alert child protective services and they might be taken away from their parents (ibid.). UN special rapporteur Catarina de Albuquerque had this to say about the situation: "I've been to rich countries like Japan and Slovenia where basically 99% of population have access to water, and I've been to poor countries where half the population doesn't have access to water . . . but this large-scale retrogression or backwards steps is new for me" (ibid.).

Regulatory Violence in Consent Decree Cities

The Detroit water experience is unprecedented in the United States, but the structural and circumstantial conditions that gave rise to it are not unique to that city alone. In the age of austerity, when social tensions and economic inequality seem to be at—or at least matching—historic highs, a number of cities with large populations living below the poverty line have seen exponential increases in their utility rates. From 2001 to 2012, Jackson, Mississippi's, water bill increased 110 percent, Chicago's by 116 percent, Cleveland's increased 130 percent, Baltimore by 140 percent, San Francisco by 211 percent, Atlanta's by 233 percent; and since 1996, Birmingham's water bill has increased by more than 329 percent, with annual rate increases scheduled for the city through to 2053 (Braun, 2013; McCoy, 2012; Smith, 2010; Wright, 2014). It is also worth noting that five out of seven of these cities (or six out of eight if including Detroit), have a majority African American population. The financial stresses under which these cities find themselves in terms of their pressing need for sewage upgrades (most major cities have several sewage lines that are more than 100-plus years old), along with heightened pressures caused by time-sensitive EPA consent decrees lodged against them, combined with austere intergovernmental fiscal relations and generalized economic stagnation that had 72 percent of the population convinced that the nation was still in a recession in 2014 (Blake, 2014), are coalescing to create the "perfect storm" of mass shutoffs and other life-threatening yet completely avoidable events in other urban areas across the nation.

The geography of austerity's lived experience is not even. Regulatory violence wrought by austerity-induced policy decision making is affecting the most vulnerable Americans first, and worst. We have already seen that children in Detroit's school districts are now at risk of being pulled into the foster care system for their family's crime of being too poor to pay the water bill. Black majority cities in general, already the historic sites of deindustrialization, white flight, and other geographies of social exclusion, now also appear to be disproportionately affected by user-fee driven increases in water bills, which are themselves often the result of cities borrowing in the municipal debt market to finance unfunded EPA mandates.

Through decades of "roll-back/roll-out" neoliberalization, Keynesian federal institutions such as the EPA have become so hollowed out and refashioned in character that they are now vehicles for a new type of "doubled-down," financialized neoliberalism and roll-back austerity. In the case of the Clean Water Act, the EPA's overwhelming reliance on litigation tactics alone (rather than a combination of court order plus federal assistance, for example) has led it to become a conduit for the debt peonage (Hudson, 2012) of cities. While at the same time, the

Superfund program has lost its ability to function in league with the spirit of the law that created it. Due to the substantive power of the PRP and neoliberal methods of accountancy, CERCLA remains severely underfunded and almost recalcitrantly slow to respond to immediate and possibly life-threatening concerns of effected residents. A neoliberalized EPA has thus contributed to the decline in power of cities within the American political-economic landscape over time, and has added to the intensity of austerity's felt effects on the most economically and ecologically vulnerable Americans.

How—or even whether, as we shall see—these affected cities and their residents are able to weather this socially constructed storm depends on a number of factors, including the structural features of the underlying debt incurred to pay for waterworks upgrades, as well as the quality and character of the relationship between the city and its state. The political-economic climate cities now face regarding both of these factors has changed substantially in the aftermath of the 2008 financial crisis. The following section compares the pre- and post-crisis experiences of Birmingham, Alabama, and Atlanta, Georgia, in their financial encounters with Clean Water Act consent decrees in order to evaluate the socioeconomic ramifications of the current context of austerity and infrastructural downloading.

The Difference a Crisis Makes:
A Tale of Two Consent Decree Cities

Jefferson County, Alabama—the county Birmingham is situated in—received an EPA Clean Water Act consent decree in 1996; while Atlanta, Georgia, received two shortly thereafter, in 1998 and 1999. The mandated upgrades in both cities were originally estimated to cost $1.5 and $2.2 billion respectively; however, the costs for repairs in both cities wound up doubling: Jefferson County accumulated more than $3 billion in debt, while Atlanta's costs shot up to $4 billion (Atlanta Department of Watershed Management, n.d; Bond Buyer, Jefferson County Timeline, n.d; Hunter & Sukenik, 2007).

Despite these similarities, the paths they took to finance the consent decrees were fundamentally different. Jefferson County financed the sewer project largely through an ill-advised combination of complex, variable interest rate bonds and swaps, and subsequently wound up filing the second largest municipal bankruptcy in U.S. history when the global financial crisis hit the municipal bond market. Atlanta, on the other hand, suffered through a botched water system privatization effort in the early 2000s, but later successfully financed its consent decree and other necessary upgrades through a patchwork of funding sources that are increasingly, and *intentionally*, being taken off the table for many metro areas by their state legislatures.

Both Jefferson County and the city of Atlanta faced corruption scandals for their political leaders' roles in mediating the swap agreements and the privatization deal respectively. Yet the combination of a $500 million loan from the state of Georgia, and a local sales tax that provides approximately 20 percent of the needed funds for the waterworks projects (Gurwitt, 2004) ultimately allowed Atlanta to repay the debt in a (relatively, given the "classic," or "pre-austerity" neoliberal context) more equitable and financially sustainable way than the debt package used by Jefferson County.

Both the loan and the local tax were difficult for the city to obtain. Shirley Franklin, mayor of Atlanta from 2002–10, faced a hostile state legislature when she first sought financial assistance for the consent decrees. President of the Georgia state senate Eric Johnson informed Atlantans via their city's major newspaper that he would "fight any effort to shift the costs of Atlanta's sewer repairs onto the taxpayers of our state" (ibid.). As a consequence of the letter, Mayor Franklin decided to hire Johnson's friend (and board member of the Georgia Christian Coalition) as a state lobbyist for the city. Happily for Atlanta, the senate president was subsequently brought around—so much so, in fact, that he even helped the city reformat the local sales tax option to bypass vested interests on the Fulton County Commission (who had voted it down three times before), so that it could be voted on directly by Atlanta residents.

Mayor Franklin also received the help of Metro Atlanta Chamber of Commerce president Lee Thomas. It was Thomas, then president of

Georgia-Pacific, a Koch Industries Paper and Pulp company headquartered in Atlanta, and former head of the U.S. EPA during the second Reagan administration, who convinced the state's governor that the financial and sewage issues facing the city of Atlanta were really "a Georgia problem" (Gurwitt, 2004). The governor subsequently agreed to package the $500 million loan for the city. However, the deal was also conditional on the city council agreeing to raise utility rates as well.

Meanwhile, in Alabama, the 1999 state legislature repealed as unconstitutional a Jefferson County tax that was historically the source of approximately 20 percent of the county's general funds. After a lengthy court battle, the state's supreme court ruled in favor of the repeal in 2009. Then, when the sewer bonds the county took out in the 1990s were refinanced in 2002–03 in an attempt to save money, municipal financial advisors to the county repackaged them into a series of complex swaps and variable interest rate deals, the specifics of which eluded even the lawyers tasked with ensuring the legality of the deals themselves:

> Neither I nor anybody in the Jefferson County Commission—or for that matter, I'm not even sure that the JPMorgan people that we deal with—really understand how swaps are priced in the global financial market. (Bill Slaughter, bond counsel for Jefferson County, quoted in Smith, 2010)

With the loss of 20 percent of its revenues, beginning in 2009, an already beleaguered Jefferson County was forced into issuing mass layoffs and service cutbacks, ultimately filing for bankruptcy two years later. In the same year, however (2009), the state legislature also passed the "Jefferson County Accountability Act," requiring the county commission to appoint a county manager, to be chosen out of "less than three" candidates selected by a nationally recognized recruiting firm. Notably, the bill was sponsored by Paul DeMarco of District 46, representing some of the wealthiest, and whitest, suburbs surrounding the Black-majority city of Birmingham.[8] The Accountability Act transfers major portions of the county commission's responsibilities to this newly appointed "chief executive officer" with no term limit.[9]

The utility rate increases demanded by the county's bankruptcy settlement disproportionately affect the county's poorest residents, as those living in the wealthier suburbs generally use septic tanks that aren't connected to the county sewer system and therefore don't pay sewage bills. Yet suburban residents with septic tanks *do* use either city or well water that is clean due to the sewage upgrades. The resulting untenable situation wherein 70 percent of those who are actually footing the bill for a universally beneficial system "reside in the commission districts with the poorest residents," is why County Commissioner George Bowman voted against the bankruptcy settlement. Sadly, he was the only commissioner to do so (Braun, 2013; Walsh, 2011).

The examples provided by Atlanta and Jefferson County not only highlight the importance of the structure of the underlying debt to the ongoing financial stability of consent decree cities, but they also emphasize the importance of the working relationship between a city and its state— the changing nature of which is one of the major differences between the pre– and post–2008 financial crisis urban-economic landscape. The ability to ply traditional, albeit elite-driven, political pressure to cut a deal is not an option for many cities in the current (fictitiously) fiscal crisis. And while Atlanta did take out municipal bonds to finance the majority of its sewer repairs, its eventual ability to pass a local area sales tax helped to reduce city residents' debt burden substantially. Moreover, it did so in a way that more evenly spreads out the cost of the tax between residents of majority-Black Atlanta proper and its visitors, as more than five hundred thousand tourists and suburbanites visit the city to work and shop every day.[10] The tax was originally passed in 2004, was reauthorized by city voters in 2008 and again in 2012, and is a key feature working to limit future utility rate rises.

Neither the sales tax option nor the $500 million state loan would have been possible for Atlanta without assistance from key players at the state level. Yet in the Jefferson County case, the state actively worked *against* the municipality—first by repealing a tax comprising 20 percent of its general funds, and then by subsequently imposing an "Orrian"-type managerial position after the county, inevitably, ran out of money.

Revenge of the Suburbs

Unfortunately, even the traditional neoliberal path that Atlanta took to finance its sewer system upgrades is no longer accessible for a growing

number of cities and metro areas. More and more states are taking their
lesson from Alabama's antiurban, hyperfinancialized austerity-driven
playbook, and actively working to prevent their consent decree cities
from raising a tax meant to offset utility rate increases or reduce their
municipalities' exposure to the debt market. With its four largest cities[11]
all in various stages of addressing their own Clean Water Act consent
decrees, for example, Tennessee enacted Senate Bill 1742 (2014), revok-
ing a municipality's right to subsidize a public works system with tax
revenues, and authorizing "financially distressed utility districts" to be
placed under the supervision of the newly created "utility management
review board."[12] Meanwhile, in Jackson, Mississippi, the city's voters
recently passed a 1 percent sales tax similar to Atlanta's, dedicated to
funding their own CWA consent decree—and did so with a massive
90 percent approval rate (Barnes, 2014). However, the Mississippi state
legislature worked steadily to hollow out the tax: first by instituting a
"sales tax commission" responsible for determining how the tax pro-
ceeds will be distributed, and on which the city itself holds a minority
position (the other seats being held by state representatives and members of the *Greater* Jackson Chamber of Commerce, i.e., the suburbs);
and then by the passage of House Bill 787 (Cleveland, 2013; Minka,
2014). HB 787 was a bond bill originally intended to provide funds
for construction of the University of Mississippi's medical center, but
in the spring of 2014 it was amended to include unrelated exemptions
for Jackson's 1 percent sales tax for "the wholesale of beer, light wine
and liquor, *as well as the delivery of goods into Jackson limits from outside
businesses*" (Barnes, 2014; emphasis added). Thus, in one move state
legislators simultaneously increased Jackson's exposure to the municipal
debt market by reducing the amount of tax it was able to collect, while
also privileging businesses located in the wealthier nearby suburbs who
are doing business inside the state capitol of Jackson. The privileging
of suburban businesses comes of course, by way of penalizing those
firms located within the Black-majority city itself, by making the latter
enterprises alone subject to the tax.

The threat of disincorporation, or revocation of all state funding to
financially "distressed," or "noncompliant" municipalities are two other
tactics that state legislators have introduced in recent years as well. In

Scranton, Pennsylvania, city employees had their salaries reduced to the state minimum of $7.25/hr. in July 2012 in an effort to pare down expenses, only to have a Clean Water Act consent decree with estimated costs of more than $140 million lodged against the city five months later, in December (Larson, 2012; U.S. Department of Justice, 2012). Meanwhile, lawmakers in the Pennsylvania state legislature introduced Senate Bill 1157 (2014) and House Bill 1773 (2014), both of which propose to disincorporate and "leave as a ward of the state" municipalities who "won't, or can't" exit financial distress within eight years (Frantz, 2014). In Ohio, where residents in at least seven municipalities[13] face CWA consent decrees (including Cincinnati, Cleveland, and Toledo), state legislators have introduced House Bill 337, which seeks to "impose sanctions" on municipalities that "fail to comply with budget, debt, or pension requirements under state law" by withholding all state funding until such compliance is met.[14] In Mississippi, the state representative from District 77, representing the second-wealthiest batch of suburbs bordering majority-Black Jackson, introduced House Bill 627, the "Municipal Government Responsibility Act," seeking to establish a replica of Michigan's financial emergency law in the Magnolia State.[15] And in Missouri, the representative of District 89, encompassing some of the wealthiest suburbs in the St. Louis metro area, proposed House Bill 1891 (2012), specifically aimed at the Black-majority city of St. Louis.[16] More to the point, District 89 represents the suburban area that houses what is by one measure the "richest community in America": Huntleigh, Missouri (pop. 369), whose median income for the top 5 percent of its residents exceeds $2.7 million per year (Holleman, 2013). It is this suburban neighborhood's representative that tabled legislation seeking to impose financial discipline on its work-worn urban center. The bill proposes, at the behest of "at least thirty % of the registered voters in the municipality who voted in the last gubernatorial election"—thus taking advantage of the filtering effect provided by low-income and minority voter suppression tactics—to give the city approximately twelve months of turn-around time under the leadership of an advisory board before the county circuit court rules on whether it is "operating below minimum standards." A court decision confirming the failure of the St. Louis city government to meet minimum service provision standards would result in the following sequential events, the autocratic breadth of which deserves extended quotation:

1. Appointment by the court of an administrative authority for the municipality including but not limited to another political subdivision, the state, or a qualified private party to administer all revenues under the name of the municipality. . . .

2. Any salaries and benefits paid to the members of the governing body shall cease from the time of appointment of the administrative authority. . . .

3. Removal from office of any or all elected officials of the municipality by the court if it believes, at the end of 180 days from the date of the court declaration, that standards are still not met. The court shall appoint new officials to fill the remainder of the terms of those removed from office. . . .

4. If the court believes that standards still are not being met at the end of ninety days from the time of the appointment of the new officials, the court will order placement on the ballot of a proposal to merge the municipality . . . with an adjacent municipality. . . .[17]

If the proposed merger is not approved by voters, then the last option is disincorporation, to be voted on at the request of 40 percent of registered voters of the subject municipality—again taking advantage of filtering effects provided by voter suppression laws and tactics.

The sort of legislation highlighted here and in the previous examples gives new meaning to everyday understandings of "rule of law." What these laws and proposed bills seek to establish is the divorce of deliberative democracy from urban governance. They seek to shunt dispossessed urban residents even farther from the realm of political decision making and power than they already are, and deliver municipalities themselves into the rule of so-called experts for the smooth operationalization of post-crisis accumulation strategies. Not the least of which has become selling money to cities in fiscal crisis.

Discussion and Conclusion: Black Cities Matter

In the ongoing and intensifying national context of urban austerity, then, the racial tension and social outrage epitomized by one word—Ferguson—continues to grow apace. Meanwhile, ten miles away from the city of Ferguson itself, the Bridgeton landfill fire continues to burn next to a Superfund site. The EPA continues to mandate that St. Louis spend $4.7 billion repairing a sewer system potentially exposed to heated and irradiated toxic waste the agency considers too expensive to move. And the representative of one of the wealthiest neighborhoods in America proposes legislation making the legal death of the Black-majority city of St. Louis itself a real possibility. Meanwhile, downriver in majority-black Jackson, Mississippi, suburban officials are citing the city's consent decree as evidence of incompetent city management: "A recently enacted U.S. EPA Consent Decree with the City of Jackson calls for repairs . . . that may exceed $400 million. This is a reflection on Jackson's ability to manage the plant," said a metro-area mayor from one of the wealthier neighboring counties, a county that, in an effort to avoid paying the increased utility fees associated with financing the consent decree, has started plans to build itself a new water processing plant just outside of Jackson's jurisdiction, ensuring the capital city's impoverished inner-city population will bear disproportionate financial responsibility for the consent decree—just as happened in Birmingham.

Yet, while state representatives from wealthy white suburbs work at hollowing out municipal tax proposals and introducing emergency manager legislation in attempts to infantilize whatever agency black-majority cities do have, and while suburban mayors levy accusations of incompetency against the material effects of generations of historical inequities, decades of neoliberalization, and years of austerity—about a mile down the road from city hall and the governor's mansion on Capitol Street in Jackson, the Chokwe Lumumba Center for Economic Democracy and

Development hosts its inaugural event: The Fire Next Time: Ferguson and the Myth of a Post-racial America (*Jackson Free Press*, 2014).[18]

Within the context of urban austerity in America, the onset and continued growth of community organizations such as the Lumumba Center for Economic Democracy and Development and social movements like Black Lives Matter is not a coincidence. The bodies made most vulnerable through successive rounds of austerity driven budget cuts, scalar dumping of regulatory responsibilities, antiurban legislation, and the crippled functionality of local government due to the absence of federal funding and mushrooming debt burdens in the municipal bond market—are the very same bodies that have always moved through life in this country via circuits laden with the accumulated detritus of previous generations of institutional inequities.

Within this context, it is important to realize that the patchwork of policies we understand and experience cumulatively as austerity urbanism are not actually focused on recovering economic production, but rather on furthering the material *reproduction* of particular lives. While, for some, the context and logic of austerity may present a new set of opportunities for accumulation through continued neoliberal governance, the lived experience of specifically *urban* austerity feels like the very worst sort of market-based transgression that Polanyi put forth in his well-known theory of dialectical social regulation, the double movement. American austerity has shown itself to pathogenically attack at racialized and classed intersections of political-economic and socioecological circuits of social reproduction. As such, the Polanyian response to protect and defend our communities against these market-borne, state-inflected, and socially encountered aggressions is lodged at these intersecting sites and circuitries as well. And it is here, at these social intersections, that organizations such as the Lumumba Center for Economic Democracy and Development and movements like Black Lives Matter have arisen and situated themselves.

Through an examination of Detroit's socially constructed water crisis; Birmingham's socially unjust bankruptcy settlement; the accounting-induced impotence of the EPA; and attempts by state legislators to render work-worn cities financially dependent on a private market in municipal debt, this chapter has aimed to show that what we are seeing on the streets—both in terms of activist protests as well as infrastructural dilapidation and other socioecological vulnerabilities—is a reflection of the violence inherent in our austerity-ridden regulatory process.

Notes

1. Point of clarification: The EPA maintains that CERCLA legislation and the Superfund are one and the same and talk about them interchangeably. However, in much of the literature surrounding them, they are conceptualized separately.

2. Figures from before 1999 unavailable.

3. The fifteen largest metro areas in the country facing CWA consent decrees are: Atlanta, Baltimore, Boston, Chicago, Cincinnati, Cleveland, Dallas, Kansas City, Miami, Pittsburgh, San Antonio, San Diego, San Francisco, Seattle, and St. Louis. Source: Pew Charitable Trusts, 2013; US Conference of Mayors, 2012.

4. The process whereby a national economy develops an accumulation pattern based on the valuation techniques of intangible financial instruments—particularly debt—rather than on the production of material goods.

5. Author's calculations, SEC figures amount to $111.3 billion increase each year over the thirty-year period, while figures from SIFMA for the same period amount to $109.19 billion.

6. SIFMA, author's calculations. Although the size of the market continued to grow throughout 2009–10, about 20–25 percent of that growth is attributed to Build America Bonds that were released by the federal government as a part of the American Recovery and Reinvestment Act of 2009. The program expired on the last day of 2010.

7. Author's calculations based on information from cited sources.

8. http://www.pauldemarco.org/about/; accessed 1/24/15.

9. Some of the primary responsibilities of the new position include: ability to hire and fire department heads; "direct oversight" of all agencies and county operations, except those duties directly assigned by law to attorneys or elected officials; control over all budgets and expenditures; and supervision over all county contracts. Act 2011-69 amending Act 2009-812; http://openstates.org/al/bills/2011rs/HB159/; accessed 2/21/15.

10. Municipal Option Sales Tax: What it Means to Atlanta, atlantaga.gov.

11. Nashville, Memphis, Knoxville, and Chattanooga, in that order.

12. S. 1742, 108th regular session, 2014.

13. Ohio cities facing CWA consent decrees include Cleveland, Toledo, Cincinnati, Akron, Youngstown, Ironton, and Lima (EPA, Civil Cases and Settlements by Statute).

14. Ohio H. 337, 130th General Assembly, regular session, 2014.

15. Mississippi H. 627, regular session, 2014.

16. District 89 was previously district 87, before redistricting took place. In 2010 the population of St. Louis was 51 percent African American. However, 2014 estimates suggest the city's Black population may be experiencing displacement, having fallen to a little more than 49 percent of the total population (a loss of more than 5,500 people), while the "white-alone" demographic has increased by more than four thousand people in the same time period (American FactFinder). The language of HB 1891 stipulates that the Act would only be relevant to any municipality located in a county with "more than nine hundred fifty thousand inhabitants." St. Louis County, which houses the metro area of St. Louis, is the only county in Missouri to match that description.

17. Missouri (State) Legislature. House. Establishes minimum standards that a municipality in St. Louis County must meet in the provision of municipal and financial services and reports. House Bill 1891, 2012 Regular Session (May 1, 2012) 96th General Assembly. https://legiscan.com/MO/text/HB1891/2012; accessed April 28, 2017.

18. Posthumously named after the city's socially activist mayor Chokwe Lumumba.

5

The Unaffordability of Recession

Housing Mobility and Recession Austerity in Providence, Rhode Island

AARON NIZNIK

Introduction

The Great Recession, beginning in late 2007 and lasting until Summer 2009, generated an increasingly precarious housing context for many Americans. Massive increases in foreclosures, unemployment, and wealth loss pushed many Americans out of their homes in search of more affordable opportunities. Given higher than average rates of eviction and job loss coupled with disproportionate decreases in wealth, people of color, particularly African Americans, exhibited higher rates of economically motivated local residential mobility (Stoll, 2013). While non-Hispanic white Americans were the largest group of borrowers driven out of their homes by foreclosure, African Americans and Hispanics were disproportionately affected given their share of mortgage originations. Much of this is largely due to lenders of subprime mortgages targeting segregated, low-income communities in search of risky borrowers (Massey & Rugh, 2010). At the same time, neighborhoods with higher than average numbers of immigrants and people of color experienced disproportionate increases in poverty, vacancy, and unemployment. These characteristics suggest that inner-city urban neighborhoods are likely to exhibit higher rates of residential mobility spurred by recessionary conditions.

In general, poor people of color exhibit higher than average rates of residential mobility, often moving within the same neighborhood or to another, similarly disadvantaged location (Coulton et al., 2009; South & Crowder, 1998). Such high rates of residential mobility are linked to a number of negative individual and neighborhood-level consequences. For example, frequent residential mobility during childhood is linked to behavioral problems and violence, risk taking, depression, lower academic achievement, and higher mortality in adulthood (Ersing et al., 2009; Leventhal, 2014; Oishi & Schimmack, 2010; Pribesh & Downey, 1999; Sharkey & Sampson, 2010). At the neighborhood level, high residential mobility decreases the likelihood that residents will develop lasting ties with their neighbors, an instrumental element in the ability of communities to solve collective problems (Kingsly, McNealy, & Gibson, 1997; Sampson, Morenoff, & Earls, 1999). As a result, the increases in residential mobility spurred by the recession work to reinforce and exacerbate the negative consequences of concentrated urban poverty.

Given the negative consequences associated with high rates of residential mobility, it is imperative that government work to maintain residential stability, particularly for low-income people. Unfortunately, the response to this instability has been largely limited due to the impact of austerity measures at all levels of government. A major negative consequence has been the decimation of funding available for affordable housing programs across the country. At the federal level, the HOME program, part of the Department of Housing and Urban Development (HUD), is a federal block grant initiative that directs funds to states to develop affordable housing for low-income Americans. Due to an austerity agenda promoted by the federal government, the HOME program has seen its budget cut by more than 50 percent since FY2010. This program, which offers crucial funding to struggling communities and local governments, is currently targeted for near elimination, as the United States Senate Committee on Appropriations voted to reduce funding from $900 million in FY2015 to merely $66 million in FY2016. Such drastic cuts make it particularly difficult for cities to achieve appropriate levels of affordable housing for low-income residents.

The retreat by the federal government in funding affordable housing, in conjunction with state fiscal crises, is part of a larger trend of "austerity urbanism" whereby cities are expected to provide basic services for their citizens while at the same time being increasingly fiscally constrained (Peck, 2015). Facing extreme budgetary conditions coupled with increasing local demand for lower cost units, many cities fail to provide appropriate levels of stable affordable housing. As a result, austerity urbanism offloads the negative consequences of fiscal crisis on the nation's most vulnerable population—the urban poor. Mass unemployment and wealth loss coupled with the retrenchment of the state in affordable housing presents a major barrier for poor people of color in search of cheaper housing in the postrecession city. The unavailability of stable affordable housing is likely to encourage more frequent mobility, exacerbating the issues faced by highly mobile disadvantaged urban neighborhoods. As a result, austerity measures work in tandem with rising residential mobility in poor communities of color to exacerbate the issues associated with concentrated urban poverty.

To gain a better sense of how residential mobility and austere housing policies are intertwined, this chapter focuses on the case of Providence, Rhode Island, a city that experienced a disproportionately high degree of foreclose and recession-related unemployment. At the same time, Providence was faced with a massive budget crisis, leading city and state leaders to impose a number of austerity measures to achieve fiscal solvency. Using a local survey from the Annie E. Casey Foundation, this chapter compares mobility patterns prior to and during the Great Recession in order to ascertain how recent economic and political shifts impacted residential stability in the city's poorest neighborhoods. Results indicate that the recession induced economically motivated residential mobility, particularly among Hispanics, who are largely concentrated within the poorest neighborhoods on the city's south side. At the same time, the south side experienced the most pronounced impacts from the foreclosure crisis in conjunction with a severe lack of affordable housing. As a result, Hispanics in the city's most disadvantaged neighborhoods are faced with increasing housing costs, decreased resources, and a local government unable to ameliorate the negative consequences due to recently enacted austerity policies. At the same time, the residential mobility induced by these changes is likely to exacerbate the negative consequences associated with neighborhood instability. In sum, higher residential mobility among the urban poor works in tandem with austerity urbanism to maintain concentrated poverty in the city's Hispanic neighborhoods.

The Recession and Housing Affordability in Providence

The state of Rhode Island, of which the Providence metropolitan area constitutes the lion's share of the state's total population, experienced a unique upsurge in housing prices in the six years prior to the start of the recession in 2007. Between the first quarter of 2000 and the first quarter of 2006, Rhode Island experienced the largest growth in housing prices in the state's history, nearly doubling the growth rates of some nearby New England states (Housing Works Rhode Island, 2012). Concurrently, between 2000 and 2008, Rhode Island had the lowest rate of new housing construction in the United States, further straining the housing supply. Compounding this problem was income stagnation, with the median income declining in the state between 2000 and 2006.[1] The combination of lower wages and increased housing costs produced a context where Rhode Island's lowest-income residents experienced a disproportionate increase in housing cost burden.[2] In 2000, 80 percent of Rhode Island's lowest-income homeowners were cost burdened, with that number jumping to 91 percent by 2012. Low-income renters experienced a similar increase in cost burden, jumping from 76 percent in 2000 to 84 percent in 2012 (Housing Works Rhode Island, 2014).

In conjunction with the housing affordability crisis, Rhode Island was hit particularly hard by the foreclosure crisis, with the majority of foreclosures taking place in the Providence metropolitan area (Housing Works Rhode Island, 2011). The consequences of foreclosure not only affect people whose mortgages have gone into default, but also the neighboring property. In a study conducted by the Center for Responsible Lending (2009), a foreclosure on a city block is directly linked to a 27 percent decrease in that home's value and a 1 percent decrease in the value of neighboring homes. Given that the foreclosure crisis disproportionately affected Hispanics and blacks, this suggests that highly segregated neighborhoods are likely to lose overall property value. Many of the housing units in the city of Providence are multifamily units, often serving as rental property owned by the same landlord. When a multifamily rental property goes into foreclosure, at least two or three families are left without housing. Given that 35 percent of the foreclosures in Providence were multifamily units, the number of displaced families dramatically increased while the number of available rental properties remained stagnant. As a result, a situation developed where displaced families were left to compete for affordable rental housing in an already shorthanded market that continued to lose even more housing to foreclosure (Housing Works Rhode Island, 2011).

The growing lack of affordable housing coupled with the foreclosure crisis further strained the housing market in Rhode Island more generally. At the same time, the labor market was disproportionately strained in the state. Rhode Island has been comparatively slow to recover from the recession, ranking seventh-worst in the nation for private sector job recovery in October 2013 since the peak of the Great Recession in 2009 (Economic Progress Institute [EPI], 2014). Rhode Island's economy was historically centered on manufacturing, particularly in the jewelry, machinery, and textile industries. As of October 2013, Rhode Island is ranked first among the states for percentage of manufacturing jobs lost since 1990. During the recession, the state lost a larger percentage of manufacturing jobs (22 percent) compared to the national average (14.5 percent). The construction industry shed 35 percent of its jobs from 2006 to 2013 in Rhode Island compared to the national average of 25 percent. This is particularly important for Hispanics, as they suffered major job losses in the construction industry nationwide (Department of Labor, 2012). Overall, we see that many of the industries directly linked to the Great Recession found disproportionately unfavorable fortunes in the wake of the recession.

The changes in Rhode Island's economic structure resulted in a higher than average rate of unemployment for the state. In 2010, Rhode Island retained an unemployment rate of 12 percent, while Providence clocked in at 14 percent, far above the national average of 9 percent.

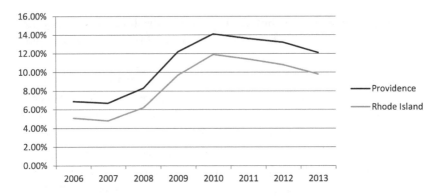

Figure 5.1. Unemployment in R.I. and Providence 2006–2013 (USDLS).

Among metropolitan areas of the United States, the Providence MSA ranked fifth in terms of unemployment in 2009. In addition, 25.2 percent of Hispanics in the Providence MSA were unemployed in 2010, compared to 11.5 percent of Hispanics nationwide. Compared to whites, Hispanics were 2.5 times more likely to be unemployed in the Providence MSA, suggesting the disproportionate impact of economic restructuring on Hispanics in the city (Austin, 2012). As a result, Hispanics in Providence are more likely to be dependent on government assistance and face increasingly constrained opportunities due to the overall lack of employment prospects and support for affordable housing. The following section outlines the changes in federal funding and the austerity measures taken by local governments to deal with changes in revenues associated with private sector shrinkage and property taxes.

Federal and Local Austerity Measures

In 2009, the Department of Housing and Urban Development released a report to Congress entitled "Worst Case Housing Needs," outlining the housing needs of the most at-risk population in the United States—very-low-income renters who contribute more than half of their income to housing and do not receive federal housing assistance. The report found that during the Great Recession, the number of cases defined as "worst case" jumped nearly 20 percent, more than any period since 1987. While all racial and ethnic groups experienced increased hardship during this time, Hispanics were disproportionately likely to be classified as worst case, as 45 percent of low-income renters fell into this category, corresponding to an eight percentage point increase between 2007 and 2009. Three major factors are argued to have been a cause of this uptick in the proportion of people identified as worst case. First, income losses among renters due to the recession's impact on unemployment and decreased wealth accumulation among people of color constrained housing opportunities. Second, federal funding for housing assistance remained stagnant despite the rapid increase in need for assistance. Third, a lack of affordable housing generated an environment of competition among renters, with those in the lowest income bracket unable to compete with those in higher brackets. Thus, during the Great Recession the most disadvantaged populations faced a context of increasing rents and competition for housing and stagnant support for affordable housing assistance, leaving them with fewer options.

The most recent version of the "Worst Case Housing Needs" report released in 2015 finds that despite improvement in private sector economic growth, worst case needs remain high. The number of those classified as worst case needs continued to grow from 2009 into 2011, but experienced modest declines by 2013 (albeit levels are still 9 percent above rates cited for 2009). These data illustrate that, overall, the national housing shortage associated with the Great Recession is still a major issue affecting the most vulnerable members of the populace. While market rebounding is attributed for bringing down the number of at-risk individuals, a large number of people remain excluded from affordable housing. With federal funding for affordable housing programs cut by 50 percent between 2010 and 2015, the most at-risk populations remain increasingly subject to the vagaries of the housing market. Inaction in tackling the affordable housing issue at the federal level shifted responsibility downward to the state and urban levels.

The changes in the availability of federally sponsored affordable housing can be traced directly to the affordable housing crisis on the ground in Providence. The Rhode Island Housing Authority (RIHA) was forced to lay off thirty employees in 2013, reducing its overall workforce by approximately 15 percent (Dunn, 2013). In addition, the RIHA lost a major source of revenue during the foreclosure crisis, as many of its borrowers failed to pay their mortgages. In general, the housing authority is operating today on a reduced budget in the context of the foreclosure crisis and reduced federal support. Thus, as federal funding for affordable housing declined, the state of Rhode Island was faced with increasing demand for affordable housing and reduced resources.

At the same time, many state-sponsored affordable housing programs lost a large amount of funding due to austerity measures. The Neighborhood Opportunities Program (NOP), started in 2001, subsidizes the cost of affordable rental housing in the state. At its inception, NOP was allocated $5 million per year until FY2006, when funding was increased to $7.5 million. However, following the Great Recession, funding was reduced from $7.5 million to $2.5 million in FY2008 to FY2010 and $1.5 in FY2011 and 2012 (redirected from federally sponsored and reduced RIHA funds). At this time, the future of the NOP is unclear, as the state no longer allocates state resources and the RIHA faces future budget cuts from the federal government. In addition, arguably the most successful affordable housing plan in the state expended all of its funds in 2015. The Building Homes Rhode Island program was funded by a voter-approved $50 million bond passed in 2006, and extended in 2012 by $25 million. This program brought 1,670 affordable homes to communities across the state, but now operates under the umbrella of the federally funded RIHA. In sum, there is a general trend toward the consolidation of local programs under the umbrella of the federally funded RIHA. At the same time, the RIHA is losing access to essential funding due to federal austerity measures. If the budget of the Department of Housing and Urban Development experiences more funding cuts, these programs face a perilous future.

The changes occurring at the federal and local levels of government are exacerbating the issue of affordable housing in the United States. In Rhode Island, successful state-sponsored programs are being defunded and federally supported programs are losing ground. At the same time, the Great Recession produced a context where already disadvantaged communities experienced higher than average rates of unemployment, wealth loss, and foreclosure. Such a context generated a situation where a tight housing market continues to push the most disadvantaged members of the population out of the housing market, increasing the risk for homelessness or habitation in substandard housing. As the Hispanic community was disproportionately affected by the unemployment and foreclosures associated with the Great Recession, it is expected that they will be disproportionately impacted by the loss of support for affordable housing. The following section turns an eye toward the sociological literature on residential mobility before developing an analysis of the most drastically affected neighborhoods of Providence in order to gain some perspective on the affordability crisis.

Residential Mobility, Or, Why People Move

Researchers have long studied the motivations behind residential mobility as a way to better understand why neighborhoods change over time. The literature on residential mobility identifies a set of common life cycle traits that influence moving decisions. Basic factors driving family mobility include life cycle factors such as household head age, marital status, housing tenure (rent or own), and the addition of children to the household (Speare, 1974). Couples recently married or divorced are likely to move due to changes in housing needs (McLanahan, 1983; Speare & Goldscheider, 1987). The number of children in the household is associated with mobility, as the addition of children, as well as children "leaving the nest," spurs moving decisions. Younger families and those recently retired are more likely to move as their housing needs shift with the changing family structure. Longer duration of residence and homeownership tend to reduce mobility as families develop stronger ties and associations within neighborhoods; at the same time, renters (who tend to be younger and less wealthy) tend to move at far greater rates than homeowners (Speare, 1974; Speare et al., 1975). In general, people consider a move when there are overall changes to a family's lifestyle, that is, as a result of marriage, retirement, or the addition of children.

Housing and neighborhood satisfaction were long considered the main driving force behind residential mobility. Speare (1974) refers to this as the "stress threshold," wherein a family's mobility decision is based upon the current household size and the subjective housing and neighborhood satisfaction. Stress thresholds vary from family to family, but typically when a family finds their housing situation to be unsatisfactory, they seek alternatives (Speare et al., 1975). However, Newman and Duncan (1979) find that there is a tenuous connection between satisfaction and mobility. Landale and Guest (1985) argue that while satisfaction may increase a family's desire to move, their actual mobility is constrained by life cycle factors. Minority residents, particularly African Americans, often cite lower satisfaction than whites, yet are far less likely to successfully move to more desirable locations due to high residential segregation and structural constraints (Deane & South, 1993; Logan & Alba, 1993). Constrained mobility out of disadvantaged neighborhoods suggests that satisfaction has limited power for explaining mobility in poor neighborhoods. At the same time, Sampson and Sharkey (2008) illustrate that poor people often move to similarly disadvantaged neighborhoods. Schacter (2001) finds that poor people and people of color are most likely to move and often move frequently, particularly because they are more likely to be renters. This suggests that, in general, mobility patterns in poor neighborhoods are unique in that they are comprised of frequent, short-distance moves between rental apartments.

These short-distance moves are inextricably tied to the precarious economic context of residents of poor neighborhoods. Throughout the latter half of the twentieth century, the federal government was active in provisioning adequate housing for the population's most disadvantaged citizens. Early attempts at massive segregated public housing complexes largely resulted in failure by further isolating poor people of color (Goetz, 2011). Following these attempts, the federal government shifted its strategy away from building massive public housing toward incentivizing private development through the use of direct-to-landlord housing vouchers and promoting the development of mixed-income housing through the HOPE VI program. However, with the recent housing crisis, these programs are losing funding, leaving many of the poorest individuals without proper assistance (Schwartz, 2014). As a result, while gains have been made in generating a stable context for low-income housing, recent austerity measures threaten the future of these programs. If residential mobility spurred by economic hardship increases and austerity measures reduce availability of assistance, already disadvantaged neighborhoods are likely to become even more unstable.

Providence, as a prime example of recessionary conditions in the context of increasing austerity, offers a unique opportunity to investigate how residential mobility in poor neighborhoods operates in the context of decreasing housing affordability and increasing economic strain. The following section introduces the data, offers an analysis, and concludes with suggestions for future policy action.

Data and Methods

The south side of Providence experienced the highest rates of foreclosure and unemployment during the Great Recession. The data for this analysis come from the *Making Connections Survey*, from the Annie E. Casey foundation housed in NORC at the University of Chicago. The survey is comprised of three waves from 2000–09: wave one, between 2002 and 2004, wave two, between 2005 and 2007, and wave three, between 2008 and 2010. In total, seven cities were included in all three waves, including Providence.[3] For each of the selected cities, a seven hundred case random digit–dialed countywide telephone survey was conducted as a control group in addition to eight hundred cases from each of the designated neighborhoods.[4] In the case of Providence, the nine census tracts that include the south side are included in the neighborhood sample.

The survey tracked only families with children over time, with single individuals or aged-out families dropped from the next wave. During followup interviews, each household was assigned a "move ID" of "mover" (out of the original Making Connections residence), "stayer" (original household that did not move), "incoming mover" (moved from a non–Making Connections neighborhood), or "new case." As the survey only followed families (and not individuals) that moved, new cases were added to the sample to compensate for attrition. These cases were also dropped as there was no information available on their mobility status. Cases for which there was no information available for key independent variables were also dropped.

The final analysis focuses on two periods: between wave one and wave two (dubbed the prerecession period) and between wave two and wave three (dubbed the recession period). The logic of focusing on people moving between these periods is that it captures mobility patterns right before the recession and follows the same people during the recession, illuminating the ways in which patterns shifted between these periods. After data manipulations, the final analyses were based upon a total of 256 cases between wave one and wave two (prerecession), and 412 cases between wave two and wave three (recession). The majority of dropped cases included single people, couples with no children, and households with more than two adults, or cases for which there were no data available on key independent variables.

The survey asks basic sociodemographic questions, along with a number of questions about housing and residential status. Wave three (postrecession) includes the addition of questions regarding a family's reason for moving, allowing for an analysis of their subjective description of their mobility.[5] Answers range from general life cycle (wanted better housing, got a new job, child added to household, wanted better neighborhood) to economic (needed cheaper housing, experienced foreclosure [both individual and landlord], and evicted). In order to discern the effect of the recession in wave three, life cycle and economic movers are separated into two categories. Eviction was a very rare occurrence and those cases are included in the economic category, as eviction is often related to nonpayment of rent. Overall, 42.72 percent of families moved during the recession, of which 16.02 percent were economic movers and 26.7 percent life cycle movers, indicating the majority of moves were spurred by life cycle factors.

Variables

This study utilizes three dependent variables: whether a family moved between wave one and wave two; whether a family moved between wave two and wave three; and a multinomial variable comparing stayers, economic movers, and life cycle movers between waves two and three. The independent variables are all factors known to induce moves: income, housing tenure (whether the family rents or owns), race, marital status, age, and the number of children in the household (see Table 5.1). In all models, the prior wave's sociodemographic characteristics are used to predict their mobility status in the next wave.

Income is associated with residential mobility, but due to many respondents' unwillingness to provide an answer for income, it is excluded from the models. Instead, welfare receipt serves as a proxy for income, as most families provided a response to this question, and its provision is determined by the household's income. In all of the waves of the neighborhood sample, between 32 and 37 percent of families were receiving welfare, lining up closely with overall levels of poverty from census tract data available on this neighborhood.

Housing tenure is associated with residential mobility in that homeowners are less likely to move than renters. The majority of the families in the sample are either renters or homeowners, but the survey includes categories for those who were staying at a home for free or were in the process of buying a home. Those who were in the process of buying a home are collapsed into the homeowner category as they were most likely homeowners by wave three, and those living at home for free were collapsed into the renter category, as they do not own their residence. Owner and renter categories are treated as dummy variables.

Race is divided into three categories: non-Hispanic whites, non-Hispanic blacks, and Hispanics. Asians and others were collapsed into the non-Hispanic white category as their presence in the sample was very limited. The sample differentiated between Hispanic identities (Cuban, Puerto Rican, other), but are collapsed into a single category as the vast majority of Providence's Hispanic community is of "other" descent, namely, due to the large number of Dominicans in the city. Non-Hispanic whites serve as the reference category as they are less likely to be affected by the recession.

The spouse variable refers to whether the respondent has a spouse living with them in the housing unit, and is included as a dummy variable. Fewer than half of household heads stated they were married. Age (of the respondent) and number of children (under eighteen and living in the same household as the respondent) were treated as integer variables and had very few unanswered dropped cases. The polynomial term for age was tested and shows the nonlinear effect of age. This is most likely due to the fact that mobility is high among young adults and those starting families, but drops off precipitously as family members leave home and householders enter retirement age.

To test the effect of the recession, employment status is included as a series of independent variables to discern any changes families experience between waves.[6] Families that were not in the labor force (retired, stay-at-home parents, self-employed, or disabled) at the time of the initial survey were dropped from the analysis. The reference category for both models is those families that remained unemployed in both waves.

The education variable is a binary one split between those with and without a high school diploma or GED. Although not a known predictor of residential mobility, education is often a marker of higher social status and income. Utilizing likelihood ratio (LR) tests comparing models, the addition of the education variable significantly improved the model fit, particularly in the absence of income. Given that approximately 30 percent of respondents have less than a high school education, they are contrasted with HS+ graduates. Through testing, I ascertained that there were no meaningful statistical differences found in moving between higher levels of education in the neighborhood after high school.

The final independent variables are based on changes in employment status between the waves. Employment status change refers to the respondent's having lost employment, gained employment, maintained employment, or remained unemployed in both waves. Constructing these alternatives was possible because respondents provided their employment status for each wave. This analysis is limited to those who were in the labor force at the time of the survey. As a result those household heads that were retired, stay-at-home parents, self-employed, or disabled are not included in the analysis, as they are out of the labor force.[7]

Methods

Logistic regression is used to predict the probability that a family will move during the prerecession and recession periods. The dependent variable is constructed so that movers are being referenced to stayers. Second, for the recession period analysis, I use multinomial logistic regression to predict whether mover families left their previous dwellings because of economic reasons relative to those who moved for life cycle reasons. Economic moves are defined as the following: needed cheaper housing, evicted, and home foreclosed. All other reasons for moving (family, addition of children, new job) are collapsed into the other category. In this regression, the dependent variable has three categories: stayers, those who moved for economic reasons, and those who moved for life cycle reasons. In this way all movers are included because they all provided a reason for moving and can easily be compared to stayers.

Results and Discussion

The descriptive statistics for the prerecessionary period and recessionary periods are found in Table 5.1 on page 118. One of the most striking differences between the prerecession and recession periods is the percentage of families that move; 27.8 percent move prerecession, while 42.72 percent move during the recession. This indicates an overall increase in residential mobility in the neighborhood during the recession, confirming expectations. The age of household heads that lost employment between the two periods doubles, from 10.42 to 19.17 percent during the recession. In addition, the age of chronically unemployed doubles from 15.38 to 31.55 percent, illustrating that families were far more likely to stay out of work during the recession, constituting approximately 50 percent of overall employment status among survey respondents (compared to approximately 30 percent prior to the recession). In sum, these numbers illustrate that South Providence experienced a large uptick in its unemployment rate along with an increase in the number of families moving going into the Great Recession.

The results from the logistic regression predicting residential mobility in the prerecession period are outlined in Table 5.2 on page 119, while the results for the recessionary period are outlined in Table 5.3 on page 120. Both sets of results offer some commonality that is predicted by the lifecycle literature discussed previously. First, renters are far more likely than homeowners to move in both periods. This is most likely due to the fact that renters tend to be younger and more apt to be going through major lifestyle changes such as moving in with

Table 5.1. Descriptive Statistics for Dependent and Independent Variables

	PANEL 1: Wave 1 to Wave 2 (N=256)				PANEL 2: Wave 2 to Wave 3 (N=412)			
	Mean or Percent	Standard Deviation	Minimum	Maximum	Mean or Percent	Standard Deviation	Minimum	Maximum
Dependent variable								
Mover	27.8		0	1	42.72		0	1
Stayer	72.2		0	1	57.28		0	1
Economic mover					16.02		0	1
Other mover					26.7		0	1
Independent variables								
Welfare receipt	32		0	1	36.65		0	1
Age (years)	42.14	15.19	18	84	40.03	14.85	18	87
Spouse	42.86		0	1	40.29		0	1
Number of children	1.49	1.23	1	5	1.55	1.29	1	5
< high school education	48.01		0	1	44.82		0	1
Employment Status								
Lost employment	10.42		0	1	19.17		0	1
Gained employment	28.57		0	1	10.44		0	1
Maintained employment	45.07		0	1	38.83		0	1
Unemployed both waves	15.38		0	1	31.55		0	1
Race								
Non-Hispanic white	15.44		0	1	12.86		0	1
Non-Hispanic black	32.82		0	1	29.37		0	1
Hispanic	51.74		0	1	57.77		0	1
Housing tenure								
Rents	64.06		0	1	70.15		0	1
Owns	32.03		0	1	26.7		0	1
Other	3.91		0	1	3.16		0	1

Source: Making Connections Survey Wave 1, Wave 2, and Wave 3 from NORC

Table 5.2. Logistic Regression Predicting Mover Families Wave 1 to Wave 2

	ß	Odds ratio
Uses Welfare	−0.164 (0.407)	0.849
Rents home	2.416*** (0.529)	11.208***
Other housing	2.588** (0.8)	13.303**
Non-Hispanic black	0.932 (0.721)	2.54
Hispanic	0.602 (0.695)	1.83
< high school education	0.017 (0.397)	1.113
Spouse in HH	0.54 (0.496)	1.53
Lost employment	0.578 (0.561)	1.782
Unemployed both waves	−0.709 (0.516)	0.492
Gained employment	−0.659 (0.557)	0.517
Respondent age+	−0.04** (0.015)	0.96**
Number of children in HH	0.74** (0.168)	2.095***
Constant	−3.683 (1.137)	.025
Log Likelihood	−108.246	−108.246
Pseudo R-Squared	0.288	0.288
Prob > chi2	0.0	0.0
Observations	256	256

Source: Making Connections Survey waves 1 and 2 from NORC
Note: Standard errors in parentheses. Reference categories: does not use welfare, Owns home, non-Hispanic white, HS+, does not have spouse, Maintained Employment
*** p<0.001, ** p<0.01, * p<0.05

Table 5.3. Logistic Regression Predicting Mover Families Wave 2 to Wave 3

	ß	Odds ratio
Uses Welfare	0.711**	2.036**
	(0.286)	(0.582)
Rents home	1.823***	6.19***
	(0.337)	(2.088)
Other housing	.999	2.718
	(0.675)	(1.834)
Non-Hispanic black	0.535	1.708
	(0.493)	(0.841)
Hispanic	0.939*	2.556*
	(0.461)	(1.179)
< high school education	0.037	0.69
	(0.29)	(0.2)
Spouse in HH	0.032	1.033
	(0.279)	(0.288)
Lost employment	1.004**	2.728**
	(0.388)	(1.059)
Maintained employment	.53	1.699
	(0.331)	(0.052)
Gained employment	0.332	1.393
	(0.448)	(0.624)
Respondent age	−0.038***	.962***
	(0.011)	(0.011)
Number of children in HH	0.573***	1.773***
	(0.12)	(0.213)
Constant	−2.487	.083
	(0.807)	(.067)
Log Likelihood	−201.209	−201.209
Pseudo R-Squared	0.284	0.284
Prob > chi2	0.0	0.0
Observations	412	412

Source: Making Connections Survey waves 2 and 3 from NORC
Note: Standard errors in parentheses. Reference categories: does not use welfare, Owns home, non-Hispanic white, HS+, does not have spouse, unemployed in wave 2 and wave 3 *** p<0.001, ** p<0.01, * p<0.05

a partner/getting married, having children, or moving for the sake of a career prospect. On a related note, families that add children are more likely to move in both periods, suggesting that the addition of children generates a need for new space, prompting a family to move (dependent upon available resources).

Given these similarities, there are major differences between the prerecession and recession period in terms of race, welfare status, and employment status. First, while race is not a statistically significant driver of residential mobility in the prerecessionary period, it becomes significant in the recessionary period. More specifically, we see that, compared to whites, Hispanics are 2.5 times more likely to move in the recessionary period. This suggests that in the recession period, Hispanics were subjected to more external pressures on mobility decisions than whites. Given that many Hispanics in Providence are engaged in the construction industry, it is likely that the housing crisis is at the root of these economically motivated mobility decisions (Austin, 2012). Due to the high levels of unemployment wrought upon Hispanics by the Great Recession, it is no surprise that they underwent higher rates of residential mobility in this period. At the same time, people who received welfare assistance (TANF) were twice as likely to move during the recession compared to those who received no federal assistance. In addition, people who lost employment during the recession were 2.7 times more likely to move than those who maintained their employment status across periods. Thus, a pattern of disadvantaged populations moving at greater rates during the recession than more advantaged populations emerges from these data. The direct impact of employment loss and dependence on government subsidies illustrates that within these neighborhoods, poor and Hispanic families suffered disproportionate disturbances of residential stability.

The effect on residential mobility for poor and Hispanic residents is further elaborated in the results for the recession period multinomial logistic regression displayed in Table 5.4 on page 122. This model is split up into three groups: stayers (those who did not move), economic movers (those who cite economic reasons as the main driver behind their mobility), and other movers (those who cite noneconomic factors as the main driver behind their move). Taken together, this model further elaborates the impact of recessionary conditions on the

Table 5.4. Logistic Regression Predicting Effects of Residential Mobility for Stayers, Economic Movers and Other Movers

	ß (Economic Move)	RRR (Economic Move)	ß (Other Move)	RRR (Other Move)
Uses Welfare	1.153**	3.169**	0.5	1.65
	(0.384)	(1.212)	(0.313)	(0.517)
Rents home	2.073***	7.946***	1.742***	5.711***
	(0.523)	(4.156)	(0.371)	(2.118)
Other housing	1.264	3.539	0.893	2.442
	(0.977)	(3.458)	(0.781)	(1.906)
Non-Hispanic black	0.211	1.235	0.628	1.875
	(0.815)	(1.006)	(0.522)	(0.998)
Hispanic	1.493*	4.45*	0.720	2.055
	(0.75)	(3.338)	(.497)	(1.021)
< high school education	−0.376	0.686	−0.371	0.689
	(0.373)	(0.256)	(321)	(0.221)
Spouse in HH	0.046	1.047	0.623	1.064
	(0.386)	(0.405)	(0.3)	(0.319)
Lost employment	1.204**	3.33**	0.958*	2.606*
	(0.388)	(1.059)	(0.429)	(1.119)
Maintained employment	0.56	1.058	0.729*	2.073*
	(0.446)	(0.472)	(0.362)	(0.751)
Gained employment	0.503	1.654	0.221	1.247
	(0.556)	(0.911)	(0.514)	(0.641)
Respondent age	−0.046**	.955**	−0.035**	0.965**
	(0.017)	(0.016)	(0.012)	(0.012)
Number of children in HH	0.707***	2.027***	0.513***	1.671***
	(0.519)	(0.324)	(0.129)	(0.215)
Constant	−4.244	.014	−2.734	0.064
	(1.245)	(.018)	(.883)	(0.057)
Log Likelihood	−305.284	−305.284	−305.284	−305.284
Pseudo R-Squared	0.232	0.232	0.232	0.232
Prob > chi2	0.0	0.0	0.0	0.0
Observations	412	412	412	412

Source: Making Connections Survey waves 2 and 3 from NORC
Note: Standard errors in parentheses. Reference categories: does not use welfare, owns home, non-Hispanic white, HS+, does not have spouse, unemployed in w2 and w3
*** p<0.001, ** p<0.01, * p<0.05

mobility patterns of vulnerable populations. More specifically, we see that for both economic movers and other movers, employment loss is a significant predictor of mobility during the recession. This suggests that a disruption in employment is a general factor spurring mobility. However, we also see that Hispanics are 4.45 times more likely than whites to cite economic reasons for their moves. These results further justify the claim that recession-era economic restructuring disproportionately affected Hispanics, resulting in increased residential instability among this group.

Conclusion

Struggling families in Providence, Rhode Island, experienced a number of negative consequences associated with the Great Recession and subsequent austerity measures enacted by government. A major restructuring of the economy resulted in a hemorrhage of jobs from the state, with Hispanics losing the most ground. These changes dramatically reshaped the availability of resources for many Hispanics, drastically circumscribing the options available for housing. Due to Rhode Island's dramatic increase in housing costs over the last decade, families that faced increasing disadvantage during the recession were subjected to an increasingly exclusionary housing market. At the same time, the stagnated resources available at the federal level shifted responsibility for affordable housing to individual state and urban governments. In Rhode Island, the loss of federal resources was compounded by the eradication of funds earmarked for affordable housing programs locally. These funds were disproportionately used in the city of Providence, where the majority of the state's low-income residents live, particularly within the south side neighborhood that is the focus of this study. Demand for assistance grew in the aftermath of the Great Recession but Providence was unable to increase access due to the imposition of austerity measures federally and the decline of local tax revenues. As a result, poor communities of color are faced with an increasingly competitive housing market and decreasing resources. These issues are compounded by the failure of government at the federal, state, and local levels to properly address these growing disadvantages.

A major consequence of austerity is the shifting of responsibility for basic services for low-income people down to the local level. In cities such as Providence, which face a number newly imposed budgetary constraints, the most vulnerable populations often fail to have their needs met. The growing trend of high residential mobility among Hispanic families in Providence is directly tied to the austerity policies enacted in the aftermath of the crisis. Skyrocketing rents coupled with a decreasing supply of locally produced affordable housing generated a context of large-scale unaffordability for the city's poorest residents, particularly those impacted by job and wealth losses from the recession. As a result, many low-income families in the city's poorest neighborhoods were forced to leave their homes in search of more affordable opportunities. The result is increasing instability among poor families and neighborhoods. In effect, austerity measures generate more housing instability by creating a large pool of churning movers that move from one low-cost unit to the next without establishing lasting ties within their neighborhoods. Such a high degree of churning movers within poor neighborhoods works to reproduce the conditions that maintain concentrated urban poverty. In sum, the austerity measures enacted in Providence are likely to generate a permanent segment of citizens that are actively excluded from the mainstream social fabric of the city. Faced with higher demands placed upon the local government, coupled with fewer available resources, the city is likely to experience higher levels of inequality and concentrated poverty in disadvantaged neighborhoods. Failure to reverse austerity measures and properly fund affordable housing will only exacerbate the already existing stark inequalities.

Notes

1. U.S. Bureau of Labor Statistics.

2. Measured as the percentage of people who contribute more than 30 percent of their income toward housing costs.

3. Beginning with wave one, the Making Connections interviewers conducted in-person interviews at randomly selected housing units within the target neighborhoods. During the wave two collection, interviewers went back to the same addresses from the first wave with the intent of reinterviewing the

same household. However, many times the original householders were no longer living at the selected address. Interviewers conducted the survey with the new family in that housing unit and added them to the data set. If the household that moved from the address was a family with children, then the interviewers attempted to get in contact with the family, wherever they currently lived, in order to reinterview them.

4. County-wide surveys were not collected for waves two and three.

5. Reasons for move are not available for wave one and wave two.

6. The survey asked employment status of the household head in each wave. There are a total of four categories: employed at time 1 and time 2 (employed), employed at time 1 and unemployed at time 2 (lost employment), unemployed at time 1 and employed at time 2 (gained employment), and unemployed at time 1 and time 2 (unemployed).

7. Self-employment is relatively rare and excluded due to its inherent ambiguity. The focus of this study is those within the formal labor market or those seeking work within it.

6

Urban Governance and Inclusionary Housing in New York City

KATHE NEWMAN

Introduction

In the context of rising land and housing costs, declining federal housing and social service assistance, the loss of assisted and unassisted affordable units, a growing population, and stagnating wages for lower-skilled workers, New York City adopted a mandatory inclusionary housing program in 2016 to produce and preserve affordable housing for households across a wide income spectrum. The program builds on the city's earlier voluntary inclusionary housing programs that, in general, allowed developers to build at greater densities in exchange for producing or preserving affordable housing units. With the mandatory program, the city hopes to increase the total supply of housing units and to produce and preserve affordable housing units. The mandatory inclusionary housing program is one piece of Mayor de Blasio's housing plan, which aims to produce or preserve two hundred thousand housing units over ten years (Goodman, 2016; NYCDCP, 2016c).

Inclusionary housing blurs the line between public and private governance. With this approach to achieve socially desirable outcomes, the public shapes the market through incentives, land-use changes, and direct subsidies, to create a context in which private actors produce affordable housing. Given the robust demand for real estate and the rapid pace of private development, New York seems like the place where policies that use real estate markets to achieve social housing outcomes could work. But designing and implementing programs that use markets and private institutions in this way is complicated in practice. The city's current mandatory housing program builds on its experiences with earlier voluntary inclusionary housing efforts that did not produce as much housing as some had hoped.

One concern is that the added profit (cross subsidy) produced by allowing developers to build at greater densities may not provide a sufficient incentive to developers to produce affordable and especially very affordable housing. To produce housing that is affordable to households with incomes that are 30 to 50 percent of the Area Median Income, the city may need to provide subsidy. Additionally, because the housing market is different in different parts of the city, the structure of the inclusionary housing program might make affordable housing development attractive in one area and not in others. One ongoing concern involves a trade-off between economic integration and the number of housing units. Areas of the city with strong markets that might support inclusionary housing development also have high land and development costs, which means that the per-unit cost of producing affordable housing is high. This translates to fewer housing units than if the subsidy was diverted to build housing in less expensive areas of the city where the economics of inclusionary housing development might not work as well. While diverting the subsidies might produce additional units, it would do less to further economic integration (Goodman & Navarro, 2016). Another concern is whether building new housing in some neighborhoods will contribute to gentrification, simultaneously increasing pressure on the affordable housing stock even as inclusionary housing programs seek to relieve it. A final concern relates to the availability of other programs that make inclusionary housing programs attractive to developers. One example is the 421-a tax exemption program. For many decades, developers have factored the tax exemption into their affordable housing development plans, but New York State suspended the program in early 2016 and it is unclear whether it will be renewed.

This chapter explores New York City's inclusionary housing programs that were created to preserve existing and produce new affordable housing units and to encourage economic integration. The city's mandatory inclusionary housing program highlights the new realities of urban governance in an age of austerity. Rather than fund housing directly, the city created a program that gives private developers incentives and guidelines to encourage, and in some cases require them, to produce housing that is affordable to households with very low to moderate incomes. The government provides subsidy to ensure the production of some housing units that are affordable to low- and very-low-income households. The effect is a mixed approach to urban governance in which the role of the state is to shape the market to achieve its outcomes with as little direct public expenditure as is possible. The shift from a voluntary inclusionary housing program to a mandatory program may suggest a shift in the public private governance arrangement with a tilt toward the public, but as yet that is unclear. It is also unclear whether the new approach will produce and preserve many affordable housing units.

The chapter begins with a discussion of some of the major trends that set the stage for the city's decision to use voluntary inclusionary housing and to later mandate it. It considers austerity politics as rooted in the response to the 1970s fiscal crisis that reset public policy expectations and reframed the role of government. The next section describes the city's inclusionary housing programs and how they changed over time. It considers the challenges facing inclusionary housing programs given the high cost of land and development and the ongoing loss of affordable units. Finally, it considers the shift to a mandatory inclusionary housing program and questions whether it is evidence of a rethinking about the public private governance relationships within the broader context of austerity politics and policymaking.

Austerity, Urbanism, and the Neoliberal Turn

While some wondered whether the global financial crisis of 2008 would challenge the fundamental assumptions of neoliberalism, the crisis instead set the stage for further cutbacks and an expansion of austerity urbanism (Peck, 2012). With fewer resources and greater certainty that federal programmatic assistance for housing and social welfare programming was not forthcoming, cities developed new and refined existing policy-making and governance approaches that embody "flexibility, innovation and entrepreneurship," which firmly replaced the logics of welfare state governance (Jessop, 2013, np). As McCann and Ward explain: "Cities and the local state have been 'entrepreneurialized' [Harvey, 1989a; Leitner 1990], and the state has, through innovations like the New Public Management, been reconceived as a facilitative, rather than regulatory, apparatus, behaving like a business to attract and support capital. As such, urban governance has been characterized by processes of downsizing, outsourcing, and privatization where services—from garbage collection, to policing, to policy expertise—are increasingly provided by the private sector" (McCann & Ward, 2011, p. xviii). In enacting this style of governance, many cities have blurred the public and private by creating hybrid governance structures (Jessop, 2013). Ward (2006) finds this in his exploration of business improvement districts in New York City and the UK. Peck (2012) is concerned that by deepening the contradictions rather than resolving them, these neoliberal governing approaches enhance the potential for future crises rather than reducing them. It might also be the case that the state, pressed by residents and community organizations that struggle, for example, to remain in place, is already modifying strictly neoliberal approaches to urban governance with expanded state engagement.

While these neoliberal transformations have been under way for decades, and seem difficult to reverse or change, Peck, Theodore, and Brenner (2013) offer an agency-inspired vision for change. Neoliberalism is a process and not a thing, and its continued existence is the result of its constant reproduction—neoliberalism exists because every day society remakes it. This realization suggests the existence of a multiplicity of opportunities to do things differently. As hopeful as Peck, Theodore, and Brenner are for the potential to change the neoliberal condition, they suggest that while policymakers are hard at work developing and rapidly exchanging new ideas, few policies address the underlying problems. As a result, they are less than effective at addressing the problems the policies are created to solve.

Inclusionary housing, in this framework, takes on the air of a pragmatic approach in a difficult context. In the midst of an affordable housing crisis, housing advocates and others have turned hopefully to New York's inclusionary housing programs and have worked with real estate organizations to create a program that all hope will be productive. The program fits well within the shift to market-based programs but it also acknowledges the need for public subsidy to achieve social objectives. Implementing it successfully raises a set of problems associated with mixed public-private governance approaches.

Crises and Governance

The precedent for these approaches dates to the 1970s and the frameworks that emerged in the wake of economic restructuring and New York's experiences through the fiscal crisis. The 1970s was a pivotal moment in New York City's history that has had long-lasting effects on how the city governs itself. The city experienced a financial crisis in the 1970s and the government all but declared bankruptcy. Before the financial crisis, New York City provided a broad array of public programs:

> It can be hard today to imagine what it was like to live in a city that provided such a rich range of social services, ones that made possible a uniquely democratic culture. The city had nineteen public hospitals in 1975, extensive mass transit and public housing, public daycare and decent schools. The municipal university system—the only one of its kind in the country—provided higher education to all, free of charge. Rent stabilization made it possible for a middle class to inhabit the city. For many, the fiscal crisis showed that it was no longer possible for New York to finance these kinds of services. (Phillips-Fein, 2013, np)

In the wake of the crisis, and with initially no assistance from the federal government (famous headline, Ford to City: Drop Dead), and pressure from state and financial actors, the city dramatically scaled back spending on health care, educational institutions, parks, libraries, labor, and many other areas (Mollenkopf, 1977). In the wake of the fiscal crisis, New York City's political leaders were responsible to the people who elected them and also to those who managed city debt (Shefter, 1985). The result was to reduce spending, to expand public private partnerships, and, for government, to use tax credits and other programs that did not require direct expenditures.

For example, to encourage developers to build as a development-led strategy out of the fiscal crisis, the city and state developed tax exemption programs and changed zoning regulations, neither of which required direct programmatic budget outlays. For example, New York State created the 421-a property tax exemption program in 1971 and, after a few modifications, and depending on property location and type and/ or amount of affordable housing, provided a ten- to twenty-five-year tax exemption with "phase out" periods for residential developments with four or more units. By 1985, amid increasing demand in Midtown Manhattan, the state modified the 421-a program to include a Geographic Exclusion Area (which covers much of Manhattan south of 96th Street and north of 14th Street and later included parts of Brooklyn, Staten Island, and Queens). To receive the tax abatement for building in those areas, developers needed to produce 20 percent of the units as housing affordable to households with incomes up to 60 percent of Area Median Income (AMI) (the U.S. Department of Housing and Urban Development's measure of affordability) (Citizens Housing and Planning Council of New York, 2002).

The strengthening housing market in the late 1990s and early 2000s increased the need for affordable housing and the city government considered new strategies to produce and preserve affordable housing. And the city, by the early 2000s, had few properties left from the one hundred thousand tax-delinquent housing units it absorbed in the wake of the 1970s fiscal crisis. The Koch administration had launched a ten-year housing plan in 1986 which gave or sold properties to private developers, some of which were used to expand affordable housing (City of New York, 2015). As the number of those units dwindled and in a context of high housing demand, strengthening markets, and reduced federal support for housing, the city created an inclusionary housing program to use the renewed strength of the city's property markets to produce affordable housing.

1980s and the Inclusionary Housing Program

Inclusionary housing programs, which can be mandatory or voluntary, offer a mixture of economic development and housing incentives designed to spur development and the production or rehabilitation of affordable housing. Developers receive a benefit such as increased density, subsidy, parking requirement reduction, tax exemption, streamlined development process, or some combination of those benefits in exchange for producing new or rehabilitating existing affordable housing. How many units, whether they are located on site or off, whether they are newly constructed or rehabilitated, the level of affordability, tenure, and the length of time units are kept affordable (i.e., temporary or permanent) vary by program rules and whether the inclusionary housing program is combined with other subsidies such as tax-exempt bond construction financing, unit or tenant subsidies, and tax exemptions (Madar, 2015; Ullman et al., 2013).

New York City created a voluntary inclusionary housing program known as the "R10" program in 1987 to increase the production of affordable housing by changing land-use rules to create more profit for developers, which could be then used to fund affordable housing. As *The New York Times* framed it at the time, "Planners have long been intrigued by the notion of using land-use controls to benefit society at no direct cost to the public" (Oser, 1987, np). With the dismantling of the welfare state and a strengthening real estate market, modifying local land-use controls to produce much needed affordable housing is an urban governance approach attuned to a time of austerity. By shaping land-use rules, the city generated money for social programs without directly taxing city residents or adding to the city's debt. The R10 program applied to areas of the city with an R10 zoning designation, which is the highest residential zoning designation and today is used mostly used in Manhattan, Downtown Brooklyn, and Long Island City (NYCP Resident Districts).

The program made it possible for developers to increase profit by building at greater density and with extra profit cross-subsidized affordable housing. Developers received up to a 20 percent floor-area ratio (FAR) density bonus in exchange for producing or substantially rehabilitating housing units that were affordable at or below 80 percent of Area Median Income. The city had already experimented with density bonuses for developers who built open plazas or donated money to parks, and this program expanded the idea to housing. In the R10 program, the affordable units could be produced within the market rate development, within the community district, or within a half-mile of the new construction to promote economic integration. The affordable housing requirement remains as long as a development with the density bonus maintains its density, which makes the affordable units quasi-permanent. Initially, some housing groups had low expectations for the program's ability to produce affordable housing and some feared that it would create new problems related to increased density (Dunlap, 1987; Furman, 2015; NYDCP, 2016a; Oser, 1987). The initial R10 program did not produce many housing units. Increasingly heated housing markets through the late 1990s and early 2000s led to calls for new programs.

The Housing Crisis This Time

While the city experienced a recession at the end of the 1980s and early 1990s, which briefly left some wondering whether the reinvestment period had run its course (Bourne, 1993), within a few years, a prolonged surge of investment moved through the Manhattan core and extended deep into the outer boroughs. The city's population exceeded eight million in 2000, and grew by another 166,855 people by 2010 (NYDCP, 2015b). Increasing population increased housing demand. Buyers from outside the city further added to housing market pressures. In a particularly dramatic turn of events considering the disinvestment of the 1970s, some individual apartments sell for tens of millions of dollars, making the ultra-luxury apartment stock a global investment commodity (*The New York Times*, Feb. 7, 2015).

To accommodate projected population growth, the Bloomberg administration rezoned approximately 40 percent of the city through 115 rezoning plans (ANHD, 2013). In some areas, the city downzoned to maintain neighborhood character, and in other places it upzoned to increase density. It also changed some land uses from nonresidential to residential, reflecting the growing residential demand and potentially higher profits (Angotti, 2008). Amid rezonings and pressures to expand housing supply, community organizations and residents grew concerned about pressures on lower income residents and the potential loss of existing affordable housing stock. Community organizations asserted that if the city changed the land-use rules, which allowed for greater profit, the city could and should capture some of that profit to benefit city residents through affordable housing development or preservation. Community organizations and residents especially were concerned about displacement related to the 2005 rezoning plans for Greenpoint-Williamsburg in Brooklyn, and Hudson Yards and West Chelsea in Manhattan.

The city responded to resident concerns by creating a modified inclusionary housing program for these areas, which it later further refined and expanded to cover thirty other rezoned areas. The 2005 Inclusionary Housing Designated Areas Program voluntary program provided a 33 percent density bonus and allowed developers to use other housing subsidies, including the 421-a tax exemption program, for developments that produce 20 percent of the floor area as permanently affordable housing at or below 80 percent AMI. The affordable housing could be developed onsite or off and developers could meet the affordable housing requirement through new construction or rehabilitation and preservation.

The inclusionary housing affordability requirement did not reach very-low-income households without additional state subsidy. There are a few reasons for this. First, the often-used U.S. Department of Housing and Urban Development's Area Median Income estimate covers metropolitan areas, and given the affluence in and around New York, the affordability requirement for the inclusionary housing program is higher than lower income household incomes in some neighborhoods (ANHD, 2015). Second, affordability depends on the mix of subsidies that developers layer to make their projects work financially, to increase the number of affordable units, and to expand affordability to lower-income households. Developments that layer the Inclusionary Housing density bonus and the 421-a tax exemption after 2006, for example, have to be affordable at 60 percent AMI and the affordable units have to be developed onsite (NYDCP, 2016b; Ullman et al., 2013). Some projects use the 80/20 tax exempt construction financing program, which provides bonds for developers that build 20 percent of their large residential rental projects as affordable housing at 50 percent AMI or 25 percent for households at 60 percent AMI. This financing also allows developers to use Low Income Housing Tax Credits (New York State Homes and Community Renewal, 2015).

Because of the city's growth since the mid-1990s, one might expect that, if neoliberal policies were to return on the promise of using markets to achieve social objectives, New York would be one place to realize that vision. But the high cost of land and development, accompanied by stagnating and decreasing wages for lower-skilled residents, present challenges to that presupposed potential. Together, the city's inclusionary housing programs produced at least 4,471 units, and more than half of those units were authorized after the implementation of the 2005 program (Furman Center, 2015).[1]

With a growing housing affordability crisis and recognition that voluntary inclusionary housing did not produce as many units as some hoped, the city recently adopted mandatory inclusionary housing.

Prosperity, Austerity, and Poverty

Even as the number of high-skilled jobs and wages in the city increased, wages for lower-skilled workers declined. The numbers of households making more than $250,000 and less than $40,000 increased between 1990 and 2012. Compounding the challenges for lower-income residents, wages for the lower-skilled jobs lost ground over the last two decades, decreasing from $26,326 in 1990 to $19,523 in 2012 (Furman Center, 2014). This is reflected in the city's stagnant median household income ($49,693 to $50,886) between 1970 and 2010. And as wages declined, housing costs increased. Median rents increased 75 percent, mean home value increased 128 percent, and the city lost about four hundred thousand apartments that rented for less than $1,000 between 2000 and 2012 (Furman Center, 2015; Stringer, 2014). With stagnating wages and increasing housing costs, nearly half of low-income households in the city paid more than half of their income for housing in 2012 (Furman Center, 2014). Between 2002 and 2014, the share of families who entered the city's shelter system after a formal eviction increased from

17 to 32 percent (Coalition for the Homeless, 2015b). In January 2015, more than sixty thousand people, including 25,459 children, stayed in homeless shelters (Coalition for the Homeless, 2015a; NYC Department of Homeless Services, 2015).

The Dismantling of the Assisted-Housing Stock

Adding further challenges, it has been difficult to retain existing assisted and unassisted below-market housing. New York City has lost some of its federal, state, and local programs that provided an array of building and tenant subsidies, low-cost financing, regulations on rent increases, and other programs that made housing available to people with low and even moderate incomes. Over time, the number of units with assistance and those that are rent-regulated has declined. For example, regulatory changes that created paths to deregulation within the Rent Control and Rent Stabilization programs resulted in a net loss of 150,000 units between 1994 and 2012 (City of New York, 2015). Units can be deregulated when rents reach $2,500 or household income exceeds $200,000 for two consecutive years. Vacancy deregulation allows annual rent increases of 18 percent for one-year leases and 20 percent for two-year leases. Rents can also be increased to reflect the costs of major capital and individual apartment improvements (Stringer, 2014). Units can be removed from these programs if they entered regulation through J-51 or 421-a tax exemption programs and those exemptions end (New York City Rent Guidelines Board, 2015). Given the demand for real estate development and the potential for increased rent revenue for landlords, the assisted-housing stock has experienced pressure to shift out of regulated status. And the revived housing markets combined with the time-delimited nature of some programs and the deregulation of others has translated into a loss of lower-cost units (City of New York, 2015).

Mandatory Inclusionary Housing

Although New York City has had a housing crisis for as long as many people can remember, the challenges discussed above created a context in which the crisis today seems to be exponentially worse than in recent memory. City council member Brad Lander emphatically stated the need for a new program to increase affordable housing: "It's a moment of crisis. . . . People are desperate for affordability, and there's a mismatch between the anxiety people have and the policy tools that are available" (quoted in Navarro, 2013, np). This is in part because demand for affordable housing is so high and yet the policy options to address it seem so limited. Mayor de Blasio responded to this crisis with a ten-year housing plan that he described as "a central pillar in the battle against inequality" (Navarro & Grynbaum, 2014). The plan proposes to produce or preserve two hundred thousand affordable housing units (60 percent preservation, 40 percent new construction) within a decade (City of New York, 2015; Stringer, 2014). The city frames the plan in a context of economic necessity and social justice: "Housing costs, quite simply, are an increasingly serious threat to the future of our City" (City of New York, 2015, p. 15). The report states that the city's diversity "drives economic growth, as employers decide to locate in the City to take advantage of its incredible and multidimensional talent pool" (ibid.).

The city included mandatory inclusionary housing as one strategy to meet the mayor's affordable housing preservation and production goal. And the intent is that strategically mandating it in areas where the city rezones to allow increased housing capacity will produce more affordable housing units than the earlier voluntary programs. "In future re-zonings that unlock substantial new housing capacity, the City must require, not simply encourage, the production of affordable housing in order to ensure balanced growth, fair housing opportunity, and diverse neighborhoods" (City of New York, 2015, p. 7). The city's mandatory inclusionary housing (MIH) program adopted in 2016 aims to expand the number of affordable housing units and to increase economic integration. Before approving it, the city council amended it to "reach lower income households while maintaining flexibility; close loopholes in the program administration; improve transparency; address safety and local hiring concerns; and address problems of displacement and tenant harassment" (New York City Council, 2016, np).

The program allows increased density in some areas that are rezoned and in private projects that increase density; it requires the production, preservation, or substantial rehabilitation of affordable housing on or off-site. The city council selects one of four options at the time of rezoning that vary in the number of affordable units and whether they are affordable to very-low, low, moderate, or middle-income households (New York City Council, 2016; NYCDCP, 2016c). The city anticipates that the program will produce twelve thousand affordable units. As the city only recently adopted mandatory inclusionary housing, its impact is as yet unclear.

There has been a wide-ranging discussion about the mandatory inclusionary housing program. Some fear that it will make housing development too expensive or cumbersome and developers will opt to build elsewhere or not at all. The suspension of the 421-a tax exemption program has strengthened these concerns. Others are concerned that mandatory inclusionary housing will have a differential effect on housing development depending on the housing submarkets within the city. Developers may continue to build in high-profit, high-density communities but might not in communities with weaker markets. The Furman Center (2015a) estimated development costs and rents for high- and mid-rise buildings in different submarkets. They found that the mandatory inclusionary housing program might produce affordable housing, even for lower-income households, in areas with strong markets and high rents, especially in high-rise developments, because the market rents are high enough to offset the costs of affordable development. In weaker markets, the rents are not high enough to generate a sufficient cross-subsidy to produce affordable housing and developers would be unlikely to build without additional subsidy.

There are also tensions between maximizing economic integration versus the number of housing units. Developing in New York City is expensive, and including affordable housing in an otherwise high-end development means high land and construction costs and therefore fewer affordable units. This suggests an implicit trade-off between applying the costs of ensuring a few units of affordable housing in some expensive communities, and thus promoting economic integration, or using the same suite of subsidies to produce more units of affordable housing in less expensive communities, which may further economic segregation. For example, in a West Chelsea building with market rents that start at $5,850 per month, 20 percent of the units will meet the IZ affordability requirements "Those apartments were granted to 19 households that make from $25,612 to $42,950 a year and won a housing lottery the city held last year. . . . The subsidy to each family getting an affordable two-bedroom unit at Abington House will be worth nearly $90,000 a year" (Barrow, 2014, np). Applying that much money to affordable housing developments in less-expensive parts of the city could potentially result in a greater number of housing units but might contribute to economic segregation. Finally, some residents and community organizations are concerned that rezoning and new development will raise the housing costs in nearby areas. This may create opposition to rezoning and proposed development.

The push to mandatory inclusionary housing is evidence of a stronger imperative to produce affordable housing. As the city's housing and community development association explains: "The City needs new tools to produce the affordable housing units that are and will be needed to keep New York a sustainable, livable city for all. New York City must follow other large U.S. cities such as Boston, Chicago, Denver, San Diego, and San Francisco all of which have adopted guaranteed inclusionary zoning laws" (ANHD, 2013, p. 8). Suggesting the lack of noninclusionary housing policy options, ANHD continues: "In order to generate the affordable housing units New York City needs, the City needs a Guaranteed Inclusionary Zoning policy. Without directly linking affordable housing production to new development production and the City's growth, New York will continue to see high housing costs climb out of reach of more New Yorkers."

The mandatory inclusionary housing program reflects more than two decades of negotiations between private market actors and local government to create a program that achieves societal and private business goals. Addressing the housing crisis within this mode of governance is challenging not only because of the above concerns but also because of the challenges involved in shaping markets by motivating private actors (McArdle, 2016). To produce housing affordable for lower-income residents, it appears necessary, at least in some cases, to add public subsidy. Doing so may mean working with state and or federal programs that may be in flux, such as the 421-a tax exemption program.

While inclusionary housing programs could be viewed as inherently neoliberal programs, New York City's programs, especially since 2005, suggest a more mixed approach to urban governance. The city government has adopted a stronger role in program development over time and has exhibited a greater commitment to creating programs that seek to produce or preserve below-market housing. Whether the city will achieve these objectives through the mandatory inclusionary housing program is unclear. The city's housing plan includes other ideas for preserving and producing new below-market-rate housing and for reducing residential displacement (City of New York, 2015, p. 7). It identifies a need to protect some of the existing affordable housing stock, including units with time-delimited subsidies and units in the state rent regulation program. Addressing this need necessitates working with the state and federal governments to ensure effective programs (ANHD, 2015; City of New York, 2015). Together, this suggests a mixed approach to addressing the city's affordable housing needs. However, the demand for affordable housing appears to outstrip the current ability to provide it even using these pragmatic mixed governance approaches. And community groups and residents continue to press the city and other governments to address the ongoing housing affordability crisis.

Supply Side Urbanism and the Urban Imagination

The 1970s fiscal crisis reset expectations for city policy. The city has adopted mixed public private governance approaches and has attempted to increase affordable housing using land-use controls, tax exemptions, and subsidies. The federal cutbacks since the 1980s further solidified the need for local action and the city adopted a pragmatic local response to producing housing through inclusionary housing. Creating growth and profit where it did not exist, the city hoped to direct money to programs and to minimize direct expenditures, but generating many units through these approaches has been challenging. Pressed by community residents and organizations, the city has strengthened its role in these market-based programs with the intent of maximizing the production of affordable housing. It is unclear whether the most recent iteration of mandatory inclusionary housing will produce more affordable units and how this mandatory inclusionary housing strategy will fit within the suite of other local, state, and federal housing programs.

The challenges raised by inclusionary housing raise anew the question of what neoliberalism governance looks like and how the boundary between public and private sectors is negotiated in the postindustrial city. The fiscal crisis of the 1970s helped to usher in the neoliberal age, a period in which cities found themselves in the throes of economic restructuring and U.S. welfare state withdrawal. The reality of roll-out neoliberalism saw government creating new mixed public private governance structures that craft market-based policy solutions (Brenner & Theodore, 2002). These public private relationships have evolved over time as social needs, and the policy and market contexts have themselves changed.

It is unclear if mandatory inclusionary housing is what Peck et al. have in mind when they suggest that it is possible to break out of the neoliberal loop and dramatically expand housing opportunities across the income spectrum, thereby helping to expand the benefits associated with New York's revival. It is clear that as demand for affordable housing as grown, communities have organized to secure programmatic and public private governance changes to protect existing and produce new affordable housing. Whether these changes will accomplish those needs is yet unclear.

Note

1. The city modified the inclusionary housing program again in 2009 to expand its potential to grow the number of affordable housing units. The 2009 modifications were intended to make the programs more attractive and useful to developers and tenants. They allow affordable limited equity homeownership units, increase the number of units produced if the developer receives additional subsidies, modified the R10 program to allow subsidies and the use of private debt, modified density rules for the earlier programs, and changed some administrative rules (NYCDCP, 2016b).

7

Homeownership in Middle America

A Case of Incidental Austerity?

DANIEL J. HAMMEL AND XUEYING CHEN

Introduction

Austerity is often understood as a set of fiscal policies focused on reducing government budgets through spending cuts, particularly in labor costs and social services (Whitfield, 2013). Such policies are often enacted in times of fiscal crisis, but far from being a rational policy response to an externally generated crisis, many urban theorists understand austerity as a tool through which neoliberal capitalism can reduce government regulation, gut social spending, and discipline labor, particularly public labor (Krugman, 2012a; Peck, 2012; Peck, 2014). Austerity then might best be understood less as policies that cut public budgets in times of crisis, and more as a tool of neoliberal capitalism. As Peck (2012) notes, austerity policy shares a neoliberal terrain. Unlike earlier rounds of austerity, such as that which followed the urban fiscal crisis of the early 1970s, this round of austerity policy is on a terrain already shaped by decades of neoliberal urban policy reform. Significant features of this policy reform include the destruction of the welfare state and the privatization of many traditional functions of urban governance.

While in Europe much focus on austerity has been at the national level, in North America there is an increasing emphasis on austerity's role in urban settings (Donald et al., 2014; Peck, 2015; Tabb, 2014). Given the complexities of the federal state system in the United States, austerity at the urban scale can be a function of national, state, and/or local policies. From 2009 through 2017, a Democratic president largely resisted national-level austerity policies, blocking many initiatives of a Republican-controlled legislature and, with the exception of the budget sequestration, he was reasonably successful. Many state governments, however, have pursued austerity with vigor, using their ability to leverage a range of deficit spending options to force through budget cuts. At the same time, state governments have also enacted tax cuts. While these practices are more common in states with Republican governors and legislatures, the Great Recession caused almost all states to make substantial budget cuts, even states with Democratic governments (Davidson & Ward, 2014). As the immediate impacts of the Great Recession have receded, some U.S. states have begun to increase spending, although others have maintained and even increased their austerity policies. Other than the short-lived federal stimulus, cities have seen little increase in federal funds to offset declining state and local-level funding.

The application and effects of austerity are therefore geographically uneven (Christopherson et al., 2013), and it is often poorer communities of color that suffer the most (Partridge & Weinstein, 2013). This is not the case simply because the poor are often the most vulnerable, but because austerity policies often target more vulnerable populations and, in some ways, have the qualities that Neil Smith identified as revanchist policies in the 1990s (Smith, 1996). This dynamic is complicated and complemented by the fact that U.S. state legislatures have traditionally been dominated by rural and suburban constituencies (Greenblatt, 2014; Smith, 2014), and the ability to focus austerity policies on government services provided in cities adds to the political appeal of austerity.[1]

The purpose of this chapter is to broaden our understanding of austerity in the context of U.S. cities. In particular, the chapter seeks to further discussions on the impact that applying austerity policies at multiple levels of government has on the overall austerity process. This concern with multilevel governmental coordination is also used to introduce the idea that government policy may empower private actors to implement austerity policies. This public/private connection in austerity is not unusual. Urban austerity policy most often involves cutting basic city services (Donald et al., 2014; Peck, 2015), firing city employees (Miller & Hokenstad, 2014), renegotiating pension obligations (Davidson & Ward, 2014; Donald et al., 2014; Peck, 2012; Reese et al., 2014) and generally scaling back the public support that cities provide, often to their poorest residents (Hackworth, 2015). These actions can involve varied forms of privatization, such as the private contracting of trash collection or the move to non-pension-based retirements for public employees. We suggest, however, that there is another type of austerity policy that works through the private sector, which we term incidental austerity. This form of austerity involves traditionally public functions, or highly regulated private functions, being used to further the goals of austerity. These policies have austere outcomes when implemented through the neoliberal marketplace, even when the original intent was unrelated to austerity policy. We suggest that incidental austerity is useful in understanding the full effects of austerity policies upon poor and minority communities.

Our research focuses on two different housing policies that are at work in Toledo, Ohio, and our analysis is set at the level of the municipality and the county, in this case Lucas County, the central county of the Toledo metropolitan area. The first policy was implemented locally and involved the use of a private contractor to address the issue of tax delinquent properties. The second involves national policies that have helped form a new and troubling landscape of mortgage finance in Toledo. In both cases government policy has set a framework for private actors to engage in what we suggest are austerity policies. In doing this we hope to broaden our understanding of the impacts of austerity policies and situate them in the wider literature on neoliberal urban governance, privatization and financialization, and the role of race and discrimination in urban housing markets.

We begin by developing the concept of incidental austerity and then turn to two examples in Toledo that illustrate different ways in which such austerity might manifest itself at the local level. Our first example is a brief examination of a plan to sell property tax liens to a private entity that resulted in a range of unintended consequences that fell heavily upon low-income families in some of the city's most troubled neighborhoods. In the second example, we examine the effects of major changes in national mortgage-lending policies upon people and places that were at the center of the recent foreclosure crisis. We outline the manner in which national policies meant to address the most egregious lending practices in the recent housing crisis, enacted through a historically discriminatory lending industry, have resulted in what we have termed a new redlining. Finally, we discuss how these policies are illustrative of incidental austerity and how this concept may alter our understanding of austerity policy in general.

Incidental Austerity

Government policies often have unintended effects, and the more complex a policy is, the wider the array of unintended effects tends to be. This proposition applies to housing policy in the United States to the extent that a strong argument can be made that despite the passage of dozens of major housing acts over the past eighty years, the most significant housing policy might have been the Interstate Highway Act of 1956. This legislation, with a clear focus on transportation, economic development, and national defense, eventually demolished hundreds of square miles of inner city neighborhoods and simultaneously made white flight and suburbanization possible at levels not before imagined (Avila, 2014). It is perhaps unsurprising then that a complex group of policies with austere outcomes might include some whose apparent intent has nothing to do with typical austerity policies and, in some cases, appear to have the opposite intent.

In the strictest sense, neither of the two policies we examine involves the cutting of public budgets, and neither was specifically designed to have the effect of disciplining the poor through the extraction of capital from low-income areas, as is typical with austerity policies. The policies themselves are not typical of austerity measures, but implemented in a context of austerity at the local, state, and federal levels the results of the policies mirror the outcomes of typical austerity policy. In both cases, the results of the policies involve the withdrawal of resources from people of color and moderate-income people in low and moderate income (LMI) neighborhoods and the transfer of some of those resources to senior officials and shareholders of large corporations. We term this incidental austerity, not to suggest that it has less impact or less importance than more typical austerity policies, but to note that either it has accidentally created these same effects or that the austerity component of the policies is incidental to the main intent. We do not mean to oversimplify austerity policies. Such policies have developed in a wide range of areas (Peck, 2015). The concern with shrinking cities, for example, developed out of an attempt to best provide important public services to decreasing populations in economically troubled cities, and was the source of significant contemplation about the role of urban planning (Pallagast, 2010). The shift from these concerns to those of right sizing, however, turned planned shrinkage policies into effective austerity tools (Hackworth, 2015). In our examples, however, we suggest that the policy intent was never to produce austere outcomes, but that implementation by private actors moved the policies in that direction.

Private actors form a key component of incidental austerity because it is often through the actions of these actors that the policy moves toward austerity. While austerity policy has clearly been understood as public policy, the emphasis on privatization in neoliberal governance has created a situation where many policies are implemented by private actors. We suggest, however, that more is at work than a simple turn to private entities to enact austerity policies. In both of our case studies we identify private entities whose implementation of policy has made the policy austere. In the case of the tax liens in Lucas County it is the manner of the implementation that moves it toward austerity. In the second case, we focus on housing provision and in the United States, a setting where there is little direct government involvement outside of various subsidies and regulations. We suggest that new government regulations have encouraged the financial industry to institute an austere lending policy, with many of the same features as public policies.

The term incidental austerity is not therefore meant to suggest that government policymakers should not have understood the potential ramifications of these actions. Policies are created in particular economic, political, and geographic contexts. In housing policy, disparate impact has long been a significant concern, and these policies clearly have a disparate impact (as do many austerity policies, e.g., Beatty & Fothergill, 2014). In addition, any housing finance policy that fails to consider the long history of discrimination in mortgage lending in the United States against both people and places is likely to extend that history.

We also note that scale forms a crucial component of our analysis. Even in countries with reasonably centralized government, such as the United Kingdom, there will be highly disparate impacts in part because of the uneven geographies of race and poverty (Beatty & Fothergill, 2014; Centre for Cities, 2014). The situation in central Toledo, however, is not only a result of policies with differential impacts, although that certainly is happening. It is also the result of local attempts to address new state-level policies, and the result of particular federal regulatory policies applied unevenly over space.

The two cases we examine provide examples of incidental austerity acting at different scales and through different public/private relationships. In the case of tax liens, policy decisions typically made at the local level by a public entity are taken over by a private entity working at a national level. We argue that the intent of this transfer of control was simply to raise revenues in a way that would not harm local residents, but that the result was quite different. In the case of mortgage lending, new regulation at the federal level allowed private operators to adopt lending strategies that have withdrawn much-needed capital from LMI areas of the city. The Dodd-Frank Wall Street Reform and Consumer Protection Act (aka Dodd-Frank) was an enormous and complex piece of legislation, but we suggest that several of the parts of the act that were specifically targeted at protecting mortgage borrowers, particularly LMI borrowers in LMI neighborhoods, have allowed financial institutions to deny mortgage capital to those same borrowers.

Austerity in Toledo

Toledo, Ohio, makes up about three-fourths of the population of Lucas County. The city sits on the Maumee River at the southwestern edge of

Lake Erie, about sixty miles southwest of Detroit. Like its neighbor to the north, the Toledo economy is heavily dependent upon auto assembly and auto parts manufacturing, and like Detroit recent crises in the auto industry have weakened the local economy (Hackworth & Nowakowski 2015; Hammel & Shetty, 2013). Toledo is losing population, but unlike Detroit the city does not have a major abandonment problem, and while the Great Recession posed significant fiscal challenges for the city, it never faced issues of insolvency.

There are few examples of austerity policy being implemented at the local level. The largely Democratic city did elect an independent mayor in the heart of the recession who made substantial cuts to the city's budget that involved some layoffs. The mayor established a hard line with city unions and managed to wring concessions out of several of the public employee unions and bridge a $48 million shortfall in 2010. Most significantly, however, the mayor sided with Ohio's Republican governor, on the antiunion Senate Bill 5, which eliminated Ohio public employee collective bargaining rights. Toledo is a union stronghold. The support of a blatantly antiunion law was not popular in the city, and may have cost the mayor in his bid for reelection. The law was not popular across the state and a petition campaign forced a statewide voter referendum in November 2011, when the law was overturned by a 62 percent majority.

While the defeat of Senate Bill 5, which was sold as a public cost savings issue, was a major setback to state-level forces of austerity, Ohio cities, particularly Toledo, face other issues. While Toledo has both a sales and income tax, it is still heavily dependent upon the State of Ohio for transfers of various types of tax revenue. City officials note that from 2008 to 2014 the city dropped from $24.3 million in state revenue to $7.7 million as the state balanced its budget during the Great Recession. State legislators note that these declines were necessary given the billions of dollars in structural budget shortfalls that Ohio faced during the recession. Those shortfalls are over, but the state has yet to increase funding to its cities. Local Republican officials wonder why, while Democratic legislators label it a war on cities (Messina & Provance, 2015). In general, however, Toledo has avoided the most severe austerity policies that have been enacted through bankruptcy in cities such as Detroit (Reese et al., 2014; Tabb, 2014) and San Bernardino (Davidson & Ward, 2014;

Peck 2014). Yet, there are examples of subtler forms of austerity, as our discussion of the tax lien situation in Lucas County makes clear.

Tax Liens

Tax-delinquent properties have presented a problem for American cities for more than a century and have attracted the attention of policy analysts since the Great Depression (Rodney, 1936). Municipalities can foreclose on tax-delinquent properties, and if the properties are abandoned, they often do. When properties are still occupied, many cities prefer to try to collect on the delinquent taxes without taking possession of the property. With particularly tight budgets, cities have explored a number of options for collecting on delinquent taxes, and selling the liens has a long history.

The fiscal crisis precipitated by the Civil War was probably the first time that property tax liens were sold to private interests in the United States (Swierenga, 1971), but recently the practice became more attractive for Rust Belt cities as revenues declined and as municipal budgets got tighter. In addition, the tradition of selling individual tax liens at auction has been replaced by the practice of selling large numbers of liens to corporations whose business is buying and selling liens. More recently, these firms have begun to secure the liens as part of the larger shift toward financialization (e.g., Rolnik, 2013). In the late 1990s, several firms were established to capitalize on the growing need to sell tax liens and one, Plymouth Park, was active in Toledo.

Plymouth Park was established in 1997 by former New Jersey governor James Florio as a service to cities trying to sell tax liens. The intent was to buy tax liens on abandoned properties in bulk, often skipping the traditional auction, and then move forward on the foreclosure process to acquire the right to the property and prepare it for new development. Municipalities had the advantage of these properties potentially being added to their tax rolls once again, but more directly, they received a payment from Plymouth Park for the lien itself.

By 2009, Plymouth Park had become one of the largest players in the tax lien business (Healey, 2009) and was operating as Xpand (although in Ohio it was still operated under the Plymouth Park name). In addition, it had been purchased by JP Morgan Chase and had begun to securitize tax liens in much the same manner as mortgages were securitized. The company was operating in seven states and had moved into the Ohio market most heavily in Cuyahoga County (Cleveland). In 2006, Lucas County had begun selling off tax liens to Plymouth Park and by 2009 had sold off more than three thousand liens for $14.7 million dollars. Eventually, the county sold 5,125 liens before halting the practice in 2010 due to its unintended consequences.

The county's experience with Plymouth Park was difficult. Local officials, including the county auditor, stated that they understood that Plymouth Park would largely concentrate on abandoned properties and that they would work with those residents in occupied properties to set up payment plans and stay in their homes. Foreclosure was to be a last resort (Parker & Blake, 2008). Stories of evictions began to mount, and created enough controversy that the situation was covered in the *New York Times* (Healey, 2009). The paper detailed the stories of several evictees and noted that Plymouth Park was allowed by state law (and the lien purchase agreement) to charge 18 percent interest on the unpaid balance, and while they agreed to work out payment plans, they required a $1,000 up-front payment. In some cases a few hundred dollars in back taxes evolved into several thousand dollars of fees and penalty payments.

The tax foreclosures were also concentrated in the same areas where large numbers of mortgage foreclosures had already been occurring (Hammel & Shetty, 2013), which accentuated the problems created by the foreclosure crisis in the city's moderate-income neighborhoods. While county officials noted that only a small percentage of people were affected, an analysis of the foreclosure data collected for another study (Hammel & Shetty, 2013) indicates that Plymouth Park may have accounted for 10 percent of all (mortgage and tax) foreclosures in Lucas County between 2004 and 2008 probably making them the most common plaintiff in foreclosure cases during that period of time (Table 7.1 on page 151). While the 95 percent confidence interval is large, conversations with local legal aid lawyers and the foreclosure magistrate provide supporting evidence that Plymouth Park was a major actor in initiating foreclosures suits.

Table 7.1. Institutions with the Largest Share of All Foreclosures in Lucas County, Ohio, from 2004–2008 Based on a 2 Percent Sample and the Range at a 0.95 Level of Confidence

Plaintiff	Number	Proportion	Max	Min
Plymouth Park Tax Services	9	0.10	0.04	0.16
Deutsche Bank	8	0.09	0.03	0.15
Fifth Third Mortgage Co.	7	0.08	0.02	0.13
Wells Fargo Bank	6	0.07	0.02	0.12
US Bank	6	0.07	0.02	0.12
Countrywide Home Loans Inc.	5	0.06	0.01	0.10

The company also developed a reputation locally of being difficult to work with. Although local officials publically praised Plymouth Park for being cooperative, legal aid lawyers (ABLE, 2009) and the foreclosure magistrate (LCFM, 2009) were not in agreement. Two Plymouth Park representatives out of the Cleveland office were highlighted for being particularly obstructionist, according to legal aid lawyers who worked daily with financial institutions and loan servicers during the height of the foreclosure crisis (ABLE, 2009).

Lucas County severed its ties with Plymouth Park as soon as the terms of the initial agreement were satisfied. A new county auditor had been elected, but if the public statements of the previous auditor are to be believed, he also would have not entered into new agreements (Parker & Blake, 2008). The sale of tax liens to Plymouth Park and their willingness to evict homeowners and file tax foreclosures ran counter to another major policy effort by the county that was aimed at keeping homeowners in their homes during what can be a one-to-three-year-long mortgage foreclosure process. At the height of the foreclosure crisis, inhabitable homes that had been abandoned by their owners were a major issue for neighborhood stabilization, and the county had established a foreclosure tax force that strongly recommended making significant efforts to keep people in their homes.

Mortgage Lending in Toledo after the Crisis

The role of the mortgage market in triggering the Great Recession is universally acknowledged if not entirely understood. From the extreme Right, it was overregulation of mortgage lending that forced bad loans (e.g., Walliston, 2009). The center and Left emphasized the lack of regulation amid a complex set of global financial conditions (Baily et al., 2008) and cited a raft of scholarship focusing on the role of the securitization of mortgage products (e.g., Aalbers 2012). Our focus, however, is on the effect that the recession has had on mortgage lending, which is beginning to become clearer. Financial institutions have become more conservative in their lending, and quickly moved away from some of the more troublesome practices that helped bring about the crisis. Subprime loans, non-amortizing loans, 100 percent loans, adjustable rate mortgages, and other "exotic" products largely disappeared from the lending landscape in the heart of the crisis, and the passage of Dodd-Frank in July 2010 ensured that some of these products are unlikely to appear in large numbers in the near future. What is not yet clear is how financial institutions will respond to these regulations, and whether some of the progress made in lending in LMI communities (despite the horrors of the years prior to the recession) will be lost. While there has been much discussion of how mortgage lending contributed to the Great Recession, as of yet there has been little formal exploration of how the Great Recession has affected subsequent mortgage lending (Wachter, 2015).

Background and Data

The Home Mortgage Disclosure Act (HMDA) of 1975 required qualifying financial institutions to report a range of data regarding mortgage applications and origins to the newly established Federal Financial Institution Examination Council (FFIEC) that would be made publically available. Modified substantially in 1992 and again in 2004, HMDA data has become a standard source of information for research on mortgage lending in the United States. Although HMDA does not cover all lending, and is particularly weak in non-MSA areas, most loans made for home purchase or refinance are included in the data. Home equity lines of credit may or may not be included (Federal Reserve, 2005; Fishbein & Essene, 2011). The data include individual loan applications and the result of the application (origination of the loan, withdrawal of the application, denial, etc.) and a range of borrower and lender characteristics. In 1992 the records began to carry census tract identifiers allowing more detailed geographic analysis. Since 2004 the records contain information on the interest rate spread for what HMDA terms "high cost" loans, defined as being three hundred basis points (three percentage points) above the prime lending rate—a reasonable definition of a subprime loan.[2] There is some ability to estimate subprime loans going as far back as 1993 by using the Department of Housing and Urban Development's subprime lender list (available at http://www.huduser.org/portal/datasets/manu.html), although it is generally thought that the use of this list results in underrepresenting subprime lending (Bradford, 2002). Despite some of its shortcomings, HMDA data have formed the basis of a large and rigorous literature on mortgage lending in the United States (Ashton, 2009; Holloway, 1998; Holloway & Wyly, 2001; Immergluck. 2004; Wyly & Hammel, 2004; Wyly et al., 2004).

We use HMDA data to analyze the pattern of lending in Lucas County, Ohio, by mapping normalized aggregate loan data. HMDA data can support more substantial statistical analysis and has often been used in logistic regression to analyze denial rates for similarly qualified candidates of different races and ethnicities and, during the peak period of subprime lending, to analyze the likelihood for those same categories of borrowers to be segmented into the subprime mortgage market (Aalbers, 2012; Chinloy & MacDonald, 2005; Dinham, 2007; Engle & McCoy, 2011; Faber, 2013; Immergluck, 2008, 2009; Lax et al., 2004; Wyly et al., 2006, 2009). Wyly et al., 2006 provide what might be the most succinct summary of this literature by noting that nationwide, African American applicants were 2.3 time more likely to have subprime loans than similarly qualified white applicants. While these types of studies are rich in their analysis of deeply problematic and enduring patterns of racial and ethnic discrimination, our intent here is to concentrate less on people and more on places, thus the focus on aggregate patterns.

We chose four years over the past two decades to examine these patterns. We use data from 2012 to provide an assessment of lending during the recovery from the Great Recession, and to put these patterns in context we chose three previous time periods at six-year intervals. The data from 2006 help us see the patterns at the height of the subprime lending boom and are the last full year of data before the beginnings of the crisis in 2007. Data from 2000 provide an overview of the situation after seven years of federal emphasis on homeownership policies and opening credit markets to "underserved" population, or greenlining, as it was termed. Subprime lending was certainly present at this point. Nationally, approximately 12 percent of all loans were subprime (Gettler et al., 2008) up from a more typical historical level of about 8 percent, but the rate paled in comparison to the levels it would obtain by 2006 when approximately 43 percent of all new loans were subprime (EOP, 2008).

While the modern era of HMDA data dates back to 1993, we chose 1994 as a time that was generally representative of the more traditional mortgage market that had been in operation since the early 1970s. Policy attempts at reducing discrimination had been in place for more than two decades, but their effects were not clear and the market and regulatory forces that created the homeownership boom of the 1990s were not yet fully in place (Squires, 1992, 2003).

In addition, we have examined the temporal patterns of lending in Lucas County from 2004 to the most recently available data in 2013 to better understand the annual dynamics of the crisis. Mapping lending patterns from this time period also allows us to track the dramatic changes in conventional prime rate lending during the buildup to the crisis, during the crisis, and in the slow recovery after the crisis.

Toledo during the Crisis

The housing market in Toledo was deeply affected by the recession (Table 7.2 on page 156). Although the home ownership rate only decreased by about 4.5 percent, the loss of 10,568 owner-occupied housing units represents an 8.8 percent decrease. In addition, although the foreclosure crisis in Toledo and other Rust Belt cities was already a decade old by

Table 7.2. Homeownership in Lucas County, Ohio, 2000 and 2010

2000	Number	Percent
Occupied housing units	128,915	100
Owner-occupied housing units	77,028	59.8

2010	Numbeer	Percent
Occupied housing units	119,730	100
Owner-occupied housing units	66,460	55.5

the beginning of the Great Recession, the general decline in the housing market meant that foreclosure sales became a much more significant part of the overall housing market, peaking at 12.3 percent of all sales in 2009.

Such a high level of foreclosures causes a range of problems in housing markets. Even one foreclosure in a neighborhood or subdivision can have a surprising effect on house prices (Immergluck & Smith, 2006). Either through short sales or sheriff's auctions, foreclosed properties can reduce the appraised value of houses in the general area. This happens either when the realtor evaluates comparable sales to suggest a sale price or, more likely, when an appraiser uses the foreclosed home as a comparable home to appraise the market value. In the latter case, a low appraisal can affect the likelihood of the mortgage loan being approved. Foreclosures also have detrimental effects on neighborhoods. In Toledo, foreclosures were highly concentrated in LMI neighborhoods (Hammel & Shetty, 2013). The city's poorest neighborhoods often avoided high concentrations of foreclosures because most homes were owned by investors. The greatest effect was on the city's working-class neighborhoods which, before the crisis, were often well maintained and mostly blight free. Foreclosures can also reduce the pool of potential home buyers. Even with somewhat more lax underwriting standards, a foreclosure would usually preclude a person from buying another home for at least seven years. In a city that was losing population, this reduction in potential home buyers was significant. By the end of the recession in mid-2009, as unemployment rates slowly began to decline and house prices showed some signs of recovery, parts of central Toledo that a decade before had been solid LMI neighborhoods were in much worse shape and in need of mortgage capital to aid in the process of recovery. That capital would be slow in coming.

Patterns over Space and Time

The magnitude of the crisis can be seen in the number of loans that were originated in the county before and during the crisis (Figure 7.1). Lending was already in decline as early as 2004 for all loans (home purchase, refinance, and a few home equity loans), but plummeted through the worst of the crisis years. Home purchase loans stayed low until 2012 and began a gradual increase while all originations including refinance loans and home equity loans were more variable. Much of that variability can be attributed to refinance loans as interest rates dropped during the recession. What is most striking, however, is the low number

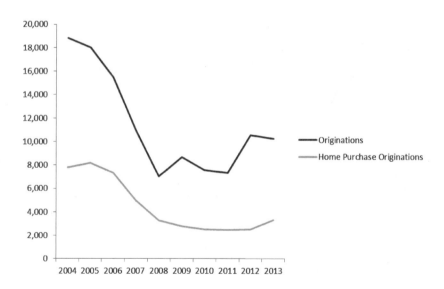

Figure 7.1. All loan originations and home purchase loan originations in Lucas County, Ohio.

of home purchase loans, which bottomed out in 2011 at 2,481. That is less than one-third of the number in 2005, and in a county with a total population of 441,815 and more than 170,000 households it indicates a housing market that had almost come to a halt.

While the numbers of home purchase loans are indicative of a market in crisis, disaggregating those loans further provides even more troubling evidence (Figure 7.2). The Federal Housing Administration (FHA) has been guaranteeing loans since the 1930s, and in recent decades FHA loans have played a relatively small role in the overall mortgage market (around 5 percent) and served largely moderate-income and first-time home purchasers. FHA loans took on much more significance during the mortgage crisis, peaking at a quarter of all loans in 2009, which, as some analysts have put it, "saved the housing market" (Griffith, 2012). In Lucas County, FHA loans accounted for just over one-half half of all home purchase loans in 2009, and in a second drop in the market in 2012 accounted for 62 percent of all home purchase loans.

The economy was well on its way toward a modest recovery in 2012, but lending in Toledo area was so weak that the conventional

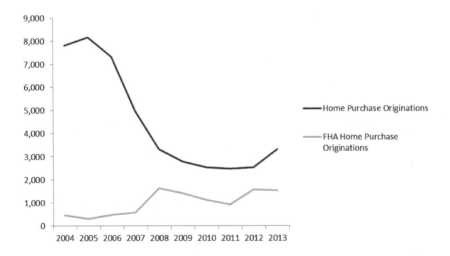

Figure 7.2. All home purchase originations and FHA home purchase originations in Lucas County, Ohio.

mortgage market made only 958 home purchase loans in a County with more than 125,000 owner-occupied housing units. Some of this can be attributed to the general weakness of the local economy, but it also is due to the unwillingness of financial institutions to make home purchase loans even when their balance sheets had almost fully recovered from the effects of the crisis.

The heavy reliance on FHA loans is also problematic because, despite their focus on LMI borrowers, FHA loans carry significantly more expense than conventional loans. FHA was established as a self-funding program that relied on an insurance fund that borrowers paid into. The insurance fund works in a somewhat similar fashion to private mortgage insurance (PMI) in that it typically is not necessary once borrowers have at least 20 percent equity in their homes. That changed, however, in 2013 when FHA expanded the insurance requirement for the entire life of the loan (de Costa, 2013). The monthly FHA insurance premium was 1.35 percent of the outstanding balance of the loan for a period of time between 2012 and 2014, but has now dropped to 1.20 percent.[3] In addition, FHA also requires an upfront prepayment of insurance at 1.75 percent of the loan balance. So, on a $100,000 home purchase with a 5 percent down payment of $5,000, the upfront premium payment, which is typically subtracted from the down payment, would result in a loan of $96,662.50. On larger loans, for example a loan of $200,000 with a 3.5 percent down payment, the costs of FHA insurance premiums for ten years would add almost $30,000 to the loan (de Costa, 2013).

The reason for these costs, which have increased substantially during and after the mortgage crisis, is related to the number of defaults that the FHA experienced and its need to stay solvent.[4] Indeed, the FHA's balance sheet was precarious enough that in September 2013 it accepted a $1.7 billion bailout from the U.S. Treasury for the first time in its eighty years of operation. With its finances in better condition, it is expected that the FHA will work to lower its insurance costs, but at least in the period of 2012–14 FHA loans were expensive. We hesitate to use the term high cost, but the final cost of some of these loans was not far from those of milder subprime loans. Thus, in a rather direct manner, the cost of increased defaults on FHA loans, largely due to the general economic conditions created by the actions of global finance, fell upon moderate- and middle-income families trying to purchase homes during a period of financial austerity. While the number of low conventional loans and the reliance on the expensive FHA products was clearly a problem, the geography of the lending presents an even more troubling pattern.

Longer-Term Patterns of Lending

While HMDA provides a wide range of data, we focus here on home purchase loans because they form the core of the housing market in any area and are less subject to fluctuations in interest rates as refinance loans. The lending pattern in 1994 (Figure 7.3) depicts a situation typical of many American cities. Downtown Toledo sits at the center of the area with the lowest levels of lending. Suburban areas lie outside of the city to the east and west, with the edges of the county in both directions being primarily rural. The area off the map to the south of downtown is northern Wood County and is largely suburban. The northern edge of the Lucas County is bounded by Monroe County, Michigan, and is largely low-density suburban.

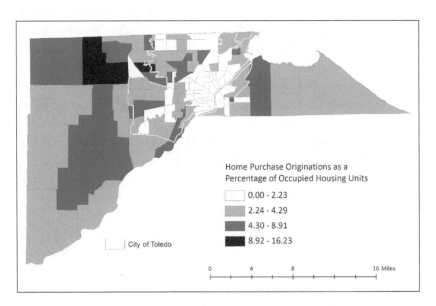

Figure 7.3. Home purchase loans in 1994 normalized by housing units.

The areas with the lowest levels of lending (fewer than 1.53 loans per 100 households) are largely poor and African American (Figure 7.4). While many homes in these areas are rentals, the edges of the area are composed of single-family homes. The pattern of home purchase loans clearly shows that large areas of central Toledo received little mortgage capital, and while this does not prove discrimination, it does raise questions about lending strategies and preferences of financial institutions, and is consistent with general nationwide trends (Listokin & Casey 1980; Listokin et al., 2000). The counterargument that people living in these areas did not have the resources necessary to purchase houses may seem compelling, but a decade later the same financial institutions were busy making hundreds of subprime loans to these same people.

The pattern in 2000 (Figure 7.5 on page 162) shows some of the effects of the prosperity of the 1990s coupled with the influence of new market initiatives by the financial institutions themselves and eight years of federal policies designed to encourage such lending. The overall level of lending has increased and specifically there were noticeable increases in the peripheral areas of the central city. The core area of low levels of lending has shrunk. Part of this increase is due to the rise of risk-based

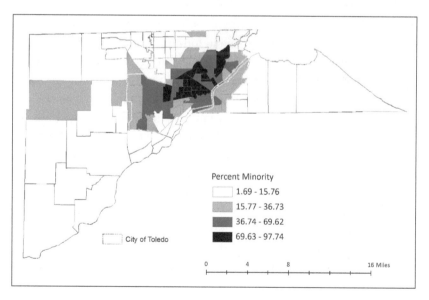

Figure 7.4. Minority population in Lucas County, Ohio, in 2010.

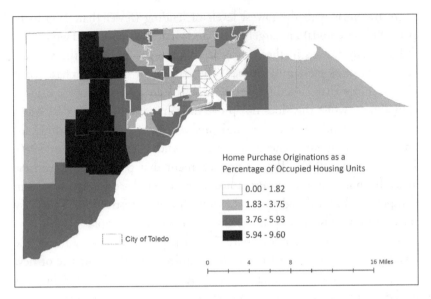

Figure 7.5. Home purchase loans in 2000 normalized by housing units.

pricing and subprime loans, but not all of it. Prime lending in these same moderate income areas increased from 1994 levels. While this cannot be termed a golden age of lending for LMI and minority communities, access to mainstream mortgage capital for home purchases had increased, and subprime and predatory lending had not yet become the problem that it would be in just a few years.

By 2006, there were clear indications of problems (Figure 7.6). While much of the country would not experience a mortgage crisis for at least another year, many Rust Belt cities were already experiencing downturns. Housing prices had begun to level off or fall, even in suburban areas, and the foreclosure rate had already begun to climb. LMI areas that had seen growth in lending in 2000 now were experiencing decline (as were suburban areas). Near downtown Toledo there are several areas of growth, but that is due to small amounts of gentrification in the city's warehouse district. In addition, by 2006, subprime lending was rampant. Figure 7.7 shows the percentage of home purchase loans that were subprime, and in many of the areas where overall home purchase lending was at its lowest levels, between 40 and 74 percent of the loans were subprime.[5]

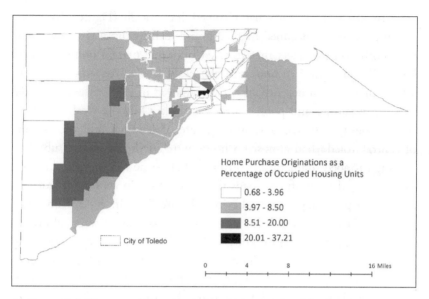

Figure 7.6. Home purchase loans in 2006 normalized by housing units.

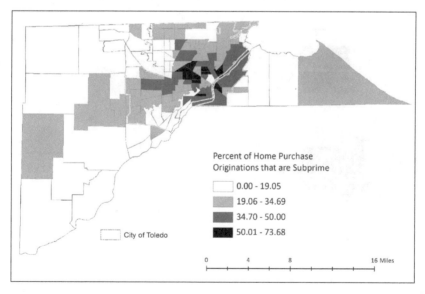

Figure 7.7. Percent of all home purchase loans that are high cost or subprime in 2006. These loans are at least 300 basis points (3 percentage points) above the going prime mortgage rate.

By 2012, the patterns had changed dramatically (Figure 7.8). Lending in general had declined markedly, and in the central city areas there were entire census tracts that received only one or two home purchase loans. The rate per 100 housing units peaked at 4.5 in suburban areas, a level that some inner city areas had achieved in 2000. The differential between wealthier and poorer areas was stark. Only the wealthiest areas in the county achieved a reasonable rate of lending, and the entirety of central Toledo had almost no home purchase loans. While subprime lending dropped dramatically during and after the recession, it does still exist and of the handful of loans that were made in central city areas, a substantial percentage were subprime (Figure 7.9). In at least one tract in largely black south Toledo, all home purchase loans were subprime.

The change in the overall number of home purchase originations in Lucas County has been dramatic (Figure 7.10) dropping well below even the 1994 levels. Lenders point to the similar decline in applications to explain the trend. To be sure, the countywide denial rate for home purchase loans was about 0.16 in 2012, which was down from the rates in 2000 and 2006 and similar to the 1994 rate, suggesting that financial institutions are willing to make loans but qualified applicants

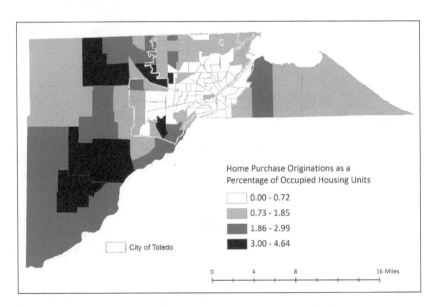

Figure 7.8. Home purchase loans in 2012 normalized by housing units.

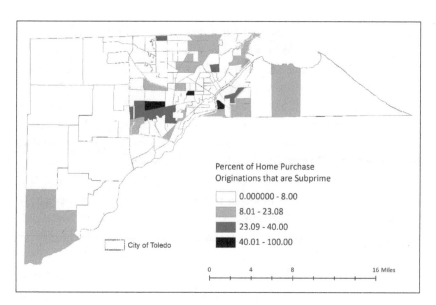

Figure 7.9. Percent of all home purchase loans that are high cost or subprime in 2012. These loans are at least 300 basis points (3 percentage points) above the going prime mortgage rate.

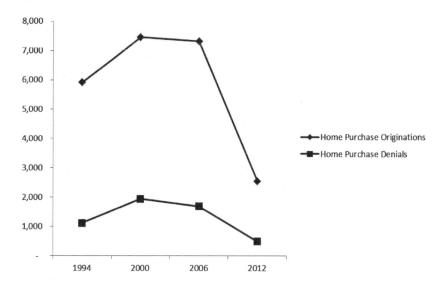

Figure 7.10. Home purchase originations and denials in Lucas County.

are not applying. However, to assume that this is simply a function of a sluggish economy would be a mistake. The mortgage market has always been plagued by self-selection issues. Historically, black home buyers have been hesitant to apply for mainstream mortgages because they knew they faced a much higher likelihood of denial, and it is likely that the same dynamic is at work in the postrecession lending landscape. This selection bias is extremely difficult to identify and document with the use of data like those in HMDA, but it can be done in specific circumstances. For example, in gentrifying neighborhoods of larger metropolitan areas it is possible to model the likelihood of minorities applying for mortgages. In the gentrified areas of Chicago, African American applicants were only three-fifths as likely to apply for loans as similarly qualified white applicants even during the heady days of the 1990s economic boom (Wyly & Hammel, 2000). While there is clearly a dynamic that is depressing applications in general in the area, it is likely to have a stronger effect in LMI and minority areas. To gain a clearer picture of these patterns we need to look more closely at the differentials in lending between poorer and wealthier areas and between minority and white areas.

We disaggregated lending data into two groups, one above and one · below the Metropolitan Statistical Area median income for the four years of our analysis (Table 7.3). We separated the data on home purchase loans into three categories: all mortgage originations that include both prime and subprime loans, and prime originations and subprime originations only. As we have noted, the 2006 and 2012, data on subprime loans are part of the HMDA data. For 1994 and 2000, loans from HUD-identified subprime lenders were coded as subprime.

In 1994 there was a clear difference between higher- and lower-income areas in the rate of mortgage originations, and there were almost no subprime originations. While there may have been some discrimination involved in the different rates between the two groups, there is reason to expect a higher origination rate in wealthier areas. If we disregard any potential discriminatory activity and use the 1994 levels as a baseline, we can begin to understand some of the changes in mortgage lending throughout this time period. The more aggressive federal regulation and the market-based greenlining initiatives of the 1990s yielded significant results in Toledo. Prime lending in lower income areas increased by more than 20 percent between 1994 and 2000—a rate that was nearly seven

Table 7.3. Prime and Subprime Mortgage Originations in Census Tracts Below and Above Msa Median Income in Lucas County

Tracts Below MSA/MD Income	1994	2000	Percent Change	2006	Percent Change	2012	Percent Change
Originations per 100 Owner Occupied Units	4.1	6.52	*59.02*	5.69	*–12.73*	1.57	*–72.41*
Prime Originations per 100 Owner Occupied Units	4.1	4.96	*20.98*	3.92	*–20.97*	1.41	*–64.03*
Subprime Originations per 100 Owner Occupied Units	0	1.56	—	1.77	*13.46*	0.16	*–90.96*
Tracts Above MSA/MD Income							
Originations per 100 Owner Occupied Units	5.82	7.17	*23.20*	6.54	*–8.79*	3.18	*–51.38*
Prime Originations per 100 Owner Occupied Units	5.8	6.56	*13.10*	5.56	*–15.24*	3.07	*–44.78*
Subprime Originations per 100 Owner Occupied Units	0.02	0.61	*2,950.00*	0.98	*60.66*	0.11	*–99.82*

percentage points greater than the increase in wealthier areas. The gap between wealthier and poorer still existed, but it had narrowed, albeit slightly. Unfortunately, many of these gains were swamped by the increase in subprime lending that had also occurred. The increase to over one and half subprime loans per 100 occupied housing units was indicative of a dramatically expanding subprime market (and recall that subprime lending at this point was concentrated in the refinance market, and not the home purchase market). The wealthier areas also experienced an increase in subprime lending (the dramatic percentage change is a function of the small numbers of subprime loans made in these areas). More importantly, the split between the concentrations of subprime lending in the poorer areas can already be seen with poorer areas having about two and one-half times the rate of subprime home purchase originations.

As we have noted, the housing crisis started in Rust Belt cities earlier than the rest of the country and the loan data from 2006 highlight this difference. While there was still a significant amount of prime lending, nearly at 1994 levels, the amount of lending had dropped from the 2000 levels. Subprime lending, however, increased in all areas. In the years before the crisis, financial institutions had begun to move their highly profitable subprime ventures into fully middle-class/middle-income neighborhoods (Aalbers, 2009; Strom & Reader, 2013). While the rate of increase in subprime lending was higher in wealthier areas, the increase in Toledo was not as extensive as it was in other areas of the country, especially Sunbelt cities. Of course, the overall rate of subprime lending still was higher in lower-income areas.

The home purchase lending numbers after the crisis in 2012 are striking. Subprime lending almost disappeared and prime lending dropped precipitously as well. The disparity between wealthier and poorer areas is greater than in any of the previous time periods, with wealthier areas having more than twice the rate of prime lending. The disparate impact of new mortgage regulations and the new geography of mortgage lending are clear. Financial institutions are applying their austere lending policies more aggressively in lower-income areas.

The patterns of lending based on racial composition of neighborhoods bear many similarities to the income patterns. We disaggregated the lending data by tracts with more than 50 percent minority population and less than 50 percent minority population (Table 7.4). In general,

Table 7.4. Mortgage Originations and Prime and Subprime Mortgage Originations in Census Tracts with More Than 50 Percent Minority Residents and Fewer Than 50 Percent Minority Residents in Lucas County

	1994	2000	Percent Change	2006	Percent Change	2012	Percent Change
Minority Dominant Tracts							
Originations per 100 Owner Occupied Units	2.59	6.49	150.58	4.44	-31.59	1.13	-74.55
Prime Originations per 100 Owner Occupied Units	2.57	4.55	77.04	2.64	-41.98	0.25	-90/53
Subprime Originations per 100 Owner Occupied Units	0.02	1.94	9,600.00	1.8	-7.22	0.88	-51.11
Non-Minority Dominant Tracts							
Originations per 100 Owner Occupied Units	5.35	7.07	32.15	6.37	-9.90	2.56	-59.81
Prime Originations per 100 Owner Occupied Units	5.33	6.36	19.32	5.01	-21.23	2.53	-49.50
Subprime Originations per 100 Owner Occupied Units	0.02	0.71	3,450.00	1.36	91.55	0.03	-97.79

minority tracts had even lower levels of prime lending in 1994 and showed a more dramatic increase in 2000, but the rate of subprime lending was higher in the minority tracts in 2000 than in any of the other disaggregated categories. The level of subprime lending in 2006 was nearly as high, while prime lending had dropped by more than 40 percent.

As bad as the situation was in 2006, it might have gotten worse by 2012. At a time when subprime lending had almost stopped, minority-dominant tracts in Lucas County have more subprime lending than prime lending. Prime lending had decreased to an astounding one home purchase loan per every four hundred owner occupied homes, a rate that is more than nine times lower than the prime home purchase lending in nonminority tracts. Of the county's 128 census tracts, thirty-nine have more than 50 percent minority residents. Of those thirty-nine tracts, in 2012, seventeen of them, with a total of 6,667 owner occupied homes, had *no home purchase loans at all*, not even a subprime loan. We should be cautious in the use the term redlining because of the well-documented specific actions and motivations involved in the process, but no matter what the actions or motivations, the result is the same. Minority areas of central Toledo are experiencing a new redlining.

A New Redlining

Why has this happened, and why do we consider it to be evidence of austerity policies at work? The mortgage-lending industry is dynamic and has shown an ability to adjust rapidly to dramatically different economic and policy environments. In addition, it is just emerging from the largest disruption since the Great Depression and adjusting to a new regulatory environment in a period of extraordinary consolidation of the industry. The forces acting on the industry and the strategies of individual institutions cannot be sorted out in a brief discussion, but we propose a basic framework for understanding some of the patterns we see in Toledo that considers the result of federal regulatory efforts in an environment of austerity.

The rhetoric surrounding the Great Recession and the financial crisis was thick. Once the questions concerning how far the crisis would proceed and what was going to happen next were settled, the focus fell on the basic question of why this had happened. It is difficult to say what explanation prevailed, but there appeared to be a "moderate" consensus that there was plenty of blame to go around and that the crisis was the result of greedy bankers and greedy borrowers (Crump et al., 2008). Columnist and pundit Leslie Marshall summed up the increasingly common view of the crisis in a *U.S. News and World Report* column in 2009. The essay is a masterpiece in apparently evenhanded criticism. She starts with a rejection of the ridiculous Right (radio commentators such as Rush Limbaugh) and moves to a discussion of the culpability of the first Bush administration. She ends, however, with the following, "Lastly, why can't we ever look in the mirror and blame ourselves? Or in this case the borrowers' and the lenders' greed? In short, our greed?" (Marshall, 2009).

While "moderates" blamed both sides, conservatives worked to deflect the blame from the financial industry and proffered some unusual conclusions. Michelle Malkin (2008) popularized the term *predatory borrower* and Thomas Sowell aggressively blamed government regulation, particularly the Community Reinvestment Act (CRA) for forcing financial institutions to make bad loans. Sowell's argument, made in dozens of columns and speeches, was adopted widely by conservatives, and continues to be repeated even now as a way of impugning Dodd-Frank (e.g., Wallison, 2015). This is despite quite a lot of careful, econometrics-based research—some of it done by Federal Reserve economists—indicating that CRA loans were not a contributing factor in the financial crisis (see Reid, 2013, for a comprehensive review).

The tenor of these arguments is much the same as the rhetoric behind austerity. Poor people, particularly poor people of color, have caused our economic problems, and as a result of this they must be disciplined in some manner. Mark Blyth (2013) provides a wide-ranging discussion and critique of the appeal of austerity. It appears to have its own logic. Belt tightening seems to make sense in times of economic contraction (even though it is not effective economic policy), and this falls neatly into the general conservative agenda of minimizing government spending, especially on social programs aimed at low-income individuals. While Blyth does not address the housing market, the basic logic that he outlines works well in the housing context. The goal of an austere mortgage-lending reform ought to be to both regulate the financial institutions and also to discipline prospective borrowers. This logic makes sense if one accepts the contention that entities on both sides of the lending equation bear blame for triggering the crisis. However, it ignores the role of a financial industry that was making record profits on subprime lending, and that had begun to aggressively move the lending tactics honed in the inner city to middle-income suburban areas because of their profitability (Schafran, 2013). It ignores the role of the securitization industry that required ever more loans to securitize, and of the Byzantine derivatives industry issuing credit default swaps that no one was able to evaluate. Thus, when the crisis had passed and policymakers attempted to sift through the rubble, the resulting regulations were as concerned with protecting the economy from poor people as they were with protecting the financial industry from itself.

Dodd-Frank was meant to address problems across all the sectors of the financial industry, from mortgage lending to the creation of derivatives. Thus, it is an immensely complex piece of legislation. It contains what are likely to be effective regulations. It deals with the some of the more disconcerting aspects of the finance industry, and it rebuilt the firewall between lending banks and investment banks. From a consumer protection standpoint, it makes subprime lending and a range of predatory credit practices much more difficult to accomplish, largely through the establishment of the Bureau of Consumer Financial Protection. However, Title XIV of the legislation, the Mortgage Reform and Anti-Predatory Lending Act, may be having some unintended consequences.

Dodd-Frank created a category of loans termed Qualified Mortgages (QMs) that have significant underwriting requirements. In short, while financial institutions are not required to issue QMs, the large federal secondary actors, Fannie Mae, Freddie Mac and Ginnie Mae will only guarantee the purchase of QMs. The QMs have a range of requirements, and many of them are quite reasonable. They allow a maximum debt-to-income ratio of 43 percent, loan fees and points cannot exceed 3 percent of the loan total, and the loan needs to be at a fixed rate (eliminating the adjustable-rate mortgage and most balloon payments). Some of the documentation requirements are more problematic. Borrowers have to prove that they have a steady consistent income, which is difficult for many self-employed individuals, and they have to explain changes or gaps in income. So, if a borrower was unemployed for a period of time, or in some cases simply changed jobs, they might fail to meet underwriting standards.

QM loans also have differential impacts. For middle-class borrowers with high credit scores, these underwriting rules might require them to provide some documentation of raises, or bonuses received at particular times that created changes to annual and monthly incomes. This type of situation makes getting a mortgage a somewhat more onerous process, but hardly constitutes a problem. In the case of borrowers with lower incomes and likely lower (but not poor) credit scores, these issues become more difficult and can dissuade financial institutions from making the loans, and even dissuade prospective borrowers from applying for them. The dearth of loans in LMI areas is in great part likely a result of the difficulties that borrowers have in becoming qualified for loans due to the very regulations meant to protect them from predatory lenders.

Private Mortgage Insurance (PMI) also may create barriers to lending. PMI has worked reasonably well to ensure that individuals could gain access to prime mortgage loans with down payments of 3, 5, or 10 percent (Neidermeyer et al., 2014). It is so important that the ability to secure PMI on a loan often determines whether or not the loan would be originated. There has long been some concern that PMI firms practiced a form of redlining (Tootell, 1995), but it is a difficult topic to investigate thoroughly due to the lack of comprehensive data on PMI. The PMI industry generally weathered the mortgage crisis quite well due to a substantial amount of careful regulation and the industry's generally conservative practices. These practices also led the industry to tread carefully into the post-recession mortgage market, and part of the need to rely so heavily on FHA loans was due to the PMI industry's reticence to insure loans during the early recovery period.

Conclusion

As these two examples show, austerity has not just happened; it is the result of decisions made at different levels of government in the context of a capitalist housing market with increasing financialization in virtually all of its segments. Even within this context, however, austerity is a process that can be resisted—bad policy can be changed. At the local level, the Lucas County tax lien policy was changed, after some negative publicity. At the national level, housing finance policy provides a more difficult target, but even federal-level policy can be resisted locally with some success. In Toledo, fair lending organizations meet with local financial institutions and discuss lending practices on occasion. While wholesale changes in lending policies are unlikely to occur, the threat of a complaint or a suit under CRA does motivate financial institutions to consider the effects of their policies on LMI borrowers and LMI neighborhoods. Real change in housing finance, however, will require action at the federal level, which appears increasingly unlikely.

These two policies also illustrate the range and reach of austerity policies. They do not involve direct government action, such as typical cutting city services or reducing government support for various social programs, but they do involve government policies that affect fiscal policies, and are meant to raise public revenues or curtail public losses. We understand that we have expanded the traditional understanding of austerity by focusing on the actions of private actors, but we note that in each case the events we describe are the result of government policy. In the case of the tax liens, it was a plan directly implemented by local government to use a private lien collector to help raise revenues in a weak economy. In the case of the Dodd-Frank bill, it was a huge federal initiative that has directly affected the pattern of mortgage lending by private financial institutions. On the surface, those policies were not intended to have the effects we have demonstrated, but in the context in which the financial industry operates, the policy outcomes should not have been hard to foresee. Nonetheless, we use the term incidental austerity to describe this more complicated path from policy development to its implementation by private actors.

The actions of Plymouth Park Tax Services after purchasing the Lucas County tax liens provide a more straightforward example of incidental austerity. The county auditor was seemingly oblivious to Plymouth Park's previous conduct, and the county severed ties with the firm as soon as they were legally able to do so because their decisions had incidentally aggravated an already serious foreclosure problem. In some respects, this could be seen as a victory over austerity, although the several hundred people who were forced out of their homes might disagree.

In the case of mortgage lending, the policies regulating the lending were meant to protect potential borrowers, particularly LMI borrowers, and they have done so in many ways. But, these regulations were implemented without any continuing emphasis on access to credit. In previous crisis periods, some policy change typically was required for any type of bailout or significant federal aid. Many of the current laws and regulations governing the lending industry were created prior to the conservative revolution of the 1980s (Fair Housing Act of 1968, Equal Credit Opportunity Act of 1974, the Home Mortgage Disclosure Act of 1975, the Community Reinvestment Act of 1977). Since that time, these laws have only been significantly updated during periods of financial crisis. The Savings and Loan Bailout of 1989 (more formally the Financial Institutions Reform, Recovery and Enforcement Act of 1989) significantly strengthened CRA and HMDA (for an insightful discussion of changes to HMDA see Wyly, 2009 and 2010). While HMDA has benefited from some changes since that time, CRA has been subject to a number of attempts to weaken or eliminate it. Ironically, most CRA advocates acknowledge that the legislation is outdated given the dramatic changes in the personal banking industry over the past two decades, and is not as effective as it once was. Nonetheless, these laws are hard-won advances in encouraging the financial industry to lend in an equitable manner that does not unduly prejudice lending decisions in LMI and minority areas.

At the end of the largest economic crisis since the Great Depression, the various financial reform bills from Dodd-Frank to the Troubled Asset Relief Program did very little to encourage lenders to be more serious about LMI and minority lending, and offered community groups who watch such lending quite closely no additional tools. The lending industry has a long history of discrimination on the basis of race, and a longstanding antipathy toward any prospective borrowers that are not solidly middle class. A set of regulations that encourage lenders to be wary of any borrowers that do not conform to the classical standards is regulation that will knowingly discourage lending in the areas that were most hurt by the foreclosure crisis and with residents still working to emerge from years of income stagnation. The result of these policies is to punish the poor for the sins of the wealthy and relieve the wealthy of any need to be concerned with the plight of the poor. This is austerity at its worst, and while we term it incidental, we do not mean to suggest that its effects are any less harsh.

Notes

1. The ongoing argument about traffic cameras in Ohio provides an odd, but instructive example. Many Ohio cities use them as a way of controlling intersections where there have been serious problems with speeding and traffic signal violations. The cameras also provide an important revenue source and are often run by private companies that split the revenue with the cities. This is exactly the type of policy that many conservatives should find appealing (law and order coupled with privatization). The Republican-controlled state government, however, has outlawed the use of cameras in part simply because the Democratic city governments are using them. The cities have sued, citing home rule rights, and won in lower courts. The case now is pending in the Ohio Supreme Court. In the interim, the state is proposing to withhold state revenues equal to the traffic camera revenues, precipitating something of a constitutional crisis.

2. We will use the more familiar term *subprime* to refer to loans that HMDA labels "high-cost."

3. FHA insurance premiums vary somewhat with the size of the loan and its length. These numbers are typical for a loan less than $600,000 and with a period of more than fifteen years.

4. It should be noted that FHA loans defaulted at a high rate during the mortgage crisis (about 7 percent), but were still much less likely to default than the myriad types of subprime and exotic loans proffered by the private sector (Griffith, 2012).

5. While subprime lending was a problem in the home purchase market, it reached its peak in refinance and home equity line of credit markets. If all loans are included in the analysis, many of the tracts in central Toledo averaged between one-half and three-quarters of all loans being subprime.

8

Conclusion

MARK DAVIDSON AND KEVIN WARD

Austerity doesn't work. Period.

—M. Blyth, *Austerity: The History of a Dangerous Idea.*

The conflicts arising out of the politics of scarcity are unrelenting. The inescapable questions becomes: who will get the short end of the stick: kids, elderly, the handicapped, government employees, single women, entrepreneurs, doctors, bankers, CEOs? The list of potential victims goes on.

—T. B. Edsall, *The Age of Austerity: How Scarcity Will Remake American Politics*

Introduction

Despite Rick Snyder, the governor of Michigan, announcing at the end of April 2015 the resolution of Flint's financial emergency, it continues to cast a long shadow on local and state finances and politics. Like a song that has ended but whose melody continues, the strategy introduced under "emergency" conditions look set to become the new normal, in the city and, on the basis of the evidence from elsewhere in urban America, across the nation. The last of the four managers appointed since December 2011, Jerry Ambrose left the city with a legislative parting gift. His final order restricts city officials from revising for a year any of the changes he made while in post. The city is tied into austerity measures, essentially. Flint may no longer constitute an "emergency" but it remains in receivership, oversight of the process passing to a Receivership Transition Authority Board that met first in June and which has continued to meet monthly through 2015.

An example of how the emergency manager–led austerity strategy continues to reveal itself can be found through looking at the example of Flint's water supply. To minimize expenditure across the city budget, Jerry Ambrose and the city council opted to switch the city's water supply from Lake Huron to the Flint River. This involved replacing Flint's contract with Detroit's sewer authority to one with the Karegnondi Water Authority (Egan, 2015). The recently founded (2010) Karegnondi Water Authority had broken ground on a $286 million pipeline designed to deliver drinking water from Lake Huron to Flint and surrounding counties in 2013. While the pipeline was under construction, the city of Flint would have its drinking water supplied from the Flint River. Given that it was widely acknowledged that the river and Flint's water infrastructure contained significant levels of lead, among other toxins and pollutants, the decision caused concerns among citizens and councilors (Fonger, 2015a, 2015b). When elevated levels of lead were detected in the city's water, concern turned to anger. With adults and children having been diagnosed with amounts over the safe level of five micrograms per deciliter of lead in their blood during late 2015, it is likely that some of Flint's residents will suffer negative health consequences (Egan, 2016a). In children, the ill effects of lead poisoning can include developmental delay, learning difficulties, weight loss, hearing loss, and fatigue. In adults, lead poisoning can cause declines in mental functioning, muscle pain, headaches, mood disorders, miscarriage. and memory loss.[1] The extent of the crisis facing the city was reflected in early 2016 with Flint mentioned both by Barack Obama and Rick Snyder within a matter of days. The former approved the governor's request for Flint to be declared a federal emergency and provided $5 million in financial assistance to cover the costs of additional water, water filters, and water test kits. In the latter's State of the State address on January 19, Snyder promised a $28 million "aid package" that included "$17.2m for bottled water and filters; $3m for city utilities for loss of revenue; and nearly $4m for behavioral health care for children with elevated blood lead levels" (Felton, 2016, np).

Flint's new water supply contract with the Karegnondi Water Authority was meant to save the city $5 million in 2015 and 2016 (Fonger, 2015a). When the new Lake Huron pipeline was completed, it was estimated that Flint and its seventeen surrounding Genesee counties would save an estimated $210 million over the course of the twenty-seven-year water contract (Johnson, 2015). It is now estimated by Flint's Mayor Karen Weaver that the cost of fixing the city's damaged water distribution system might reach $1.5 billion (Egan, 2016a). The damage to the infrastructure relates to both the toxic contamination of the system and the corrosive effects of the Flint River water (ibid.). The city, state government, and EPA are currently working to assess the extent of the damage. As a result of the water contamination, Flint's residents will be required to use bottled water and lead filtration systems for the foreseeable future. Collective consumption has become individualized. Class action law suits have already been filed against the city as a result of the health costs inflicted by the usage of highly polluted drinking water from the Flint River (Fonger, 2015b). The suit, filed on November 13, 2015, in the U.S. District Court in Detroit on behalf of Flint's residents, claims that fourteen state and city officials were responsible for replacing safe water with water that was dangerous and inadequately treated (ibid.).

If Michigan's use of technocratic emergency management has placed it at the forefront of U.S. austerity (Peck, 2014), it is also becoming an exemplar of the social costs of austerity. In Detroit, stories about the city's much-heralded "comeback" (Tomlinson, 2015) are just that: fiction not fact. They conceal the new austere reality, sometimes deliberately, in order to promote the city to potential investors and tourists. At its most extreme, these stories invoke a sense of playfulness, as if the future of the city is safe in the hands of hipsters. Indeed, those charged with designing and delivering the city's economic future seem to believe their own stories, heading to New York and launching a marketing campaign to attract young residents to the city (Willett, 2014). This campaign even had its own hashtag: #movetodetroit!

Echoing the cut of a hipster's jeans, Detroit is now described as a skinny or minimal city: "What we have here is a minimal city. . . . A whole range of services from recreation to public health to neighborhood improvement are not available in the same ways that they are available if you just cross 8 Mile" (Hammer, quoted in Dolan et al., 2015, np). Detroit's immediate fiscal future is a little more secure thanks to its bankruptcy. In July 2015, the credit rating agency Moody's upgraded its rating and outlook for Detroit, although the city retained "junk status" (Shields, 2015, np). Commentators have praised the city's positive budget progress a year on from the end of bankruptcy (ibid.), although some have cautioned against any long-term predictions: "Detroit is on the road to recovery but it would be shortsighted to say it has recovered. Recovery for a distressed municipality like Detroit is better determined five or ten years later and judged by the extent of addressing the systemic problems that led to the financial distress" (Spiotto, quoted in Shields, 2015, np). But for the thousands who still rely on city services and schools, signs of recovery have been more difficult to identify. It is these folks and others like them in many urban centers around the United States that will get "the short end of the stick," to quote Thomas Edsall (2012) in *The Age of Austerity*, with which we began this concluding chapter.

The alarming stories of Michigan's experience of "austerity on steroids" have had two seemingly contradictory effects on the wider ideological and political landscape. On the one hand, Detroit does appear to have stemmed decades of decline. At least for some inside (and outside of) the city, the future seems a little brighter as capital is reinvested in the industrial and physical environment (Tomlinson, 2015). The city has also managed to restructure onerous elements of its budget that were once thought untouchable. For some, then, particularly on the right of the political spectrum, Detroit represents a story of recovery: all of us like a comeback kid, do we not? And, what happens in Michigan no longer looks set to stay in Michigan, not with Governor Rich Snyder going out on his own "Making Government Accountable: The Michigan Story" tour, funded through the establishment of a new, nonprofit organization, the underwriters of which are undisclosed (Gottesdiener,

2015). Rather, the experiments pursued in the state may yet prove to be models for fiscal and political restructuring across U.S. urban centers. On the other hand, the restructuring introduced across the state's public sectors—education, health care, policing, welfare, and so on—and the associated consequences for those most disadvantaged and marginalized in American society—promises a more unequal and unjust set of urban futures (Edsall, 2012; Peck, 2013).

Beyond the headline-grabbing traumas of Flint and Detroit, austerity remains a pernicious logic across the United States, as many of the contributions in this collection illustrate. Efforts to shrink expenditures remain in place as the economic outlook remains uncertain. In 2015, the National League of Cities (NLC, 2015) reported that some cities were starting to see a modest recovery in annual budgets. This has enabled some U.S. cities to replace staffing positions and assets that had been cut or delayed in preceding years. But the recovery of capacity within the U.S. urban system remains geographically uneven and slow, indicating that commitments to austerity will likely remain in place. Without a significant shift in political discourse, something that looks unlikely given the prominence of issues such as deficit reduction and shrinking government and a continued reluctance to implement substantive tax increases, austerity appears to have become something more than an immediate response to financial crisis and recession. Not cyclical, it is looking as if austerity has morphed into an ideological project that is altogether more systemic. It appears to be the new normal. It is therefore worth reflecting on some of the major conclusions of this collection.

Austerity Statecraft

All of the contributions to the collection make a commentary on what the state is doing, or not doing, in an era of austerity. Indeed, a major part of Hammel and Chen's contribution demonstrates that through the strategies employed by the state, others have become increasingly responsible for the "doing" of austerity. Its edges have been redefined, both internally and externally (Peck, 2001). Yet, as Kirkpatrick and Bolton, and Ponder and Hinkley, all show, there are clearly identifiable characteristics of austerity statecraft. This is no rolling back of the state but is, rather, its qualitative restructuring from within and without. Perhaps the single most important characteristic of postrecession austerity is its insistence on a smaller state. As Peck (2012, p. 626) explains:

> Austerity represents a historic opportunity to press for yet smaller small state settlements at the urban scale; in defining government downsizing and rolling privatization as fiscal necessities, it is neoliberal terrain. It is not the same terrain, of course, because this latest austerity offensive is being prosecuted under historically and geographically distinctive conditions, and in the context of already neoliberalized configurations of (local) state power and (urban) politics.

However insistent the demand to shrink the state is at the current moment, it is not without its contradictions and inconsistences. As Kirkpatrick and Bolton's examination of Detroit's new hockey stadium negotiations shows, austerity, even at its most extended articulations, does not necessarily mean minimal state spending. Austerity statecraft is not simply concerned with the goal of a minimal state. Detroit's extensive state spending appears perfectly justifiable so long as it has a speculative component. That is, so long as those private and public, local, state, federal, and international stakeholders *believe* in these sorts of redevelopment strategies delivering growth—defined through a relatively narrow form of benchmarks and indicators. In part, this belief stems from the sort of economic analysis that is conducted in the planning of these projects, as consultancies of various stripes run econometric models and generate supportive data. However, they also involve something more. That is, the enrolling of certain emotions, for there is a rather ethereal and hard to pin down aspect to these sorts of speculative large-scale cultural and sporting projects.

Crucially, this speculative state spending does not necessarily demand a strong empirical justification. The example of stadia development has indeed become symbolic of the fantastic nature of entrepreneurial governance (Baade, 1996; Flyvberg & Stewart, 2012). It has been shown repeatedly that the state subsidization of sports stadia rarely produces a return on investment and where revenue is generated this is most clearly captured by private interests (Baade, 1996). And, yet it remains popular among city government policymakers. The promise of revenue growth sometime in the future is hard for many to resist. Under increasingly austere conditions there appear still more examples of this form of speculative urbanism, such as in the case of Detroit, where subsidies provided to the private sector continue.

If austerity is about the targeted qualitative downsizing of the state, then the issue of employee remuneration and benefits has become a defining area of concern. Hinkley's explanation and analysis of San Jose's austerity drive gives an example of the new limits of neoliberalism:

> Speculative urbanism under austerity is creating a turbulent and insecure political landscape. Whilst those cities that have pursued bankruptcy have brought crisis to retirees in ill-health (i.e., Vallejo) and slashed the value of bond holdings (i.e., San Bernardino and Stockton), these cases are also changing the stakes of municipal politics. What were once sacred cows are now fair game, enabling cities in fiscal crisis to threaten creditors with unilateral changes that would, a short time ago, have been unthinkable. (Davidson & Ward, 2014, p. 95)

Austere statecraft has made the unthinkable thinkable. In San Jose, a city in one of the most prosperous regions in the United States, a mayor-led restructuring exercise has focused on the salaries, pensions, and health benefits of employees and retirees. Outside of the select group of bankrupt cities that have used court powers to restructure collective bargaining agreements (GMUSLGLC, 2012; Trotter, 2011), San Jose is one of a growing number of cities that has attempted to reform its public employment contracts and public services in order to divest the city of significant expenditure obligations. As cities such as Detroit and San Bernardino have descended into bankruptcy, they have therefore provided the likes of San Jose with a prospective future. It is argued that without austerity the future is one of public service chaos, unlimited restructuring of employment contracts, and perpetual fiscal crisis (*Kansas City Star*, 2016; Mathewson, 2015). As Peck (2012, pp. 631–32) notes:

The neoliberal proclivity for downloading, by way of responsibility dumping and devolved discipline, assumes an increasingly radical and regressive form in an environment of austerity, as both budget cuts and responsibility for their management is handed down to local authorities, actors and agencies—where the capacity to respond is uneven at best. Systemic conditions of fiscal restraint serve to reinforce the hierarchical powers of budget chiefs and audit regimes, inducing instrumentalism, entrepreneurialism and muscular modes of management at subordinate scales. Moreover, the long term rollback of fiscal transfer regimes, automatic stabilizers, revenue sharing, and both redistributive and investment based programming means that there is little option but to (crisis) manage budgetary crises at the local scale.

Perversely, this type of Hobson's choice urban governance has not meant a necessary rethinking of intergovernmental relations. Rather, the neoliberal downloading of governmental responsibility has continued apace. As Ponder's discussion of the EPA's imprint on U.S. cities vividly shows, the neoliberalization of federal agencies continues to generate implications farther down the governmental hierarchy. What this has meant in places such as Alabama and Missouri is that cities have become ever more financially responsible for environmental management and cleanup. In the context whereby the fiscal capacities of cities are ever more eroded, such requirements have meant city administrations have become open to using more complex financial tools to deal with burdensome remediation responsibilities. To extend this contradiction, they have become participants in complex financial deals at the same time that their capacity to understand and favorably negotiate these deals has become reduced. Were it that there was ever parity between the public and private sectors in terms of financial expertise and numeracy, this period seems to have passed.

Such contradictions of austere statecraft warn against a simplistic understanding of austerity. Although Mark Blyth (2013, p. 13) describes austerity as "a form of voluntary deflation in which the economy adjusts through the reduction of wages, prices, and public spending to restore competitiveness, which is (supposedly) best achieved by cutting the state's budget, debts, and deficits," at the urban level such a description can be misleading. In the chapters both by Ponder and by Kirkpatrick and Bolton, the story of austerity is about significant increases in debts, despite all efforts to remove these obligations from budget statements. Austerity at the federal or state level therefore means something different than at the local level. It is open to mediation and translation. Consequently, a different type of statecraft appears to continue to be emerging across U.S. localities.

Hinkley's discussion of San Jose illustrates some of the distinctiveness of urban statecraft under austerity. Where calls for fiscal reform at the national level are dominated by issues of deficits and burgeoning interest payments (Congressional Budget Office, 2014), at the urban level fiscal reform is discussed in the context of utter failure. The specter of governmental failure, whether symbolized by Detroit's decline or California's urban dysfunction, has proven a powerful device in the entrepreneurial governance system (Peck, 2014). The stakes of austerity at the urban level can therefore appear profound. Compared to the federal level, where the discourse is often about long-term decline, at the urban level it is therefore easier to put the case for more urgent reform. Without immediate intervention, as the San Jose argument goes, life and death fiscal problems will rapidly emerge.

Austerity Public Service Reform

Against this backdrop of targeted intervention and seeming urgency stands a remarkably static landscape of service reform. Since austerity does involve a certain neoliberalizing of neoliberalism, it may not be surprising that the repertoire of policy reform has not been revolutionized under austerity. As we have previously noted, the story is better encapsulated by the idea that now-long-standing reform agendas have been dramatically extended under austerity (Davidson & Ward, 2014; Peck, 2012). Of course, playing out the same policy reform agendas in a new institutional and macro context holds the potential to deliver a different set of outcomes.

Kathe Newman provides an insightful example of this process in her discussion of inclusionary zoning in New York City. She situates New York City's current engagement with inclusionary zoning in a long-term perspective. Inclusionary zoning, according to Newman, is an initial iteration of austerity urban politics, originating from the late 1970s fiscal crisis of New York. From this seminal event in the history of neoliberalism (Harvey, 2005), inclusionary zoning emerged as the "only" option for provisioning "affordable" housing under the neoliberal conditions. With the ability of governments to build housing removed, private market actors have to be incentivized to produce below-market rent housing, it is argued. The failure of this policy mechanism to produce the number of necessary units has become evident in cities such as New York, where overcrowding, homelessness, and insecure tenure are near endemic (Smith, 2015; Stewart and Yeejan, 2016). The response from progressive New York City mayor Bill di Blasio has been to consider making inclusionary zoning mandatory. Austere housing policy may therefore go through a future iteration in New York City. Although this would strengthen affordable housing policy, it would do so in an austere context. Such a context contributes to Newman's questioning of why other forms of affordable housing provision remain so taboo in the context of a city in which most people cannot afford to live.

The continuities of austerity that Newman makes central to her discussion of New York City stand in sharp contrast to the account of Toledo offered by Hammel and Chen. Whereas it would appear that little is new in the context of austere policymaking in New York City, the Toledo case makes it clear that in some localities new policy innovations are part of the wider restructuring associated with austerity. However, it may be that the traditional policy actors we associate with neoliberal public service reform are not responsible for the latest restructuring. Hammel and Chen illustrate two different examples of what they call "incidental austerity." The first, a local tax lien collection arrangement, where the city outsourced the revenue collection exercise, created an unexpected austerity process. The second, the federal government's re-regulation of mortgage lending, changed geographies of mortgage lending in Toledo. Although both policy reforms appeared to be intent on progressive outcomes, they have had the opposite effect.

What unites these two examples of "incidental austerity" is their ideological commitment to private market solutions. Both public service reforms were intent on having the state play a marginal role in governance, and instead focused on directing private market actors. Such policy reforms fall in line with the renewed commitment to neoliberal principles under austerity. However, what Hammel and Chen persuasively argue is that it was the very commitment to light-touch state action and privatization that generated austere outcomes. Austerity was not an added dimension to neoliberal public service reform. Rather, austerity was integral to that very form of reform. Here, Hammel and Chen find agreement with Newman's own critique of New York City's recent housing policies. Austerity becomes manifest not in new types of governmental reform, but in the continued implementation of long-standing forms of restructuring.

Austerity Subject Making

Neoliberalism is merely the most recent development of such techniques that govern human life, that is, governmentality that relies on market knowledge and calculations for a politics of subjection and subject-making that continually places in question the political existence of modern human beings. (Ong, 2006, p. 13)

If austerity can be understood through the notion of neoliberalism plus neoliberalism, then one might expect the idea of subject (re)making to be at the core of austerity reform (England & Ward, 2007). From the very origins of the neoliberal movement in the inner discussions of the Austrian School economists (Brown, 2015; Mirowski & Plehwe, 2009; Peck, 2010), the idea that humans were particular kinds of beings requiring certain types of state forms to condition them was central. For Hayek (1945, pp. 6–7), optimal social and economic conditions could not be arrived at through centralized planning (i.e., a strong state), since the ability of a select group of bureaucrats to possess and manipulate the necessary knowledge to coordinate affairs was impossible:

> Planning in the specific sense in which the term is used in
> contemporary controversy necessarily means central plan-
> ning—direction of the whole economic system according to
> one unified plan. Competition, on the other hand, means
> decentralized planning by many separate persons. . . . Which
> of these systems is likely to be more efficient depends mainly
> on the question under which of them we can expect that
> fuller use will be made of the existing knowledge. And this,
> in turn, depends on whether we are more likely to succeed
> in putting at the disposal of a single central authority all
> the knowledge which ought to be used but which is initially
> dispersed among many different individuals, or in conveying
> to the individuals such additional knowledge as they need in
> order to enable them to fit their plans with those of others.

The way to coordinate a society was therefore to enable individual subjects
to deploy their own knowledges in such a way to optimize the most
effective deployment of societal knowledge at any one moment. The
individual was therefore to be empowered and state severely restricted.
This creed has been subject to all kinds of manipulation and abuses
by politicians since Margaret Thatcher declared allegiance to Hayek's
economics (Bourne, 2013). Whether it is housing vouchers instead of
public housing, at-will employment contracts rather than contractual
commitment, or 401K pensions over guaranteed pension formulas,
the neoliberal transformation of states in the Global North has often
embodied Hayek's idea about the subject and its relationships to society.

What Nitzik's detailed examination of housing mobility in Providence demonstrates is the next iteration of the neoliberalization of the
neoliberal city (Hackworth, 2006). Providence has been undergoing a
rapid transformation since 2008. As a result of the city's downturn,
unemployment rose sharply and this rise was most concentrated in the
Hispanic population. Nothing particularly new here, perhaps, given what
we know about those groups who have been disproportionately affected
by the combination of the financial crisis and the austerity responses
of government. As a consequence, the social costs of the recession were
being concentrated in some of the city's most vulnerable communities.

Some of these social costs are implicated in rising rates of housing mobility. The sudden uptake of housing mobility during the recession is a direct result of neoliberal doctrine. Leaving people to make their own decisions about housing, enabling markets to respond accordingly, and the reduction of state involvement from this process all have shaped the experience of Hispanics in Providence.

The most important element of this subject remaking is noted by Nitzik when he lists the consequences of multiple housing moves on life chances: "frequent residential mobility during childhood is linked to behavioral problems, risk taking, depression and lower academic achievement. . . . At the same time, frequent residential mobility in childhood is linked to higher mortality in adulthood." As cities such as Providence undergo austerity drives, they therefore expose their most vulnerable populations to the more violent consequences of market housing.

The subject making described by Nitzik takes us a long way from Hayek's optimal society. Yet it does look like those of other people who are also subject to the other dimensions of austerity. Whether it is the retired public employees in Vallejo, California, who had their healthcare benefits slashed by, on average, 80 percent and capped (Davidson & Kutz, 2015), the retirees in Detroit who now must repay tens of thousands of dollars out of shrinking pensions (Tompor, 2015), the thousands of public workers who have been laid off since 2008 (Bivens, 2015), or the thousands who unwittingly hold municipal bonds in their maturing pension savings (Slavin, 2015), the urban subject under austerity is marked by an increasing proximity to the turbulence of the crisis-ridden economy.

U.S. Urban Futures under Austerity

Recent revelations in Flint suggest that the longer-term consequences of austerity urbanism à la the United States are only just beginning to reveal themselves. Since in the United States austerity has been devolved through its federalist system (Peck, 2014), unlike European national level iterations (A. Newman, 2012), it appears that some of the outcomes of U.S. austerity are delayed and, certainly, variegated. That is, they vary, but in interconnected and relational ways. On the one hand, there are some discernible patterns and regularities, as reading across the chapters in this collection reveal. For Peck (2012, pp. 628–629):

> Clearly, the situation is far from uniform, for uneven spatial development is also part of the story, but the generalized manifestations of devolved austerity are becoming increasingly evident at the urban scale across the country. In important respects, this represents an incipient fiscal crisis for the local government sector as a whole in the USA, but it is also a distinctively urban crisis in the sense that the cities have been hit especially hard by the housing slump and the parallel wave of mortgage foreclosures; in the sense that cities are disproportionately reliant on public services; and in the sense that they are "home" to many of the preferred political targets of austerity programs—the "undeserving" poor, minorities and marginalized populations, public-sector unions and "bureaucratized" infrastructures.

On the other hand, while one or two U.S. states, particularly California and Michigan, have garnered attention through their high-profile restructuring, even to the point of being cast (or casting themselves) as models from which other states might learn, across the United States there are a range of less prosaic but no less important ways in which the lives of urban residents have been damaged through austerity programs. Seemingly mundane and ordinary changes to the services delivered across U.S. urban government have had a profound effect on people's lives, even if the precise implications vary from city to city and state to state. In this collection we have attempted to survey some of this emergent urban landscape. By sketching out how statecraft, policy reform, and subject remaking are all constituent and defining features of the austerity program, we can begin to understand its vast and varied impacts.

If one were attempt to distill public discourse on austerity to its most simple element, one might arrive at the idea that there is simply "not much to go around." Across the United States, we have seen an assessment of city budgets where constituents have been pitched against one other. In Vallejo, California, unionized employees were accused of having been given unfairly generous contracts at the expense of citizens. In Detroit, Michigan, the bankruptcy proceedings featured stakeholders constantly positioning to receive a more favorable deal in the plan of readjustment. In other cities facing lesser degrees of fiscal crisis, the same negotiations have taken place in less dramatic circumstances; whether it be city departments fighting over cuts, unions outmaneuvering each other, or citizens fighting for different city services. As a consequence of this type of urban politics, austere cities can be absent of more collective concerns; a politics that revolves around what is best for the city as a whole.

If austerity urban politics have a tendency to be tribal, then one tribe is clearly winning. Throughout the course of city reforms and court-mediated bankruptcy cases, many of the losers of austerity have been the most at-risk and disadvantaged groups. In this contribution, we have seen vulnerable populations in Toledo (see Hammel and Chen) and Providence (see Nitzik) facing the brunt of austerity restructuring. In places such as Detroit (see Kirkpatrick and Bolton) we have seen a differential treatment of unionized employees, a pattern repeated in other distressed cities (Davidson & Kutz, 2015). In these cases, police and fire union contracts have tended to receive more favorable outcomes in renegotiations, even if their contracts are more onerous for the city compared to other employees. In terms of those with municipal debt (i.e., bondholders), some have fared poorly in bankrupt cities, but generally city and state governments have moved to protect this class of creditors. This can be explained by the desire of all involved to maintain the ability to borrow in capital markets. If there is less to go around in our austere times then those with the greatest wealth appear to have been successful in protecting their privilege (http://www.aflcio.org/Corporate-Watch/Paywatch-2015). Returning to the quote with which we began this chapter, and of those listed by Edsall (2012, p. 23), it would seem the "entrepreneurs, doctors, bankers and CEOs" have done rather better than the "kids, elderly, the handicapped, government employees, [and] single women" through what he terms the "politics of scarcity."

Austerity politics in the United States have therefore tended to see one group pitched against another. But throughout these battles, the dominant story features the most vulnerable being made even more vulnerable, those already marginal being further marginalized. In a tribal politics that has engaged lawyers in complex cases, relied on funded lobbyists, and is stitched into established structures of city governance, this is an entirely predictable outcome. The consequence is, of course, a reinscribing of already deep class distinctions, ones that have been generated, maintained, and nurtured since the late 1970s through a neoliberalizing economic and social system premised on social and spatial inequality and unevenness. As Campbell (2015, np) argues:

> Stories about austerity measures in the EU don't get much attention in the States, mainly because austerity is already our reality. Our safety net is knit together by charities and faith groups which do the work that government could more easily and efficiently accomplish.

The production of an even less progressive and an even more unjust urban landscape would not seem to suggest a particularly promising set of futures for residents of urban America. There are alternatives of course, as there have been under neoliberalization. These have not been the focus of this collection, although they are present in some of the chapters. This is important. For the delivery of on the ground austerity urbanism involves a degree of everyday pushback and resistance. This can be both low-key and mundane and more high-profile and spectacular, of course. Allowing for the limits associated with dissonance and particularism, another city remains possible if not probable.

In their edited collection on contesting neoliberalism Leitner et al. (2007, p. 326) end by making the following statement:

> [The] recognition that local, regional, national, and global scales of governance are radically intertwined means confronting the challenges of a different kind of politics. The eruption and persistence of challenges to neoliberal rule, in cities across the globe; the proliferation of translocal and transnational networks, and of alliances among diverse social groups and movements; are each suggestive of such innovation, providing hope and inspiration that alternatives to the market and consumer monoculture are alive and thriving.

Fast forward a decade and in general the macrocontext would seem to have gotten worse, not better, particularly in the United States, where despite two terms of office for a Democratic president, the popular and political mainstream seems to have moved rightward. Alternatives remain alive and thriving, of course. These include the various living wages ordinances that have emerged in U.S. cities over the last couple of decades through to the specifics of place-based initiatives such as Cooperation Jackson (http://www.cooperationjackson.org/), which themselves draw their ideological nourishment from longer histories of significant geographical reach. For sure, then, in some U.S. cities the politics of austerity has included contestation and pushback against the wide program. There is an element of co-production, as what city governments are able to achieve in terms of budget cuts or service restructuring is the product of a range of stakeholders, some of whom have sought to challenge the new orthodoxy. And these localized examples of the sorts of trajectories about which Leitner et al. (2007) wrote might become the building blocks for a more interconnected and upscaled set of progressive projects. Maybe. However, with the conditions for transformation becoming less, not more, conducive, this seems a stretch. Even if there is an acknowledgment that a more just urban future might be best fashioned through the DIY politics espoused by some on the Left, there is some way to go in the United States at least before the various good work currently being done in cities around the country might be able to be translated into a more systemwide program of progressive reform. Or, maybe that is a version of a more progressive future rooted in a set of social relations from the past. To write of a "system-wide" program may be to cede ground unnecessarily to those on the Right and to misunderstand movements and the societies out of which they emerge.

Note

1. Mayo Clinic (n.d.) Lead Poisoning. Retrieved from http://www.mayo clinic.org/diseases-conditions/lead-poisoning/basics/symptoms/con-20035487.

Postscript

MARK DAVIDSON AND KEVIN WARD

Definitions belong to the definer not the defined.

—Toni Morrison, *Beloved*

Urban renewal means . . . Negro renewal.

—James Baldwin

Nobody needs to tell African Americans in this country that the old new deal from the Democratic Party isn't working for them. In election after election, Democratic Party leaders take African American voters for granted and year after year the condition of Black America gets worse. The conditions in our inner cities today are unacceptable. Too many African Americans have been left behind.

—Donald J. Trump, 2016

At the time of writing, it is now just over forty days since Donald Trump won the forty-fifth U.S. presidential election. It will be just over another thirty days until he is sworn in as President of the United States. It is thus early—to say the least—to speculate with any certainty on what his presidency might mean for U.S. cities. His campaign was, as many have observed, not one strong on coherence and consistency. Policy often gave the impression of being poorly thought through, even made up as it was introduced, and with scant regard for the existing program-matic landscape. Nevertheless, in ending this volume it is worth offering some tentative remarks on how five years of Trump might restructure the ways in which government is involved in cities, in light of the last decade or so of austerity urbanism and the longer-term neoliberalization of U.S. cities under successive Democratic and Republication govern-ments. For while he might have run his campaign as an alternative to the two main political parties, early cabinet appointments suggest what we are likely to see unfold is a speculative variant of the mainstream neoliberal theme, with future cuts in social budgets, an increased role for the private sector, and the stigmatizing of those rendered "undeserving" (Monbiot, 2016), paired with deficit spending on infrastructure and military, revenue-neutral tax reform (at least at inception!) focused on boosting corporate profitability and on-shoring, and a host of "choice" initiatives that promise routes toward social mobility.

Back to the Future (but without Michael J. Fox)?

On October 26, 2016, just under two weeks before the end of cam-paigning, Trump's plane touched down in Charlotte, North Carolina. In the fastest-growing U.S. city, according to some indicators, with the largest financial sector in the country outside of New York, he used his speech to launch his *New Deal for Black America, With a Plan for Urban Renewal*. It did not come out of nowhere, of course. Over the campaign, his language had moved back and forth between inner cities and black America as if the two were one and the same. Trump responded to a question asked from the floor by an African American in the town hall–style debates by talking about the inner cities, even though nothing related to the topic was asked. This was taken and satirized by *Saturday Night Live*, as part of its series of sketches with Alec Baldwin playing Donald Trump and Kate McKinnon as Hillary Clinton.

Trump's *New Deal* consisted of three and a half pages "stuffed with items that don't make much sense," according to Covert (2016, np). It contained a list of ten points. These were a combination of general claims already made about "Trade That Works for American Workers" and "America First Foreign Policy" and a set of only loosely connected points about different aspects of urban America. A strategy it was not. It said rather less about Trump's possible approach to "the inner city" and more about his probable approach to race. Its title and its opening paragraph were both instructive.

Of course, the term *New Deal* was borrowed from the 1930s slogan coined by Franklin D. Roosevelt in reference to his strategy for dealing with the Great Depression. This centered on the 3Rs—relief, recovery, and reform. More recently, the term was used by Bill Clinton as he introduced a wholesale restructuring of the U.S. welfare state, which included the demonizing of young African American women as "welfare queens." So it has recent history in terms of its targeting of African Americans. The history and usage of the term *renewal* is even more problematic. It was put to work during the 1950s as a means of justifying and legitimizing the razing of large swathes of urban housing. Urban renewal laws gave city governments the money and the power to exercise eminent domain, as communities were dismantled and dispersed. In their place were built hotels, higher-end housing, shopping centers, and roads, as cities sought to retain the middles class and their spending power in the face of widespread suburbanizing. The irony, of course, was that city governments were also active in making suburbanization possible by changing financial, land, and zoning regulations.

In light of this, Trump's most explicit urban policy says as much about his stance on race as it does his plan for cities. For this understanding of "the urban" characterizes it as a site of danger and threat to the (white) American way of life. It is rooted in the material and political relations of the 1970s wherein "the urban" serves to symbolize all contemporary African American experiences. This is despite evidence that "Many 'Inner Cities' Are Doing Great" (Badger, 2016, np), although they are not doing great for everyone.

Tout change, rien ne change pas?

While some have argued that "the GOP's urban agenda need not solely focus on inner cities" (Borelli, 2016, np), it is this spatial signifier that has figured most prominently in the Trump campaign. Although not included in its title, it is nevertheless mentioned four times in the *New Deal* document. Its use is far from neutral, of course. As Badger (2016, np) notes:

> Inner city, in short, is imprecise in describing today's urban reality. It captures neither the true geography of poverty or black America, nor the quality of life in many communities in central cities. But politically, its 1970s-era meaning lingers.

According to Massie (2016, np), the term has "more to do with how racism has shaped America's cities than simply identifying where black and brown people live." More than a geographical reference, its use by Trump's campaign was a cultural and social signifier for a largely white audience. It sat nicely with Trump's wider call to "Make America Great Again," which invokes a return to a period before the inner cities became synonymous with deprivation and poverty. That they became this was attributed to those who lived there, African Americans for the most part. This line of thinking on social pathology has been pushed by, among others, Dr. Ben Carson, the new secretary for housing and urban development, whose appointment despite zero experience in either housing and urban development or policy has caused a mixture of anger, amusement, bewilderment, and confusion to some, while others have been more supportive:

> HUD has made many mistakes over the years. Instead of pursuing yet another scheme to rebuild America's inner cities, HUD should instead do what it can to make poor neighborhoods safe and attractive to private investment. The agency should cease ordering banks to make such investments and roll back disincentives for upward mobility. Ben Carson is just the man for that job. (Huscok, 2016, np)

So, after a decade of austerity targeting the most marginalized groups in the city, and in turn consigning a growing proportion of the population to this category, the revival of the term *inner city* and all that goes with it in terms of cultural, racial, and social meaning does not bode well for the production of a more inclusive and progressive city. This is speculation at this point, of course, but the signs are not good, while the stakes for those who live in U.S. cities could not be higher.

Trumpian Urban Austerities?

If Donald Trump's campaign rhetoric converts into presidential politics—and this is a big if—the future of austerity urbanism, as with almost all facets of American society, remains unclear. The Trump campaign featured tax and spending promises that many budget experts have dismissed as unreasonable and unworkable (Timiraos & Rubin, 2016). Yet if the Republican-majority Congress can be convinced to back large-scale infrastructure investment, some parts of the United States will likely experience renewed and/or heightened growth. It seems improbable that this infrastructure investment will replicate the national scope of Eisenhower's 1956 Federal Aid Highway Act (McNichol, 2006), since most existing propositions are, at best, local and regional schemes. In the Trump era, infrastructure policy will therefore likely be defined by clientelism, with consequent uneven geographies of urban and regional renewal. In this regard, it is not clear who the beneficiaries of Trump's infrastructure plans might be, since so much of the incoming administration has little or no record of holding public office.

Of the existing clues as to how urban investment might unfold under Trump, two stand out. First, the proposed expenditure is intended to be revenue-neutral and organized through public-private partnerships (DeGood, 2016). Some degree of existing economic activity and associated growth is therefore a prerequisite for most schemes if sufficient user fees are to be collected and private capital investment is to be profitable. The prospect of Trump's infrastructure plans producing some kind of progressive redistribution across the U.S. urban landscape therefore seem, at this stage, remote. Second, if campaign rhetoric is any guide, the forthcoming administration will have little reluctance in naming winners and losers. If certain cities lose out on infrastructure investments, or fail to follow the line of the Republican-dominated administration, the campaign has suggested that economic "losers" will find little in the way of recompense. Failure, it again seems, will likely be the victim's fault.

In this collection's preface, Jamie Peck describes austerity urbanism as having a checkerboard-like geography. Far from being a uniform process, austerity has been differentially applied across the U.S. urban landscape. Recession and state cutbacks barely registered in some thriving cities, while for others, recession meant budgetary collapse. When the Trump administration begins its work, it is likely that this checkerboard will be rearranged yet again. Spending has been promised, but it is unlikely to be ameliorative for most troubled cities. Rather, a push for economic growth rates of 4–5 percent will ensure that return of capital dictates geographical location and accentuates the existing unevenness in economic development. There will also be little sympathy for those unwilling or unable to join this quest for remade greatness. In an urban system defined by speculative urban governance (Davidson & Ward, 2014), the situation is poised to produce an even higher-stakes game of entrepreneurial urban competition. Win big or die trying may become the norm for cities under Trump's casino-like economic policy.

To finish, then, by asking where this leaves the idea of austerity urbanism is to lay another speculation atop existing layers of speculation. Things are undoubtedly poised to change under Donald Trump and a Republican-controlled Washington, D.C., with his emphasis on empowering states. Trump's campaign rhetoric and policy prescriptions are unprecedented in their lack of consistency and reasoned argument. Early signs, such as the appointment of Ben Carson to HUD or the emerging infrastructure plan, signify a continuation and mutation of neoliberal norms, yet Trump is far from a traditional small-state conservative or doctrinaire neoliberal. He is, however, acutely aware of his political base and the antiestablishment sentiments he has come to represent. How he manages this contradiction will likely define his presidency, and it remains impossible to predict how he will manage those situations where the contradiction becomes unavoidable.

The ongoing story of austerity urbanism will therefore be imposed on this uncertain political landscape over the next four years. Dramatic changes to economic policy and tax codes under Trump will have both predictable and unpredictable impacts. A highly charged and divided national political landscape will likely also shape the next president's term in unforeseeable ways. Yet what seems less uncertain is that workable economic and fiscal solutions will remain difficult to achieve for many U.S. cities. Decades of neoliberal reform have deeply marked U.S. cities and any reversal of this trend will require a sustained and painfully long effort. After the Great Recession, many cities find themselves with even fewer resources to take up this task. Austerity will, therefore, almost certainly remain an agonizing reality for many. This effort will now play out in perhaps the most unpredictable presidency in the history of the union. The future might be orange, but is does not look bright.

References

Aalbers, M. (2009). Geographies of the financial crisis. *Area, 41*(1), 34–42.

Aalbers, M. (2012). *Subprime cities: The political economy of mortgage markets.* Hoboken, NJ: Wiley-Blackwell.

Advocates for Basic Legal Equality (ABLE). (2009). Interview with members of the legal staff of Advocates for *Basic Legal Equality.* Toledo, OH, February 5.

Aguilar, L. (2013a). State OKs bonds for arena project—Gov: Approval shows Detroit's woes won't halt new development. *The Detroit News*, June 25, p. B4.

Aguilar, L. (2013b). Red Wings arena deal faces critics—$650M proposal is subject of public hearing today amid city bankruptcy. *The Detroit News*, September 5, p. B4.

Aguilar, L. (2013c). Weighing in on $650M proposal: Red Wings arena effort wins support, scorn at hearing. *The Detroit News*, September 6, p. A11.

Aguilar, L. (2013d). Ilitches own half of arena's land—Family has spent $48M so far on property for proposed Wings' home, entertainment district. *The Detroit News*, November 26, p. A1.

Aguilar, L. (2013e). Land swap next step for arena—Detroit council may vote today on Wings deal. *The Detroit News*, December 20, p. A19.

Aguilar, L. (2014a). Ilitch project ignites land rush. *The Detroit News*, January 16, p. A1.

Aguilar, L. (2014b). Motor City may start to turn from freeways—Plans to connect downtown neighborhoods expected next year. *The Detroit News*, December 30, p. A1.

Aguilar, L., & Ferretti, C. (2014b). State OKs money to raze Joe—Cost expected to be $6M; Detroit officials must first approve final 5-year lease. *The Detroit News*, March 26, p. A3.

Aguilar, L., & Ferretti, C. (2014a). Wings arena project picks up steam—Council OKs land swap. *The Detroit News*, February 5, p. A1.

Alba, R., & Logan, J. (1993). The changing neighborhood contexts of the immigrant metropolis. *Social Forces, 79*(2), 587–621.

Alcaly, R. E., & Mermelstein, D. (Eds.) (1977). *The fiscal crisis of American cities.* New York, NY: Vintage.

Alesina, A., & Ardagna, S. (2010). Large changes in fiscal policy: Taxes versus spending. In J. R. Brown (Ed.), *Tax policy and the economy, Volume 24* (pp. 35–68). Chicago, IL: University of Chicago Press.

Algernon, A. (2010). Unemployment by metropolitan area and race. Washington, DC: Economic Policy Institute. Retrieved from http://www.epi.org/publication/ib278/.

Algernon, A. (2012). Hispanic metropolitan unemployment in 2011. Washington, DC: Economic Policy Institute. Retrieved from http://www.epi.org/publication/ib336-hispanic-metropolitanunemployment/.

Allen, R. (2013). Costly Sewer Project Lumbers On, *The Advocate.* Retrieved from http://www.sewageclaims.com/category/costly-sewer-project-lumbers-on/.

Anderson, M. W. (2012). Democratic dissolution: Radical experimentation in state takeovers of local governments. *Fordham Urban Law Journal, 39,* 577–623.

Anderson, R. (2007). Who pays for the water pipes, pumps, and treatment works? Local government expenditures for sewer and water 1991–2005, United States Conference of Mayors, Mayors Water Council.

Anderson, R. (2013, February 28). City to pay hundreds of millions in EPA fines and improvements, *Fox19Now.* Retrieved from http://www.msnewsnow.com/story/19768707/city-to-pay-hundreds-of-millions-in-epa-fines-and-improvements.

Angotti, T. (2008). *New York City for sale: Community planning confronts global real estate.* Cambridge: MIT Press.

ANHD. (2013). Guaranteed inclusionary zoning. Retrieved from http://www.anhd.org/wp-content/uploads/2013/08/ANHD-2013-Guaranteed-Inclusionary-Zoning_Online.pdf.

Ankeny, R. (2003, March 10). Lions still working out stadium financing. *Crain's Detroit Business.*

Ashton, P. (2009). An appetite for yield: The anatomy of the subprime crisis. *Environment and Planning A, 41*(6), 1420–1441.

Ashton, P., Doussard, M., & Weber, R. (2012). The financial engineering of infrastructure privatization. *Journal of the American Planning Association, 78*(3), 300–312.

Associated Press. (2012). EPA: Municipalities need $300 billion in sewer, water upgrades, *Syracuse.* Retrieved from: http://www.syracuse.com/news/index.ssf/2012/02/epa_us_needs_300_billion_in_se.html.

Atlanta Department of Watershed Management. (2015). *Water & sewer rates.* Retrieved from http://www.atlantawatershed.org/customer-service/rates/.

Atlanta Department of Watershed Management. (nd). *Water & sewer rates.* Retrieved from http://www.atlantawatershed.org/customer-service/rates/.

Auletta, K. (1979). *The streets were paved with gold.* New York: Monthly Review Press.

Avalos, G. (2014). Santa Clara County has highest median household income in nation, but wealth gap widens, *San Jose Mercury News.* Retrieved from http://www.mercurynews.com/business/ci_26312024/santa-clara-county-has-highest-median-household-income.

Avila, E. (2014). *The folklore of the freeway: Race and revolt in the modernist city.* Minneapolis, MN: University of Minnesota Press.

Baade, R. A., & Dye, R. F. (1988). Sports stadiums and area development: A critical review. *Economic Development Quarterly, 2*(3): 267–275.

Baade, R. (1996). Professional sports as catalysts for metropolitan economic development. *Journal of Urban Affairs, 18*(1), 1–17.

Badger, E. (2016). Why Trump's use of the words "urban renewal" is scary for cities. *New York Times*, December 7 [online]. Retrieved from: http://www.nytimes.com/2016/12/07/upshot/why-trumps-use-of-the-words-urban-renewal-is-scary-for-cities.html.

Baily, M. N., Litan, R. E., & Johnson, M. S. (2011). *The origins of the financial crisis.* Washington, DC: Brookings Initiatives on Public Policy.

Baker, D. (2010). *The myth of expansionary fiscal austerity.* Washington, DC: Center for Economic and Policy Research.

Bakker, K. (2010). The limits of "neoliberal natures": Debating green neoliberalism. *Progress in Human Geography, 34*(6), 715–735.

Baldwin, J. (1963). Interview with Kenneth Clark. Retrieved from: https://www.youtube.com/watch?v=T8Abhj17kYU.

Banfield, E. (1974). *The unheavenly city revisited.* Boston, MA: Little, Brown.

Barker, J. (2015a). West Lake Landfill may be more contaminated than previously thought, company says. *St. Louis Post-Dispatch.* Retrieved from http://www.stltoday.com/business/local/west-lake-landfill-may-be-more-contaminated-than-previously-thought/article_9bbbe6c5-7fa2-5272-9d44-8a81a3eb61a8.html.

Barker, J. (2015b). Calls mount for corps of engineers to take over West Lake. *St. Louis Post-Dispatch.* Retrieved from http://www.stltoday.com/business/local/calls-mount-for-corps-of-engineers-to-take-over-west/article_909c65d9-5ca8-5dfc-9c31-0b505776b888.html.

Barkholz, D. (1997, November 24). Ford says Lions can build stadium at discount price. *Crain's Detroit Business*, 38.

Barnes, D. (2014, June 2). One-cent sales tax change could hurt city projects, *The Clarion-Ledger.*

Barrow, J. (2014). Affordable housing that's very costly. *The New York Times.* Retrieved from http://nyti.ms/1oIrhlj.

Batini, N., Callegari, G., & Melina, G. (2012). Successful austerity in the United States, Europe and Japan. *IMF Working Papers, 12*/190. Washington, DC: International Monetary Fund.

Baudrillard, J. (1988). *America.* Translated by Chris Turner. New York, NY: Verso.

Beatty, C., & Fothergill, S. (2014). The local and regional impact of the UK's welfare reforms. *Cambridge Journal of Regions, Economy and Society, 7*(1), 63–79.

Bélanger, A. (2000). Sports venues and the spectacularization of urban spaces in North America: The case of the Molson Centre in Montreal. *International Review for the Sociology of Sport, 35*(3), 378–397.

Bélanger, A. (2002). Urban space and collective memory: Analyzing the various dimensions of the production of memory. *Canadian Journal of Urban Research, 11*(1), 69–92.

Bélanger, A. (2009). The urban sports spectacle: Towards a critical political economy of sports. In B. Carrington & I. McDonald (Eds.), *Marxism, Cultural Studies, and Sport* (pp. 51–67). London: Routledge.

Bellant, R., Cabil, L., Coffey, S., Damaschke, M., Howell, S., Levy, K., & Orduno, S. (2014). *Timeline: The story of Detroit's water.* Retrieved from http://www.d-rem.org/timeline-the-story-of-detroits-water/.

Benjamin, W. (1969). Paris: Capital of the nineteenth century. *Perspecta,* 165–172.

Bivens, J. (2015). Government layoffs are a major cause of persistent unemployment, *The New York Times.* Retrieved from http://www.nytimes.com/roomfordebate/2013/02/06/are-government-layoffs-the-problem/government-layoffs-are-a-major-cause-of-persistent-unemployment.

Blake, A. (2014, September 25). Americans think we're still in a recession. They're wrong. But still. . . . *The Washington Post.*

Blyth, M. (2013). *Austerity: The history of a dangerous idea.* New York, NY: Oxford University Press.

Blyth, M. (2013b). The austerity delusion: Why a bad idea won over the West. *Foreign Affairs, 92*(3), 41–50.

Bomey, N. (2016). *Detroit resurrected: To bankruptcy and back.* New York, NY: W. W. Norton.

Bomey, N., & Gallagher, J. (2013). How Detroit went broke: The answers may surprise you—and don't blame Coleman Young. *Detroit Free Press.* Retrieved from http://archive.freep.com/interactive/article/20130915/

NEWS01/130801004/Detroit-Bankruptcy-history-1950-debt-pension-revenue.

The Bond Buyer. (n.d.). *Jefferson County Timeline*. Retrieved from http://cdn. bondbuyer.com/media/pdfs/BB111011JEFFCO_TIMELINE.pdf.

Borelli, J. (2016, November 14). Trump, GOP must develop an urban agenda to stay on offense. *The Hill*. Retrieved from http://thehill.com/blogs/pundits-blog/the-administration/305862-trump-gop-must-develop-an-urban-agenda-to-stay-on.

Bourne, L. (1993). The demise of gentrification? A commentary and prospective view. *Urban Geography, 14*(1), 95–107.

Bourne, R. (2013, January 13). Lady Thatcher's relationship with Frederich Hayek and Milton Friedman, *Pieria.com*. Retrived from http://www.pieria. co.uk/articles/lady_thatchers_relationship_with_friedrich_hayek_and_milton_friedman.

Boyer, R. (2012). The four fallacies of contemporary austerity policies: The lost Keynesian legacy. *Cambridge Journal of Economics, 36*(1), 283–312.

Boyes, R. (2009). *Meltdown Iceland: Lessons on the world financial crisis from a small bankrupt island*. New York, NY: Bloomsbury.

Boyle, P., & Haggerty, K. D. (2009). Spectacular security: Mega-events and the security complex. *International Political Sociology, 3*(3), 257–274.

Bradford, C. (2002). *Risk or race? Racial disparities and the subprime refinance market*. Washington, DC: Center for Community Change.

Bradley, B. (2015). *Has Detroit found an answer to the publicly financed stadium scam?* Retrieved from http://deadspin.com/has-detroit-found-an-answer-to-the-publicly-financed-st-1684944648.

Bradley, B. (2014). *Red Wings stadium upset! Why taxpayers are losing—again—in Detroit*. Retrieved from http://nextcity.org/features/view/red-wings-stadium-upset-subsidies-arena-taxpayers.

Braun, M. (2013, November 23). Jefferson County's bankruptcy leaves legacy of higher fees. *Bloomberg Businessweek*.

Brecher, C., & Horton, R. D. (1985). Retrenchment and recovery: American cities and the New York experience. *Public Administration Review, 45*(2), 267–274.

Brenner, N., & Theodore, N. (2002). Cities and the geographies of "actually existing neoliberalism." *Antipode, 34*(3), 349–379.

Brenner, N., Peck, J., & Theodore, N. (2010). Variegated neoliberalization: Geographies, modalities, pathways. *Global Networks, 10*(2), 188–222.

Brown, W. (2015). *Undoing the Demos: Neoliberalism's stealth revolution*. Cambridge, MA: Zone Books.

Bull, A., & Bohan, C. (2012). Obama pins recovery hopes on Europe's leaders. *Reuters*. Retrieved from http://www.reuters.com/article/2012/06/09/us-usa-whitehouse-obama-idUSBRE8570PV20120609.

Burchell, R. W., & Listokin, D. (1981). Issues in city finance: Overview and summary. In R. W. Burchell & D. Listokin (Eds.), *Cities under stress: The fiscal crises of urban America* (xi–li). Piscataway, NJ: Center for Urban Policy Research, Rutgers, the State University of New Jersey.

Business Week. (2012). Moody's targets California cities for downgrades. *MNLABOR*. Retrieved from https://mnlabor.wordpress.com/2012/10/10/moodys-targets-calif-cities-for-downgrades-businessweek/.

Byrne, P. (2005). Strategic interaction and the adoption of tax increment financing. *Regional Science and Urban Economics, 35*(3), 279–303.

Calcagno, A. (2012). Can austerity work? *Review of Keynesian Economics, 1*(1), 24–36.

California State Auditor. (2012). *City of San Jose: Some retirement cost projections were unsupported although rising retirement costs have led to reduced city services (No. 2012-106)*. Sacramento, CA: Bureau of State Audits.

Callinicos, A. (2012). Contradictions of austerity. *Cambridge Journal of Economics, 36*(1), 65–77.

Campbell, S. (2015). Americans live with the austerity you Europeans are so concerned about. *The Guardian*. Retrieved from http://www.theguardian.com/commentisfree/2015/jun/06/american-austerity-europeans-concerns-safety-net.

Carlson, J. (2012). *Public pensions under stress (forefront)*. Cleveland, OH: Federal Reserve Bank of Cleveland.

Carson, B. S. (2015, July 23). Experimenting with failed socialism again. *Washington Times*. Retrieved from http://www.washingtontimes.com/news/2015/jul/23/ben-carson-obamas-housing-rules-try-to-accomplish-/.

Cassidy, J. (2014, February 24). Obama's unpopular stimulus won't be the last. *New Yorker*. Retrieved from http://www.newyorker.com/news/john-cassidy/obamas-unpopular-stimulus-wont-be-the-last.

Cecchetti, S., & Kharroubi, E. (2015). Why does financial sector growth crowd out real economic growth? *BIS Working Papers 490*. Basel: Bank for International Settlements.

Center for Responsible Lending. (2009). *Soaring spillover: Accelerating foreclosures to cost neighbors $502 billion in 2009 alone*. Durham, NC: CRL.

Center for the Human Rights of Children. (2015). *UN special rapporteurs visit Detroit regarding water shutoffs*. Retrieved from http://blogs.luc.edu/chrc/2014/10/30/un-special-rapporteurs-visit-detroit-regarding-water-shut-offs/.

Centre for Cities. (2014). *Cities outlook.* Retrieved from http://www.centreforcities. org/wp-content/uploads/2014/01/14-01-27-Cities-Outlook-2014.pdf.

Chappatta, B. (2012). Muni bankruptcies foreshadow "disturbing" trend, Schotz Says. *BusinessWeek.* Retrieved from http://www.businessweek.com/ news/2012-10-19/muni-bankruptcies-foreshadow-disturbing-trend-schotz-says.

Chiang, J. (2011). *California Controller's Office annual report FY 2009–10.* Sacramento, CA: California State Controller.

Chinloy, P., & Macdonald, N. (2005). Subprime lenders and mortgage market completion. *Journal of Real Estate Finance and Economics, 30*(1), 153–165.

Christopherson, S., Martin, R., & Pollard, J. (2013). Financialisation roots and repercussions. *Cambridge Journal of Regions, Economy and Society, 6*(3), 351–357.

Church, S., & Raphael, S. (2014, September 29). Detroit bankruptcy judge refuses to halt water shutoffs. *Bloomberg Businessweek.*

Citizens Research Council of Michigan. (1996). *CRC memorandum No. 1040.* Retrieved from http://crcmich.org/PUBLICAT/1990s/1996/memo1040.pdf.

City of Atlanta. (n.d.). The Municipal Option Sales Tax (MOST): What it means to Atlanta. Retrieved from *http://www.atlantaga.gov/index.aspx?page=755.*

City of New York. (n.d.). Housing New York: A five-borough, ten-year plan. *City of New York: Housing and Economic Development.* Retrieved from http://www.nyc.gov/html/housing/assets/downloads/pdf/housing_plan.pdf.

City of New York. (2015). *Housing New York: A five-borough ten-year plan.* New York, NY: City of New York.

Clark, T., & Ferguson, L. (1983). *City money: Political processes fiscal strain and retrenchment.* New York, NY: Columbia University Press.

Clarke, J., & Newman, J. (2012). The alchemy of austerity. *Critical Social Policy, 32*(3), 299–231.

Clavel, P., Forrester, J., & Goldsmith, W. W. (Eds.). (1980). *Urban and regional planning in an age of austerity.* New York, NY: Pergamon Press.

Cleveland, T. (2013, September 17). Lumumba, chamber break sales-tax impasse. *Jackson Free Press.*

Coalition for the Homeless. (2015a.). *New York City homeless municipal shelter population, 1983–present.* Retrieved from http://www.coalitionforthehome-less.org/wpcontent/uploads/2014/04/NYCHomelessShelterPopulation-Worksheet-1983-Present.pdf.

Coalition for the Homeless. (2015b). *State of the homeless.* Retrieved from http://www.coalitionforthehomeless.org/wp-content/uploads/2015/03/SOTH2015.pdf.

Coates, D., & Humphreys, B. R. (2000). The stadium gambit and local economic development. *Regulation, 23*(2), 15–20.

Cohen, N. (2013). U.S. states need $980bn to fill pension gap, says Moody's. *Financial Times.* Retrieved from http://www.ft.com/intl/cms/s/0/b763a6f8-de91-11e2-b990-00144feab7de.html#axzz2XWOdPJAy.

Congressional Budget Office. (2014). *Options for reducing the deficit: 2015 to 2024.* Retrieved from https://www.cbo.gov/budget-options/2014.

Cooper, M. (2002). City gets budgeting tips, down to turning off lights. *The New York Times.* Retrieved from http://www.nytimes.com/2002/12/05/nyregion/city-gets-budgeting-tips-down-to-turning-off-lights.html.

Cooper, M. (2012). In San Jose, budget woes take a toll. *The New York Times.* Retrieved from http://www.nytimes.com/2012/02/19/us/in-san-jose-budget-woes-take-a-toll.html.

Copeland, C. (2002). *Clean Water Act: A summary of the law.* Washington, DC: Congressional Research Service.

Corsetti, G. (2012). Has austerity gone too far?, *Voxeu.* Retrieved from http://www.voxeu.org/article/has-austerity-gone-too-far-new-vox-debate.

Covert, B. (2016). Trump's very strange ideas for urban renewal. Retrieved from https://thinkprogress.org/trump-urban-renewal-ee58654aaa75#.dud3isiy1.

Crotty, J. (2012). The great austerity war: What caused the U.S. deficit crisis and who should pay to fix it? *Cambridge Journal of Economics, 36*(1), 79–104.

Crouch, C. (2013). *The strange non-death of neo-liberalism.* Oxford: Polity Press.

Crump, J., Newman, K., Belsky, E. S., Ashton, P., Kaplan, D. H., Hammel, D. J., & Wyly, E. (2008). Cities destroyed (again) for cash: Forum on the U.S. foreclosure crisis. *Urban Geography, 29*(8), 745–784.

Cwiek, S. (2014a, March 19). Lease proposal: Joe Louis Arena to be darkened, demolished after Red Wings leave. *Michigan Public Radio.*

Cwiek, S. (2014b, December 8). House bill would ban local minimum wage laws, community benefits agreements. *Michigan Public Radio.*

Davidson, J. (2015). "Mandatory inclusionary zoning": The dullest, most important phrase in New York. *New York.* Retrieved from http://nymag.com/daily/intelligencer/2015/08/dullest-most-important-phrase-in-new-york.html.

Davidson, M., & Iveson, K. (2014). Recovering the politics of the city: From the "post-political city" to a "method of equality" for critical urban geography. *Progress in Human Geography, 39*(5), 543–559.

Davidson, M., & Kutz, W. (2015). Grassroots austerity: municipal bankruptcy from below in Vallejo, California. *Environment and Planning A, 47*(7), 1440–1459.

Davidson, M., & Ward, K. (2014). "Picking up the pieces": Austerity urbanism, California, and fiscal crisis. *Cambridge Journal of Regions, Economy and Society, 7*(1), 81–97.

De Costa, P. (2013). FHA mortgage loans no longer best option after rule change. *Newsday*. Retrieved from http://www.newsday.com/classifieds/real-estate/fha-mortgage-loans-no-longer-best-option-after-rule-change-1.6481166.

Deane, D. D., & South, S. J. (1993). Race and residential mobility: Individual determinants and structural constraints. *Social Forces, 72*(1), 147–167.

Debord, G. (1970). *Society of the spectacle*. New York, NY: Black & Red.

DeFilippis, J. (Ed.). (2016). *Urban policy in the time of Obama*. Minneapolis, MN: University of Minnesota Press.

DeGood, K. (2016). How Donald Trump's infrastructure plan fails America. *Centre for American Progress*. Retrieved from https://www.americanprogress.org/issues/economy/reports/2016/12/01/293948/how-donald-trumps-infrastructure-plan-fails-america/.

della Porta, D. (2015). *Social movements in times of austerity*. Cambridge, UK: Polity.

Dembosky, A., & Bullock, N. (2012). City pensions thrust to fore in U.S. *Financial Times*. Retrieved from http://www.ft.com/cms/s/0/df97b2fc-ad66-11e1-97f3-00144feabdc0.html#axzz1wqtlszWP.

Democracy Now. (2013). Civil rights veteran Chokwe Lumumba elected mayor of Jackson, Miss., once a center of racial abuses. *Democracy Now*. Retrieved from http://www.democracynow.org/2013/6/6/civil_rights_veteran_chokwe_lumumba_elected.

Department of Planning, City of New York. (2015a). *Population: Historical population information. Total and foreign-born population New York City, 1790–2000*. Retrieved from http://www.nyc.gov/html/dcp/html/census/1790_2000_hist_data.shtml.

Department of Planning, City of New York. (2015b). *Population 2010 demographic tables*. Retrieved from http://www.nyc.gov/html/dcp/html/census/demo_tables_2010.shtml.

Detroit Water Project. (2015). *Detroit water project*. Retrieved from www.detroitwaterproject.org.

Detroit Works Project. (2012). *Detroit future city: Detroit strategic framework plan*. Detroit, MI: Detroit Works Project.

Devitt, C. (2014a, February 5). Detroit council advances bond-funded downtown hockey venue. *The Bond Buyer*.

Devitt, C. (2013, August 5). Detroit's current pension assumptions fall within standards: Morningstar. *The Bond Buyer*. Retrieved from http://www. bondbuyer.com/issues/122_149/detroits-current-pension-assumptions-fall-within-standards-morningstar-1054319-1.html.

Dinham, H. (2007). Prepared testimony of Harry Dinham on "Preserving the American dream: Predatory lending practices and home foreclosures." *Committee on Banking, Housing, and Urban Affairs, U.S. Senate*. Retrieved from http://www.gpo.gov/fdsys/pkg/CHRG-110shrg50309/html/CHRG-110shrg50309.html.

Dolan, M., Temper, S., & Gallagher, J. (2015). Detroit rising: Life after bankruptcy. *Detroit Free Press*. Retrieved from http://on/freep.com/1NBalMV.

Donald, B., Glasmeier, A., Gray, M., & Lobao, L. (2014). Austerity in the city: economic crisis and urban service decline. *Cambridge Journal of Regions, Economy and Society, 7*(1), 3–15.

Dreier, P. (2011, February 4). Reagan's real legacy. *The Nation*. Retrieved from https://www.thenation.com/article/reagans-real-legacy/.

Duncan, G. J., & Zuberi, A. (2006). Mobility lessons from Gautreux and moving to opportunity. *Northwestern Journal of Law and Social Policy, 1*(1), 110–126.

Dunlap, D. (1987). Mixed reviews for Upper East Side rezoning. *The New York Times*. Retrieved from http://www.nytimes.com/1987/12/10/nyregion/mixed-reviews-for-upper-east-side-rezoning.html?smid=pl-share.

Dunn, C. (2013). Rhode Island Housing lays off 30, citing aid cutbacks and foreclosure fallout. *Providence Journal*. Retrieved from http://www.providencejournal.com/article/20130826/NEWS/308269982.

Economic Progress Institute. (2014). Rhode Island's jobs deficit and the changing economy: Jobs Deficit fact sheet 2012/2013. Retrieved from http://www.economicprogressri.org/FactsStats/JobsDeficit1213/tabid/305/Default.aspx.

Edsall, T. B. (2012). *The age of austerity: How scarcity will remake American politics*. New York, NY: Doubleday.

Egan, P. (2015). Flint water mystery: How was the decision made? *Detroit Free Press*. Retrieved from http://on.freep.com/1HfnEBN.

Egan, P. (2016a). Flint mayor: Cost of lead fix could hit $1.5 billion. *Detroit Free Press*. Retrieved from http://on.freep.com/1RbRjPE.

Egan, P. (2016b). Snyder declares emergency as feds probe Flint water. *Detroit Free Press*. Retrieved from http://on.freep.com/1R9rwal.

Eide, S. (2013). *Defeating fiscal distress. Civic Report No. 78*. New York, NY: Center for State and Local Leadership, Manhattan Institute.

Eide, S. (2016). Caesarism for cities. *City Journal, 26*(1), 70–75.

Emergency Manager, City of Atlantic City. (2015). *60 day report of the emergency manager.* Trenton, NJ: Department of Community Affairs, State of New Jersey.

Emergency Manager, City of Atlantic City. (2016). *Update report of the emergency manager.* Trenton, NJ: Department of Community Affairs, State of New Jersey.

Emshwiller, J. (2014, July 25). U.S. News: Worries over St. Louis landfill are heating up. *The Wall Street Journal.*

Engel, K. C., & McCoy, P. A. (2011). *The subprime virus.* New York, NY: Oxford University Press.

England, K., & and Ward, K. (Eds.). (2007). *Neoliberalization: Networks, peoples, states.* Oxford: Wiley Blackwell.

Ersing, R. L., Sutphin, R. D., & Loeffler, D. N. (2009). Exploring the impact and implications of residential mobility: From the neighborhood to the school. *Advances in Social Work, 10*(1), 1–18.

Ewen, L. A. (2015) [1978]. *Corporate power and urban crisis in Detroit.* Princeton, NJ: Princeton University Press.

Executive Office of the President (EOP). (2008). *Economic report of the president.* Retrieved from www.gpoaccess.gov/eop/2008/2008_erp.pdf.

Executive Office of the President (EOP). (2016). *Investing in a safer, stronger Baltimore.* Washington, DC: Executive Office of the President.

Faber, J. W. (2013). Racial dynamics of subprime mortgage lending at the peak. *Housing Policy Debate, 23*(2), 328–349.

Farmer, L. (2013). Detroit's pension is actually well-funded, So what's all the fuss? *Governing.* Retrieved from http://www.governing.com/topics/finance/gov-detroits-pension-is-actually-well-funded——so-whats-all-the-fuss.html.

Fausset, F., Blinder, A., & Eligon, J. (2016, August 25). Blacks beg to differ with Trump's depiction. *New York Times,* p. A12.

Federal Reserve (2005). *Frequently asked questions about the new HMDA data.* Retrieved from http://www.federalreserve.gov/boarddocs/press/bcreg/2005/20050331/attachment.pdf.

Felton, R. (2014a, May 6). How Mike Ilitch scored a new Red Wings arena: Hockeytown's Caesar gets a sweet deal. But what's in it for Detroit? *Detroit Metro Times.*

Felton, R. (2014b, September 24). Financing the new Detroit Red Wings arena could include an interest rate swap. *Detroit Metro Times.*

Felton, R. (2014c, September 10). WTF is TIF? *Detroit Metro Times.*

Felton, R. (2016, January 23). How Flint traded safe drinking water cost-cutting plan that didn't work. *The Guardian.* Retrieved from http://www.theguardian.com/us-news/2016/jan/23/flint-water-crisis-cost-cutting-switch-water-supply.

Ferretti, C. (2014a, March 24). Arena deal limits city to $5.2M in cable fees—Issue settled for a fraction of estimates in Wings lease plan. *The Detroit News.*

Ferretti, C. (2014b, November 26). Council delays new arena rezoning—Questions remain about traffic, parking, and preservation. *The Detroit News.*

Fishbein, A., & Ren, E. (2011). The Home Mortgage Disclosure Act at thirty-five: Past history, current issues. In N. Retsinas and E. Belsky (Eds.), *Moving forward: the future of consumer credit and mortgage finance* (150–188). Washington, DC: Brookings Institution Press.

Fitzgerald, J. (2011). Foley turns to private security firm in cost-cutting move, *Innpost.* Retrieved from https://www.minnpost.com/politics-policy/2011/11/foley-turns-private-security-firm-cost-cutting-move.

Flint, A. (2016, November 9). How to start thinking about what a Trump presidency means for cities. *Citylab.* Retrieved from http://www.citylab.com/politics/2016/11/what-a-trump-presidency-means-for-cities/507125/.

Flyvbjerg, B., & Stewart, A. (2012). *Olympic proportions: Cost and cost overrun at the Olympics 1960–2012.* Saïd Business School Working Papers, Oxford: University of Oxford. Retrieved from http://ssrn.com/abstract=2238053.

Fong, A. M. P. (2011). Investigation into City of San Jose fiscal emergency declaration. *Assembly California Legislature.* Retrieved from http://www.mef101.org/Resources/11-0520%20-%20CA%20AG%20Investigation%20into%20City%20of%20SJ%20Fiscal%20Emergency%20Declaration.pdf.

Fonger, R. (2015a). Flint water problems: Switch aimed to save $5 million—but at what cost? *MLive.com.* Retrieved from http://www.mlive.com/news/flint/index.ssf.

Fonger, R. (2015b). Class action lawsuit claims Snyder, Flint put water cost above safety, *MLive.com.* Retrieved from http://www.mlive.com/news/flint/index.ssf/2015/11/class_action_lawsuit_claims_sn.html.

Ford, Z. (2015). *Extreme bill would override all local employment laws, including LGBT protections.* Retrieved from http://thinkprogress.org/lgbt/2015/05/13/3658201/michigan-death-star-employment-bill/.

Frantz, J. (2014, April 10). Bill aims to get Pa.'s financially distressed municipalities through Act 47, or else. *The Patriot-News.*

Friedhoff, A., & Kulkami, S. (2013). Metro monitor—June 2013. Washington, DC: Brookings Institution. Retrieved from http://www.brookings.edu/newsletters/metroupdate/2013/0710.

Fritze, J. (2016, December 14). Federal task force on Baltimore winds down as Trump's urban policy remains uncertain. *Baltimore Sun*. Retrieved from http://www.baltimoresun.com/news/maryland/baltimore-city/bs-md-white-house-report-baltimore-20161214-story.html.Fujita, K. (2013). Introduction: Cities and crisis: New critical urban theory. In K. Fujita (Ed.) *Cities and crisis: New critical urban theory* (1–50). London: Sage.

Furman Center (2011). *State of New York City's subsidized housing: 2011*. Retrieved from http://furmancenter.org/research/publications/c/state-of-new-york-citys-subsidized-housing.

Furman Center. (2014). *Understanding affordable housing*. Retrieved from http://furmancenter.org/institute/directory/understanding.

Furman Center. (2015a). *Creating affordable housing out of thin air: The economics of mandatory inclusionary zoning in New York City*. Retrieved from http://furmancenter.org/files/NYUFurmanCenter_CreatingAffHousing_March2015.pdf.

Furman Center. Mandatory Zoning. (n.d.). *Should the next mayor adopt a mandatory inclusionary zoning program that requires developers to build or preserve affordable housing whenever they build market-rate housing?* Retrieved from http://furmancenter.org/files/publications/NYChousing_Mandatory-InclusionaryZoning.pdf.

Galbraith, J. K. (2008). *The collapse of monetarism and the irrelevance of the new monetary consensus, 25th Annual Milton Friedman Distinguished Lecture at Marietta College, Marietta, Ohio*. Retrieved from http://utip.gov.utexas.edu/papers/CollapseofMonetarismdelivered.pdf.

Gallagher, J., & Egan, P. (2012, December 5). Ilitch proposes new entertainment district. *The Pioneer*.

George Mason University's State and Local Government Leadership Center. (GMUSLGLC). (2012), Local government fiscal crises: The crisis facing local governments and why it matters. Retrieved from http://s3.amazonaws.com/chssweb/documents/12810/original/GMU_Fiscal_Lit_Review.pdf?1379616883.

Getter, D. E., Jickling, M., Labonte, M., & Murphy, E. V. (2007). Financial crisis? The liquidity crunch of August 2007. *Report for Congress*. Washington, DC: Congressional Research Service. Retrieved from http://assets.opencrs.com/rpts/RL34182_20070921.pdf.

Giles, C., Fleming, S., & Spiegel, P. (2015). Christine Lagarde dashes Greek hopes on loan respite. *Financial Times*. Retrieved from http://www.ft.com/cms/s/0/7032744e-e452-11e4-a4de-00144feab7de.html#axzz3eViG3m8m.

Gilman-Opalsky, R. (2011). Reconsidering situationist praxis. In R. Gilman-Opalsky (Ed.), *Spectacular capitalism: Guy Debord and the practice of radical philosophy* (63–88). London: Minor Compositions.

Glaeser, E. (2011). *Triumph of the city*. New York, NY: Penguin Press.

Glaeser, E. (2013, July 23). Bad policies bear bitter fruit. *Boston Globe*, p. A11.

Goetz, E. (2011). Where have all the towers gone? The dismantling of public housing in U.S. cities. *Journal of Urban Affairs, 33*(3), 267–287.

Gonzalez, S., & Oosterlynck, S. (2014). Crisis and resilience in a finance-led city: Effects of the global financial crisis in Leeds. *Urban Studies, 51*(15), 3164–3179.

Gopnik, A. (2012, May 7). Vive la France. *The New Yorker*, 17–18.

Gotham, K. F. (2002). Marketing Mardi Gras: Commodification, spectacle, and the political economy of tourism in New Orleans. *Urban Studies, 39*(10), 1735–1756.

Gotham, K. F. (2005). Theorizing urban spectacles. *City, 9*(2), 225–246.

Gotham, K. F. (2009). Creating liquidity out of spatial fixity: The secondary circuit of capital and the subprime mortgage crisis. *International Journal of Urban and Regional Research, 33*(2), 355–371.

Gotham, K. F., & Krier, D. A. (2008). From the culture industry to the society of the spectacle: Critical theory and the situationist international. In H. Dahms (Ed.), *Current perspectives in social theory Vol. 25: No social science without critical theory* (155–192). United Kingdom: JAI Press.

Gottdiener, M. (1986a). Introduction. In M. Gottdiener (Ed.), *Cities in stress. Urban Affairs Annual Reviews, Volume 30* (7–15). Beverly Hills, CA: Sage.

Gottdiener, M. (1986b). Retrospect and prospect in urban crisis theory. In M. Gottdiener (Ed.), *Cities in stress. Urban Affairs Annual Reviews, Volume 30* (277–291). Beverly Hills, CA: Sage.

Gottdiener, M. (1987). *The decline of urban politics: Political theory and the crisis of the local state*. Newbury Park, CA: Sage.

Gottesdiener, L. (2014, October 20). UN officials "shocked" by Detroit's mass water shutoffs. *Aljazeera America.*

Gottesdiener, L. (2015). Michigan is in the midst of a "massive experiment in unraveling U.S. democracy." *Inthesetimes.com.* Retrieved from http://inthesetimes.com/article/18032/a-magical-mystery-tour-of-american-austerity-politics.

Government Accounting Standards Board. (GASB). (2012). *Statement no. 68 accounting and financial reporting for pensions—an amendment of GASB statement No. 27*. Retrieved from http://www.gasb.org/jsp/GASB/Document_C/GASBDocumentPage?cid=1176160220621.

Graff, G. M. (2016, December 12). The urban inheritance Trump stands to squander. *Next City*. Retrieved from https://nextcity.org/features/view/obama-urban-policy-donald-trump-inherits.

Greenblatt, A. (2014). Rural areas lose people but not power. *Governing*. Retrieved from http://www.governing.com/topics/politics/gov-rural-areas-lose-people-not-power.html.

Greenhut, S. (2012). They can't be serious. *City Journal*. Retrieved from http://www.city-journal.org/2012/cjc0905sg.html/.

Greenspan, A. (2013). *The map and the territory: Risk, human nature, and the future of forecasting*. New York, NY: Penguin.

Griffith, J. (2012). *The Federal Housing Administration saved the housing market*. Washington, DC: Center for American Progress. Retrieved from https://cdn.americanprogress.org/wp-content/uploads/2012/10/Griffith_FHA.pdf.

Groothuis, P. A., Johnson, B. K., & Whitehead, J. C. (2004). Public funding of professional sports stadiums: Public choice or civic pride? *Eastern Economic Journal, 30*(4), 515–526.

Guajardo, J., Leigh, D., & Pescatori, A. (2014) Expansionary austerity? International evidence. *Journal of the European Economic Association, 12*(4), 949–968.

Guarjardo J., Leigh, D., & Pescatori, A. (2014). Expansionary austerity? International evidence—fiscal consolidation and the overstated expansionary impact. *IMF Working Papers 11/158*. Washington, DC: International Monetary Fund.

Guillen, J., & Reindle, J. C. (2014, March 2). Ilitches to get all revenues from new publicly financed Red Wings arena. *Detroit Free Press*.

Gurwitt, R. (2004). How to win friends and repair a city. *Governing*.

Hackworth, J. (2006). *The neoliberal city: Governance, ideology, and development in American urbanism*. Ithaca, NY: Cornell University Press.

Hackworth, J. (2015). Right-sizing as spatial austerity in the American Rust Belt. *Environment and Planning, A, 47*(4), 766–782.

Hackworth J., & Nowakowski, K. (2015). Using market-based policies to address market collapse in the American Rust Belt: the case of land abandonment in Toledo, Ohio. *Urban Geography, 36*(4), 528–549.

Hall, S., & Jonas, A. G. J. (2014). Urban fiscal austerity, infrastructure provision, and the struggle for regional transit in "Motor City." *Cambridge Journal of Regions, Economy and Society, 7*(1), 189–206.

Hammel, D. J., & Shetty, S. (2013). Complexity and change in the foreclosure process in Toledo, Ohio. *Housing Policy Debate, 23*(1), 35–58.

Harrison, B., Markusen, A., Massey, D., Walker, R., Gertler, M., Glasmeier, A., Landau, M., Luger, M., O'Malley, R., Mayer, N., Ong, P., Saxenian, A., Schoenberger, E., Shapira, P., Storper, M., Widess, E., Weiss, M., & Wilmoth, D. (1979). *President Carter's national urban policy: A critical analysis*. Berkeley, CA: National Urban Policy Collective.

Harvey, D. (1989a). From managerialism to entrepreneurialism: The transformation in urban governance in late capitalism. *Geografiska Annaler, 7B*(1), 3–17.

Harvey, D. (1989b). *The condition of postmodernity: Enquiry into the origins of cultural change*. Cambridge: Blackwell.

Harvey, D. (2005). *A brief history of neoliberalism*. Oxford: Oxford University Press.

Hawkins, E. (2013, December 12). The election victory of Chokwe Lumumba—part one of two. *Socialist Alternative*.

Hayek, F. (1945). The use of knowledge in society. *American Economic Review, XXXV*(4), 519–530.

Healey, J. (2009, August 18). Tax bills put pressure on struggling homeowners. *The New York Times*. Retrieved from http://www.nytimes.com/2009/08/18/business/18taxes.html?pagewanted=all&_r=0.

Hempel, G. H. (1971). *The postwar quality of state and local debt*. New York, NY: Columbia University Press.

Hobsbawm, E. (2008). Is the intellectual opinion of capitalism changing? Today Program, BBC Radio 4, 20 October. Retrieved from www.news.bbc.co.uk/today/hi/today/newsid_7677000/7677683.stm.

Holeywell, R. (2012). New clean water regulations leave localities skeptical. *Governing*.

Holland, D., & Portes, J. (2013). *Self-defeating austerity*. Retrieved from http://niesr.ac.uk/sites/default/files/publications/ofcefiscal2013.pdf.

Holleman, J. (2013, August 8). Huntleigh ranks as richest U.S. community, *St. Louis Post-Dispatch*.

Holloway, S. R. (1998). Exploring the neighborhood contingency of race discrimination in mortgage lending in Columbus, Ohio. *Annals of the Association of American Geographers, 88*(2), 252–276.

Holloway, S. R., & Wyly, E. K. (2001). "The Color of Money" expanded: Geographically contingent mortgage lending in Atlanta. *Journal of Housing Research, 12*(1), 55–90.

Housing Works Rhode Island. (2011). *Foreclosures in Rhode Island Winter 2011*. Barrington, RI: Roger Williams University.

Housing Works Rhode Island. (2008). *Foreclosures in Rhode Island Winter 2008*. Barrington, RI: Roger Williams University.

Housing Works Rhode Island. (2012). *2012 housing fact book.* Barrington, RI: Roger Williams University.

Housing Works Rhode Island. (2014). *2014 housing fact book.* Barrington, RI: Roger Williams University.

Hsieh, S. (2013, May 10). St. Louis is Burning, *Rolling Stone.*

Hudson, M. (2012). The road to debt deflation, Debt peonage, and neofeudalism. *Levy Economics Institute of Bard College Working Paper* 708. New York, NY: Bard College.

Hula, R., & Cynthia, J. E. (Eds.). (2000). *Nonprofits in urban America.* Westport, CT: Quorum Books.

Hunter, R. J., & Sukenik, W. H. (2007). Atlanta's consent decrees drive a substantial commitment to trenchless sewer rehabilitation. In M. Najafi & L. Osborn (Eds.), *Pipelines 2007: Advances and experiences with trenchless pipeline projects.* Boston, MA: American Society of Civil Engineers.

Husock, H. (2016, December 5). Laying a new foundation at HUD. *City Journal Online.* Retrieved from http://city-journal.org/html/laying-new-foundation-hud-14884.html.

Ignazzio, M., & Provance, J. (2015). State cuts, city transfers, funding affect Toledo roads, schools. *Toledo Blade.* Retrieved from http://www.toledoblade.com/Economy/2015/05/17/City-transfers-funding-affect-roads-schools.html.

Immergluck, D. (2004). *Credit to the community.* Armonk, NY: M. E. Sharpe.

Immergluck, D. (2008). From the subprime to the exotic: Excessive mortgage market risk and foreclosures. *Journal of the American Planning Association, 74*(1), 1–18.

Immergluck, D. (2009). *Foreclosed: High-risk lending, deregulation, and the undermining of America's mortgage market.* Ithaca, NY: Cornell University Press.

Immergluck, D., & Smith, G. (2003). *Risky business: An econometric analysis of the relationship between subprime lending and foreclosures.* Chicago, IL: Woodstock Institute. Retrieved from http://Woodstock.org/documents/risky/business.pdf.

Immergluck, D., & Smith, G. (2006). The external costs of foreclosure: The impact of single-family mortgage foreclosures on property values. *Housing Policy Debate, 17*(1), 57–80.

Independent Budget Office (IBO). (2013). *What program is the largest source of income support grants for low-income New York City residents.* Retrieved from http://ibo.nyc.ny.us/cgi-park2/?cat=15.

Independent Budget Office (IBO). (2013). *With the rise in the city's homeless shelter population, how much has shelter spending increased?* Retrieved from http://ibo.nyc.ny.us/cgi-park2/?cat=15.

Jennings, E. (1975). Wildcat! The wartime strike wave in auto. *Libcom.org*. Retrieved from https://libcom.org/history/wildcat-wartime-strike-wave-auto-industry.

Jessop, B. (2013). *The entrepreneurial city: Re-imaging localities, re-designing economic governance, or re-structural capital?* Retrieved from http://bobjessop. org/2013/12/02/the-entrepreneurial-city-re-imaging-localities-re-designing-economic-governance-or-re-structuring-capital/.

Johnson, J. (2015). Flint water crisis doesn't change KWA pipeline plan to finish in June or July. *MLive.com*. Retrieved from http://www.mlive.com/news/flint/index.ssf/2015/10/kwa_crews_still_working_tpo_bri.html.

Johnson, S. P. (2010). *The city's credit ratings and the rating agencies ratings recalibration process*. San Jose, CA: City of San Jose.

Jonas, A. E. G., & Wilson, D. (Eds.). (1997). *The urban growth machine*. Albany, NY: State University of New York Press.

Kansas City Star. (2016). Kansas shrivels under more budget cuts, proposed efficiency measures. *Kansas City Star*. Retrieved from http://www.kansascity. com/opinion/editorials/article54555120.html.

Karmasek, J. M. (2012). Calif. court to cut staff, close courtrooms in wake of budget crisis. *Legal Newsline Legal Journal*. Retrieved from http://legalnewsline.com/stories/510526947-calif-court-to-cut-staff-close-court-rooms-in-0wake-of-budget-crisis.

Katz, B. (2016, December 15). Believe it or not, age of Trump is an opportunity for cities like Chicago. *Crain's Chicago Business*. Retrieved from http://www.chicagobusiness.com/article/20161215/OPINION/161219951/chicago-and-cities-in-the-age-of-trump-bruce-katz.

KBRA. (2011). *An analysis of historical municipal bond defaults*. New York, NY: KBRA.

Kear, M. (2012). Governing Homo Subprimicus: Beyond financial citizenship, exclusion, and rights. *Antipode, 45*(4), 926–946.

Kear, M. (2014). The scale effects of financialization: The Fair Credit Reporting Act and the production of financial space and subjects. *Geoforum, 57*(1), 100–109.

Kellogg, C. (2012). Louisiana state library funding has been eliminated. *Los Angeles Times*. Retrieved from http://latimesblogs.latimes.com/jacketcopy/2012/06/louisiana-eliminates-state-funding-for-libraries.html.

Kelman, S., Clavel, P., Forrester, J., & Goldsmith, W. W. (1980). New opportunities for planners. In P. Clavel, J. Forrester, & W. W. Goldsmith (Eds.), *Urban and regional planning in an age of austerity* (1–22). New York, NY: Pergamon Press.

Kinsella, S. (2012). Is Ireland really the role model for austerity? *Cambridge Journal of Economics, 36*(1), 223–235.

Kirkpatrick, L. O., & Smith, M. (2011). The infrastructural limits to growth: Rethinking the urban growth machine in times of fiscal crisis. *International Journal of Urban and Regional Research, 35*(3), 477–503.

Kirkpatrick, L. O. (2015). Urban triage, city systems, and the remnants of community: Some "sticky" complications in the greening of Detroit. *Journal of Urban History, 41*(2), 261–278.

Kirkpatrick, L. O., & Smith, M. P. (2011). The infrastructural limits to growth: rethinking the urban growth machine in times of fiscal crisis. *International Journal of Urban and Regional Research, 35*(3), 477–503.

Kitson, M., Martin, R., & and Tyler, P. (2011). The geographies of austerity. *Cambridge Journal of Regions, Economy and Society, 4*(3), 289–302.

Kleniewski, N. (1986). Triage and urban planning: A case study of Philadelphia. *International Journal of Urban and Regional Research, 10*(4), 563–579.

Knox, J., & Levinson, M. (2009). *Municipal bankruptcy.* San Francisco and Sacramento, CA: Orrick.

Koehn, J. (2012). Fiscal emergency report cost $222K. *San Jose Inside.* Retrieved from http://www.sanjoseinside.com/news/entries/3_16_12_fiscal_emergency_pension_reform_mayor_chuck_reed_don_rocha/.

Kohn, M. (2008). Homo spectator: Public space in the age of the spectacle. *Philosophy and Social Criticism, 34*(5), 467–486.

Krippner, G. (2005). The financialization of the American economy. *Socio-Economic Review, 3*(2), 173–208.

Krippner, G. (2011). *Capitalizing on crisis: The political origins of the rise of finance.* London: Harvard University Press.

Krugman, P. (2012a, 27 April). Death of a fairy tale. *The New York Times,* p. A27.

Krugman, P. (2012b, June 1). The austerity agenda. *The New York Times.* Retrieved from http://www.nytimes.com/2012/06/01/opinion/krugman-the-austerity-agenda.html?_r=0.

Krugman, P. (2012c, January 30). The austerity debacle. *The New York Times.* Retrieved from http://www.nytimes.com/2012/01/30/opinion/krugman-the-austerity-debacle.html?_r=0.

Krugman, P. (2013). How the case for austerity has crumbled. *The New York Review of Books.* Retrieved from http://www.nybooks.com/articles/2013/06/06/how-case-austerity-has-crumbled/.

Krugman, P. (2014). The stimulus tragedy. *The New York Times.* Retrieved from http://www.nytimes.com/2014/02/21/opinion/krugman-the-stimulus-tragedy.html?_r=0.

Lacapra, V. (2014a). Confused about the Bridgeton and West Lake landfills? Here's what you should know. *St. Louis Public Radio.* Retrieved from http://news.stlpublicradio.org/post/confused-about-bridgeton-west-lake-landfills-heres-what-you-should-know#stream/0.

Lacapra, V. (2014b, March 31). EPA analysis: Neighbors could be at risk if landfill fire reaches radioactive waste in Bridgeton. *St. Louis Public Radio.*

Lacapra, V., & Skiöld-Hanlin, S. (2013, November 21). Nuclear analyst: Radioactive waste at West Lake landfill must go. *St. Louis Public Radio.*

Landale, N., & Guest, A. M. (1985). Constraints, satisfaction, and residential mobility: Speare's model reconsidered. *Demography, 22*(2), 199–222.

Langley, P. (2006). Securitising suburbia: The transformation of Anglo-American mortgage finance. *Competition and Change, 10*(3), 283–299.

Larson, A. (2012). Cities in the red: Austerity hits America. *Dissent.* Retrieved from https://www.dissentmagazine.org/online_articles/cities-in-the-red-austerity-hits-america.

Lax, H., Manti, M., Raca, P., & Zorn, P. (2004). Subprime lending: An investigation of economic efficiency. *Housing Policy Debate, 15*(3), 533–571.

Leitner, H. (1990). Cities in the pursuit of economic growth: The local state as entrepreneur. *Political Geography Quarterly, 9*(2), 146–170.

Leitner, H., Sheppard, E., Sziarto, K., & Maringanti, A. (2007). Contesting urban futures: Decentering neoliberalism. In Leitner, H., Peck, J., & Sheppard, E. (Eds.), *Contesting neoliberalism: Urban frontiers* (1–25). New York, NY: Guilford Press.

Leventhal, T., Anderson, S., Dupere, V., & Newman, S. (2014). Residential mobility among children: A framework for child and family policy. *Cityscape: A Journal of Policy Development and Research, 16*(1), 5–36.

Levine, C. H., Rubin, I. S., & Wolohojian, G. G. (1981). *The politics of retrenchment: How local governments manage fiscal stress.* Beverly Hills, CA: Sage.

Levitas, R. (2012). The just's umbrella: Austerity and the bog society in coalition policy and beyond. *Critical Social Policy, 32*(3), 320–342.

Lichten, E. (1986). *Class, power, and austerity: The New York City fiscal crisis.* South Hadley, MA: Praeger.

Liner, B. E. (Ed.). (1989). *A decade of devolution: Perspectives on state-local relations.* Washington, DC: Urban Institute Press.

Lipietz, A. (1987). *Mirages and miracles.* London: Verso.

Lipman, P. (2011). *The new political economy of urban education: Neoliberalism, race, and the right to the city.* London: Routledge.

Liptak, A. (2013). Supreme Court invalidates key part of Voting Rights Act. *The New York Times.* Retrieved from http://www.nytimes.com/2013/06/26/us/supreme-court-ruling.html.

Listokin, D., & Casey, S. (1980). *Mortgage lending and race.* New Brunswick, NJ: Center for Urban Policy Research.

Listokin, D., & Wyly, E. K. (2000). *Making new mortgage markets.* Washington, DC: Fannie Mae Foundation.

Liu, G. (2012). Municipal bond insurance premium, credit rating, and underlying credit risk. *Public Budgeting and Finance, 32*(1), 128–156.

Livengood, C. (2014, December 10). Community benefit pacts take hit—House panel bans requiring developers to provide benefits. *The Detroit News.*

Lobao, L. (2016). The rising importance of local government in the United States: Recent research and challenges for sociology. *Sociology Compass, 10,* 893–905.

Lobao, L. M., & Adua, L. (2011). State rescaling and local governments' austerity policies across USA, 2001–2008. *Cambridge Journal of Regions, Economy and Society, 4*(3), 419–435.

Lomax, J. (2015). No, Sharpstown, Texas, did not fire its police force and bring about a huge drop in crime. *Texas Monthly.* Retrieved from http://www.texasmonthly.com/the-daily-post/no-sharpstown-texas-did-not-fire-its-police-force-and-bring-about-a-huge-drop-in-crime/.

Long, J. G. (2005). Full count: The real cost of public funding for major league sports facilities. *Journal of Sports Economics, 6*(2), 119–143.

Long, J. G. (2013). *Public/private partnerships for major league sports facilities.* New York, NY: Routledge.

Lowenstein, R. (2011). Broke town, U.S.A. *The New York Times.* Retrieved from http://www.nytimes.com/2011/03/06/magazine/06Muni-t.html.

Lowndes, V., & Pratchett, L. (2012). Local governance under the coalition government: Austerity, localism, and the "Big Society." *Local Government Studies, 38*(1), 21–40.

Lucas County Foreclosure Magistrate (LCFM). (2009, February 5). Interview with staff of the Lucas County Foreclosure Magistrate's Office. Toledo, OH.

Lyman, R., & Walsh, M. W. (2013). Struggling, San Jose tests a way to cut benefits. *The New York Times.* Retrieved from http://www.nytimes.com/2013/09/24/us/struggling-san-jose-tests-a-way-to-cut-benefits.html.

MacLeod, G. (2011). Urban politics reconsidered: Growth machine to post-democratic city? *Urban Studies, 48*(12), 2629–2660.

Madar, J. (2015). *Inclusionary housing policy in New York City: Assessing new opportunities, constraints, and trade-offs.* NYU Furman Center whitepaper. Retrieved from http://furmancenter.org/files/NYUFurmanCenter_InclusionaryZoningNYC_March2015.pdf.

Magnet, M. (1993). *The dream and the nightmare*. San Francisco, CA: Encounter Books.

Malkin, M. (2008). The subprime whiners: Ignoring reality. *New York Post*. Retrieved from http://www.nytimes.com/2015/04/05/realestate/revisiting-subprime.html.

Mallach, A. (2016, November 28). Malign neglect? Urban policy in the Trump era. *Rooflines*. Retrieved from http://www.rooflines.org/4691/malign_neglect_urban_policy_in_the_trump_era/.

Management Partners Incorporated. (2008). *City of San Jose—Development of strategies to address the city's general fund structural budget deficit*. San Jose, CA: Office of the City Manager.

Marcuse, P., Medoff, P., & Pereira, A. (1982). Triage as urban policy. *Social Policy, 12*(3), 33–37.

Marshall, L. (2009). Greed caused the subprime mortgage crisis, not ACORN. *U.S. News and World Report*. Retrieved from http://www.usnews.com/opinion/articles/2009/10/16/greed-caused-the-subprime-mortgage-crisis-not-acorn.

Massey, D., & Rugh, J. (2010). Racial segregation and the foreclosure crisis. *American Sociological Review, 75*(5), 629–651.

Massey, D., & Denton, N. (1987). Trends in the residential segregation of blacks, Hispanics, and Asians. *American Sociological Review, 52*(6), 802–825.

Massie, V. (2016). Donald Trump's "inner city" has nothing to do with where black people live. *Vox*. Retrieved from http://www.vox.com/identities/2016/9/28/13074046/trump-presidential-debate-inner-city.

Mathewson, J. (2016). Bankruptcy is the only way out. *Chicago Sun Times*. Retrieved from http://chicago.suntimes.com/opinion/7/71/887897/opinion-bankruptcy-way.

Mayer, M. (2013). First world urban activism: Beyond austerity urbanism and creative city politics. *City, 17*(1), 5–19.

McCann, E., & Ward, K. (Eds.). (2011). *Mobile urbanism: Cities and policymaking in the global age*. Minneapolis, MN: University of Minnesota Press.

McCoy, K. (2012). USA Today analysis: Nation's water costs rushing higher. *USA Today*. Retrieved from http://usatoday30.usatoday.com/money/economy/story/2012-09-27/water-rates-rising/57849626/1.

McGeehan, P. (2016, February 16). "A crisis every day" for the mayor trying to rescue Atlantic City. *The New York Times*.

McLanahan, S. (1983). Family structure and stress: A longitudinal analysis of male and female headed households. *Journal of Marriage and Family, 45*(2), 34–57.

McNichol, D. (2006). *The roads that built America: The incredible story of the U.S. Interstate system.* New York, NY: Sterling.

Merriam-Webster. (2010). *2010 word of the year.* Merriam-Webster press release. Retrieved from https://www.merriam-webster.com/press-release/2010-word-of-the-year.

Merrifield, A. (2013). *Metromarxism: A Marxist tale of the city.* New York, NY: Routledge.

Merrifield, A. (2014). Against accountancy governance: Notes towards a new urban collective consumption. *City, 18*(4–5), 416–426.

Miller, D. B., & Hokenstad, T. (2014). Rolling downhill: Effects of austerity on local government social services in the United States. *Journal of Sociology and Social Welfare, 16*(2), 93–108.

Minka, A. (2014). Mayor: Answer questions about tax law change, *Jackson Free Press.* Retrieved from http://www.jacksonfreepress.com/news/2014/nov/05/mayor-answer-questions-about-tax-law-change/.

Mirowski, P., & Plehwe, D. (Eds.). (2009). *The road from Mont Perelin: The making of the neoliberal thought collective.* Cambridge, MA: Harvard University Press.

Mollenkopf, J, (1977). The crisis of the public sector in America's cities. In R. Alcaly (Ed.), *The fiscal crisis of American cities.* New York, NY: Vintage Books.

Monbiot, G. (2016). Neoliberalism: The deep story that runs beneath Donald Trump's victory. *The Guardian* (on-line). Retrieved from https://www.theguardian.com/commentisfree/2016/nov/14/neoliberalism-donald-trump-george-monbiot.

Monkkonen, E. H. (1987). The sense of crisis: A historian's point of view. In M. Gottdiener (Ed.), *Cities in stress. Urban Affairs Annual Reviews, Volume 30* (20–38). Beverly Hills, CA: Sage.

Moody's Investors Service. (2010). *Governmental pension contributions may increase due to new guidance (special comment).* Retrieved from http://www.ct.gov/opm/lib/opm/secretary/opeb/gasbpensionchangesmoodys7-6-10.pdf.

Moody's Investors Service. (2012). *Moody's downgrades San Jose g.o. and lease revenue bonds to Aa1 and Aa3 respectively; Outlook remains stable (rating action).* Retrieved from https://www.moodys.com/research/MOODYS-DOWNGRADES-SAN-JOSE-GO-AND-LEASE-REVENUE-BONDS-TO—PR_241695.

Moody's Investors Service. (2009). *Employee pension-costs pressure state and local governments.* New York, NY: Moody's Investors Service.

Moody's Investors Service. (2013). *Adjustments to U.S. state and local government reported pension data (cross sector rating methodology)*. Retrieved from https://assets.documentcloud.org/documents/686623/moodys-pensions-final-adjustments-sc.pdf.

Morrison, T. (2005). *Beloved*. London: Vintage.

Munnell, A. H., Aubry, J. P., Hurwitz, J., & Cafarelli, M. (2013). Are city fiscal woes widespread? Are pensions the cause? *Center for Retirement Research at Boston College*. Retrieved from http://crr.bc.edu/briefs/are-city-fiscal-woes-widespread-are-pensions-the-cause/.

National Association of State Budget Officers. (2014). *State expenditure report: Examining fiscal 2012–2014 state spending*. Washington, DC: The National Association of State Budget Officers.

National League of Cities. (2010). *National League of Cities city fiscal conditions*. Retrieved from http://www.nlc.org/Documents/Find%20City%20Solutions/Research%20Innovation/Finance/city-fiscal-conditions-research-brief-rpt-oct10.pdf.

National League of Cities. (2014). *National League of Cities fiscal conditions*. Retrieved from http://www.nlc.org/find-city-solutions/city-solutions-and-applied-research/finance/city-fiscal-conditions-report-2014.

National League of Cities. (2015). *City fiscal conditions 2015*. Retrieved from http://www.nlc.org/Documents/Find%20City%20Solutions/Research%20Innovation/Finance/CSAR%20City%20Fiscal%20Conditions%202015%20FINAL.pdf.

Navarro, M. (2013). Report finds a city incentive is not producing enough affordable housing. *The New York Times*. Retrieved from http://www.nytimes.com/2013/08/16/nyregion/report-finds-a-city-incentive-is-not-producing-enough-affordable-housing.html.

Navarro, M., & Grynbaum, M. (2014). De Blasio sets a 10-year plan for housing, putting the focus on sffordability. *The New York Times*. Retrieved from http://www.nytimes.com/2014/05/06/nyregion/de-blasio-affordable-housing-plan.html?_r=0.

Neidermeyer, A. B., Boyd, N. E., & Neidermeyer, P. (2014). PMI: Mortgage backstop from the Alger Report to Dodd-Frank. *Journal of Financial Regulation and Compliance, 22*(1), 43–48.

Nelson, K. L. (2012). Municipal choices during a recession bounded rationality and innovation. *State and Local Government Review, 44*(1), 44–63.

New York City Department of Homeless Services. (2015). *Daily Shelter Report*. Retrieved from http://www.nyc.gov/html/dhs/downloads/pdf/dailyreport.pdf.

New York City Planning. (n.d.). *Inclusionary housing.* Retrieved from http://www.nyc.gov/html/dcp/html/inclusionary_housing/index.shtml.

New York City Planning. (n.d). *DCP history project. Rezonings 2002–2013.* Retrieved from http://www.nyc.gov/html/dcp/html/rezonings/rezonings.shtml.

New York City Rent Guidelines Board. (2015). *New York City RGB.* Retrieved from http://www.nycrgb.org/.

New York City Rent Guidelines Board. (2015). *421a and J-51 housing FAQ.* Retrieved from http://www.nycrgb.org/html/resources/faq/421a-J51.html#my.

New York State Homes and Community Renewal. (2015). *80/20 housing program.* Retrieved from http://www.nyshcr.org/Topics/Developers/MultifamilyDevelopment/8020HousingProgram.htm.

The New York Times. (2014, February 23). What the stimulus accomplished, p. SR10.

The New York Times. (2015). A summary: The hidden money buying condos at the Time Warner Center. *The New York Times.* Retrieved from http://www.nytimes.com/2015/02/08/nyregion/the-hidden-money-buying-up-new-york-real-estate.html.

The New York Times. (2016, November 14). Atlantic City, symbol of big bets gone bad, p. A24.

Newman, A. (2012, May 1). Austerity and the end of the European model. *Foreign Affairs.* Retrieved from http://users.dickinson.edu/~mitchelk/readings/newman%20-%20Austerity%20and%20the%20End%20of%20the%20European%20Model.pdf.

Newman, S., & Duncan, G. J. (1979). Residential problems, dissatisfaction, and mobility. *Journal of the American Planning Association, 45*(2), 154–166.

Nichols, D. A. (2014, April 1). Council narrowly approves deal for Wings' lease—Move starts clock for Joe Louis Arena's eventual demolition. *The Detroit News.*

O'Conner, A. (1999). Swimming against the tide: A brief history of federal policy in poor communities. In R. Ferguson and W. T. Dickens (Eds.), *Urban problems and community development* (77–137). New York, NY: Routledge.

O'Connor, A. (2008). The privatized city: The Manhattan Institute, the urban crisis, and the conservative counterrevolution in New York. *Journal of Urban History, 34*(2), 333–353.

O'Connor, B. J. (2012, December 6). Public funds key to Ilitch's plan for $650M arena. *The Detroit News.*

Oates, W. E. (1999). An essay on fiscal federalism. *Journal of Economic Literature, 37*(3), 1120–1149.

Office of Mayor Chuck Reed. (2014). *San Jose general fund deficits (October)*. San Jose, CA: City of San Jose.

Office of the City Manager. (2008). *General fund structural deficit elimination plan*. San Jose, CA: City of San Jose.

Oishi, S., & Schimmack, U. (2010). Residential mobility, wellbeing, and mortality. *Journal of Personality and Social Psychology, 98*(6), 980–994.

Oliff, P., Mai, C., & Palacios, V. (2012). *States continue to feel recession's impact*. Washington, DC: Center on Budget and Policy Priorities.

O'Neill, P. (2013). The financialisation of infrastructure: The role of categorisation and property relations. *Cambridge Journal of Regions, Economy and Society, 6*(3), 441–454.

Ong, A. (2006). *Neoliberalism as exception. Mutations in citizenship and sovereignty*. Durham, NC: Duke University Press.

Oosterlynck, S., & Gonzalez, S. (2013). Don't waste a crisis: Opening up the city yet again for neoliberal experimentation. *International Journal of Urban and Regional Research, 37*(3), 1075–1082.

Oser, A. S. (1987). Perspectives: Low-income housing; the "inclusionary-zoning" experiment. *The New York Times*. Retrieved from http://www.nytimes.com/1987/03/15/realestate/perspectives-low-income-housing-the-inclusionary-zoning-experiment.html.

Ostry. J. D., Loungani, P., & Furceri, D. (2016). Neoliberalism: oversold? *Finance and Development, 53*(2), 38–41.

Pacewicz, J. (2013) Tax increment financing, economic development professionals and the financialization of urban politics. *Socio-Economic Review, 11*(3), 413–440.

Pagano, M. A., Hoene, C. W., & McFarland, C. (2012). *City fiscal conditions 2012. National League of Cities*. Retrieved from http://www.nlc.org/find-city-solutions/city-solutions-and-applied-research/finance/city-fiscal-conditions-in-2012.

Pallagast, K. (2010). The planning research agenda: shrinking cities—a challenge for planning cultures. *Town Planning Review, 81*(5), i–vi.

Parker, A., & Blake, E. (2008). Debt collector drowns Lucas County court with tax-lien foreclosures. *Toledo Blade*. Retrieved from http://www.toledoblade.com/local/2008/12/25/Debt-collector-drowns-Lucas-County-court-with-tax-lien-foreclosures.html.

Partridge, M. D., & Weinstein, A. L. (2013). Rising inequality in an era of austerity: The case of the U.S. *European Planning Studies, 21*(3), 388–410.

Passantino, G., & Summers, A. B. (2005). *The gathering pension storm: How government pension plans are breaking the bank and strategies for reform.* Los Angeles, CA: Reason Foundation.

Pauldemarco.org. (n.d.). Paul DeMarco, About. *Pauldemarco.* Retrieved from Pauldemarco.org.

Peck, J. (2001). Neoliberalizing states: Thin policies/hard outcomes. *Progress in Human Geography, 25*(3), 445–455.

Peck, J. (2010). Zombie neoliberalism and the ambidextrious state. *Theoretical Criminology, 14*(1), 104–110.

Peck, J. (2011). Neoliberal suburbanism: Frontier space. *Urban Geography, 32*(6), 884–919.

Peck, J. (2012). Austerity urbanism: American cities under extreme economy. *City, 15*(6), 626–655.

Peck, J. (2013). For Polanyian economic geographies. *Environment and Planning A, 45*(7), 1545–1568.

Peck, J. (2014). Pushing austerity: State failure, municipal bankruptcy, and the crises of fiscal federalism in the USA. *Cambridge Journal of Regions, Economy and Society, 7*(1), 17–44.

Peck, J. (2015). *Austerity urbanism: The neoliberal crisis of American cities.* New York, NY: Rosa Luxemburg Stiftung.

Peck, J. (2015). Framing Detroit. In M. P. Smith & L. O. Kirkpatrick (Eds.), *Reinventing Detroit: The politics of possibility.* New York, NY: Transaction Publishers.

Peck, J. (2016). Economic rationality meets celebrity urbanology: Exploring Edward Glaeser's city. *International Journal of Urban and Regional Research, 40*(1), 1–30.

Peck, J. (2017a). Transatlantic city, part 1: Conjunctural urbanism. Urban Studies 54(1), online early. Retrieved from http://journals.sagepub.com/doi/abs/10.1177/0042098016679355.

Peck, J. (2017b). Transatlantic city, part 2: Late entrepreneurialism. Urban Studies 54(2), online early. Retrieved from http://journals.sagepub.com/doi/abs/10.1177/0042098016679355.

Peck, J., Theodore, N., & Brenner, N. (2009). Neoliberal urbanism: Models, moments, mutations. *SAIS Review, 29*(1), 49–66.

Peck, J., Theodore, N., & Brenner, N. (2010). Postneoliberalism and its malcontents. *Antipode, 41*(S1), 94–116.

Peck, J., Theodore, N., & Brenner, N. (2013). Neoliberal urbanism redux? *International Journal of Urban and Regional Research, 37*(3), 1091–1099.

Peck, J., Theodore, N., & Brenner, N. (2017). Actually existing neoliberalism. In D. Cahill, M, Cooper, & M. Konings (Eds.), *The Sage handbook of neoliberalism*. London: Sage.

Peck, J., & Tickell, A. (2002). Neoliberalizing space. *Antipode, 34*(3), 380–404.

Peck, J., & Whiteside, H. (2016). Financializing Detroit. *Economic Geography, 92*(3), 235–268.

Pecorella, R. F. (1984). Coping with crises: The politics of urban retrenchment. *Polity, 17*(2), 298–316.

People's Initiative to Limit Property Taxation. (1978). Pub. L. No. Proposition 13.

Perlman, B. J., & Benton, E. (2014). Devolutionary realignment: Shedding services, ad hoc collaboration, and political reconfiguration. *State and Local Government Review, 46*(3), 205–210.

Perotti, R. (2012). The "austerity myth": Gain without pain? In A. Alesina and F. Giavazzi (Eds.), *Fiscal policy after the financial crisis* (307–354). Chicago, IL: University of Chicago Press.

Peters, M. (2015). *New York City Department of Investigation: Probe of Department of Homeless Services' shelters for families with children finds serious deficiencies*. NYC Department of Investigation. Retrieved from http://www.nyc.gov/html/doi/downloads/pdf/2015/mar15/pr08dhs_31215.pdf.

Pettit, B., & McLanahan, S. (2003). Residential mobility and children's social capital: Evidence from an experiment. *Social Science Quarterly, 84*(3), 632–649.

Pew Charitable Trusts. (2012). *The local squeeze*. Washington, DC: Pew Charitable Trusts.

Phillips-Fein, K. (2013). The legacy of the 1970s fiscal crisis. *The Nation.* Retrieved from http://www.thenation.com/article/173873/legacy-1970s-fiscal-crisis?page=0,1.

Pickoff-White, L. (2014). San Jose City Council rejects sales tax measures, *KQED News Fix.* Retrieved from http://ww2.kqed.org/news/2014/08/05/san-jose-measures-november-ballot/.

Pike, A., & Pollard, J. (2010). Economic geographies of financialization. *Economic Geography, 86*(1), 29–51.

Plant, R. (2012). *The neo-liberal State*. Oxford: Oxford University Press.

Pribesh, S., & Downey, D. (1999). Why are residential and school moves associated with poor school performance? *Demography, 36*(4), 521–534.

Polak, B., & Schott, P.K. (2012, June 11). America's hidden austerity program. *New York Times.* Retrieved from http://economix.blogs.nytimes.com/2012/06/11/americas-hidden-austerity-program/?_r=0.

Pollin, R., & Thompson, J. (2011). State and municipal alternatives to austerity. *New Labor Forum, 20,* 22–30.

Purcell, M. (2012). Insistent democracy: Neoliberal governance and popular movements in Seattle. In M. P. Smith & M. McQuarrie (Eds.), *Remaking urban citizenship.* London: Transaction Publishers.

Raphael, R. (2012). U.S. state interventions on local governments vary widely. *Fitch Wire.* Retrieved from http://www.fitchratings.com/web/en/dynamic/articles/U.S.-State-Interventions-on-Local-Governments-Vary-Widely.jsp.

Raudenbush, S., Sampson, R. J., & Earls, F. (1997). Neighborhoods and violent crime: A multilevel study of collective efficacy. *Science, 277*(5328), 918–924.

RealtyTrac. (2014). *1.4 million U.S. properties with foreclosure filings in 2013, down 26% to lowest annual total since 2007.* Retrieved from http://www.realtytrac.com/content/news-and-opinion/2013-year-end-us-foreclosure-report-7963.

Reed, M. C. (2007). *2007 State of the City address.* Retrieved from http://www.sanjoseca.gov/ArchiveCenter/ViewFile/Item/452.

Reed, M. C. (2008). *March budget message for Fiscal Year 2008–2009.* San Jose, CA: City Council.

Reed, M. C. (2010). *June budget message for Fiscal Year 2010–11.* San Jose, CA: City Council.

Reed, M. C. (2012a). *March budget message for Fiscal Year 2012–13.* San Jose, CA: City Council.

Reed, M. C. (2012b). *Mayor Chuck Reed's 2012 State of the City address February.* San Jose, CA: City Council.

Reese, L. A., Sands, G., & Skidmore, M. (2014). Memo from Motown: is austerity here to stay? *Cambridge Journal of Regions, Economy & Society, 7*(1), 99–118.

Reid, C. (2013). *Debunking the CRA myth—again.* Chapel Hill, NC: UNC Center for Community Capital. Retrieved from http://ccc.unc.edu/contentitems/debunking-the-cra-myth-again/.

Reinhart, C. M., & Rogoff, K. S. (2010). Growth in a time of debt. *American Economic Review, 100*(2), 573–578.

Reschovsky, A. (2016, July 28). Convention cities highlight economic challenges the next president will face. *Next City.* Retrieved from https://nextcity.org/daily/entry/convention-cities-philadelphia-cleveland-economic-challenges.

Rivas, R. (2014). Mothers outraged at EPA's response on West Lake Landfill. *The St. Louis American.* Retrieved from http://www.stlamerican.com/news/local_news/article_fede1aa8-71ad-11e4-b287-0be5be584fff.html.

Rodney, A. U. (1936). The tax lien investor's relation to the collection of delinquent taxes. *Law and Contemporary Problems, 3*(1), 429–435.

Rojas, R. (2016, May 28). Christie signs a financial rescue plan, and an ultimatum, for Atlantic City. *New York Times*, p. A18.

Rolnik, R. (2013). Late neoliberalism: The financialization of homeownership and housing rights. *International Journal of Urban and Regional Research*, *37*(3), 1058–1066.

Rudd, K. (2009, February). The global financial crisis. *The Monthly*, 20–29.

Sampson, R., & Sharkey, P. (2008). Neighborhood selection and the social reproduction of concentrated racial inequality. *Demography*, *45*(1), 1–29.

Sbragia, A. M. (1996). *Debt wish*. Pittsburgh, PA: Pittsburgh University Press.

Schacter, J. (2001). *Geographic mobility: Population characteristic*. Washington, DC: United States Census Bureau.

Schafran, A. (2013). Origins of an urban crisis: The restructuring of the San Francisco Bay area and the geography of foreclosure. *International Journal of Urban and Regional Research*, *37*(2), 663–688.

Schönig, B., & Schipper, S. (Eds.). (2016). *Urban austerity: Impacts of the global financial crisis on cities in Europe*. Berlin: Theater de Zeit.

Schuessler, R. (2015). St. Louis landfill fire could reach radioactive waste in months. *AlJazeera America*. Retrieved from http://america.aljazeera.com/articles/2015/9/18/missouri-st-louis-landfill-fire-could-reach-radioactive-waste-in-months.html.

Schwartz, A. (2014). *Housing policy in the United States*. New York, NY: Routledge.

Scorsone, E. A. (2013). *Depopulating cities and chronic fiscal stress: The Detroit story*. PhD Thesis. Michigan State University.

Scorsone, E. A. (2014). *Municipal fiscal emergency laws: Background and guide to state-based approaches*, Working Paper 14-21, Mercatus Center, George Mason University. Washington, DC: George Mason University.

Securities Industry & Financial Markets Association. (2015). *U.S. bond market issuance and outstanding*. Retrieved from http://www.sifma.org/uploadedFiles/Research/Statistics/StatisticsFiles/CM-US-Bond-Market-SIFMA.xls?n=49566.

Segall, E. (2012). San Jose begins preliminary steps to hike business taxes. *Silicon Valley / San Jose Business Journal*. Retrieved from http://www.bizjournals.com/sanjose/print-edition/2012/01/27/san-jose-to-hike-business-taxes.html.

Shea, B. (2013b, July 22). Bankruptcy filing should not affect arena district, M1 Rail projects. *Crain's Detroit Business*.

Shea, B. (2013d, December 9). Council puts check on arena financing, wants details first. *Crain's Detroit Business*.

Shea, B. (2014, September 22). On cost, financing of Wings arena: Here are answers. *Crain's Detroit Business*.

Shea, B. (2014a, July 20). Detroit rink city: Ilitches' grand plan to supersize the entertainment district. *Crain's Detroit Business.*

Shefter, M. (1985). *Political crisis, fiscal crisis: The collapse and revival of New York City.* New York, NY: Basic Books.

Shields, Y. (2015). Detroit, a year out of bankruptcy, still faces long road back. *The Bond Buyer.* Retrieved from http://www.bondbuyer.com/news/regionalnews/detroit-a-year-out-of-bankruptcy-still-faces-long-road-back-1091868-1.html.

Silicon Valley Community Foundation. (2012). *The City of San Jose's budget crisis.*

Skocpol, T., & Williamson, W. (2012). *The Tea Party and the remaking of Republican conservatism.* Oxford: Oxford University Press.

Slavin, R. (2015). Defaults reached record in 2014. *The Bond Buyer.* Retrieved from http://www.bondbuyer.com/news/markets-buy-side/defaults-reached-record-in-2014-1069491-1.html.

Smith, G. (2015). Rise in overcrowded NYC apartments shows need for more housing, says Controller Scott Stringer. *New York Daily News.* Retrieved from: http://www.nydailynews.com/new-york/exclusive-surge-number-overcrowded-nyc-apartments-article-1.2385078.

Smith, J., & Douglas, J. (2014). *On democracy's doorstep: The inside story of how the Supreme Court brought "one person, one vote" to the United States.* New York, NY: Hill and Wang.

Smith, M. (2015). A water dilemma in Michigan: Cloudy or costly? *The New York Times.* Retrieved from http://www.nytimes.com/2015/03/25/us/a-water-dilemma-in-michigan-cheaper-or-clearer.html?_r=0.

Smith, N. (1996). *The new urban frontier: Gentrification and the revanchist city.* New York, NY: Routledge.

Smith, R. (2010). Southern discomfort: An examination of the financial crisis in Jefferson County, Alabama. *Houston Business and Tax Law Journal, 10*(3), 363–395.

Somers, M. R., & Block, F. (2005). From poverty to perversity: Ideas, markets, and institutions over 200 years of welfare debate. *American Sociological Review, 70*(2), 260–287.

Sorkin, M. (1992). *Variations on a theme park: The new American city and the end of public space.* London: Macmillan.

South, S. J., & Crowder, K. D. (1998). Leaving the 'hood: Residential mobility between black, white, and integrated neighborhoods. *American Sociological Review, 63*(1), 17–26.

Speare, A. (1974). Residential satisfaction as an intervening variable in residential mobility. *Demography, 11*(2), 173–188.

Speare, A., & Goldscheider, F. (1987). Effects of marital status change on residential mobility. *Journal of Marriage and Family, 49*(2), 455–464.

Speare, A., Goldstein, S., & Frey, W. H. (1975). *Residential mobility, migration, and metropolitan change.* Cambridge, MA: Ballinger Press.

Squires, G. D. (1992). *From redlining to reinvestment.* Philadelphia, PA: Temple University Press.

Squires, G. D. (2003). *Organizing access to capital.* Philadelphia, PA: Temple University Press.

Stegman, M. (1982). *The dynamics of rental housing in New York City.* New Brunswick, NJ: CUPR Press.

Sternlieb, G., & Hughes, J. W. (1981). New dimensions of the urban crisis. In R. W. Burchell & D. Listokin (Eds.), *Cities under stress: The fiscal crises of urban America* (51–75). Piscataway, NJ: Center for Urban Policy Research, Rutgers, the State University of New Jersey.

Stewart, N., & Yeejan, V. (2016). As Cuomo acts on homeless problem, New York City blames state cuts. *The New York Times.* Retrieved from http://www.nytimes.com/2016/01/13/nyregion/as-cuomo-acts-on-homelessness-problem-city-and-state-are-often-at-odds.html?_r=0.

Stiglitz, J. E. (2008, July 7). The end of neo-liberalism? *Project Syndicate Commentary.* Retrieved from https://www.project-syndicate.org/commentary/the-end-of-neo-liberalism.

Stoll, M. (2013). Residential mobility in the U.S. and the Great Recession: A shift to local moves. *US2010 Project.* Retrieved from http://www.russellsage.org/blog/great-recession-and-residential-mobility.

Stringer, S. (2014). *The growing gap: New York City's housing affordability change.* Office of the Comptroller, City of New York. Retrieved from http://comptroller.nyc.gov/wp-content/uploads/documents/Growing_Gap.pdf.

Strom, E., & Reader, S. (2013). Rethinking foreclosure dynamics in a Sunbelt City: What parcel-level mortgage data can teach us about subprime lending and foreclosures. *Housing Policy Debate, 23*(1), 59–79.

Stuckler, D., & Basu, S. (2013). *The body economic: Why austerity kills.* New York, NY: Basic Books.

Sugrue, T. (2016, December 6). Donald Trump says he wants to fix cities. Ben Carson will make them worse. *Washington Post.* Retrieved from https://www.washingtonpost.com/posteverything/wp/2016/12/06/donald-trump-says-he-wants-to-fix-cities-ben-carson-will-make-them-worse/?tid=pm_opinions_pop&utm_term=.6fdf53861322.

Swierenga, R. (1971). The odious tax title: A study in nineteenth century legal history. *American Journal of Legal History, 15*(2), 124–139.

Swyngedouw, E. (2009). The antinomies of the postpolitical city: In search of a democratic politics of environmental production. *International Journal of Urban and Regional Research, 33*(3), 601–620.

Tabb, W. (1982). *The long default: New York City and the urban fiscal crisis.* New York, NY: Monthly Review Press.

Tabb, W. K. (2014). The wider context of austerity urbanism. *City, 18*(2), 87–100.

Tabb, W.K. (2014). If Detroit is dead, some things need to be said at the funeral. *Journal of Urban Affairs, 37*(1), 1–12.

Timiraos, N., & Rubin, R. (2016, September 15). Donald Trump promises tax cuts, offset by robust growth. *Wall Street Journal.* Retrieved from http://www.wsj.com/articles/donald-trump-lays-out-more-details-of-economic-plans-1473955537.

Tomich, J. (2013a). EPA says West Lake radiation is "contained." *St. Louis Post-Dispatch.* Retrieved from http://www.stltoday.com/news/epa-says-west-lake-radiation-is-contained/article_536df835-7b9d-5c23-82f0-c1166a9a3488.html.

Tomich, J. (2013b). Angry residents tell EPA officials to remove West Lake nuclear waste. *St. Louis Post-Dispatch.* Retrieved from http://www.stltoday.com/news/local/angry-residents-tell-epa-officials-to-remove-west-lake-nuclear/article_48b128e2-18dd-547f-9fb9-a0d85b14e72e.html.

Tomlinson, M. (2015). A millennial paradise: How once-bankrupt Detroit is making a comeback. Elitedaily.com. Retrieved from http://elitedaily.com/users/mtomlinson/.

Tompor, S. (2015). Detroit retirees to see pension cuts starting Monday. *Detroit Free Press.* Retrieved from http://www.freep.com/story/money/personal-finance/susan-tompor/2015/02/27/detroit-orr-pension-checks-cuts/24144513/.

Tonkiss, F. (2013). Austerity urbanism and the makeshift city. *City, 17*(3), 312–324.

Tootell, G. (1995). *Discrimination, redlining, and private mortgage insurance.* Boston, MA: Federal Reserve Bank of Boston.

Trotter, R. (2011). *Running on empty: Municipal insolvency and rejection of collective bargaining agreements in Chapter 9 bankruptcy.* Retrieved from http://works.bepress.com/richard_trotter/1.

Trump, D. (2016a). In Charlotte, Trump proposes urban renewal agenda for America's inner cities. Trump-Pence campaign press release. Retrieved from https://www.donaldjtrump.com/press-releases/in-charlotte-trump-proposes-economic-renewal-for-americas-inner-cities1.

Trump, D. (2016b). Trump's New Deal for black America, With a plan for urban renewal. Retrieved from https://www.donaldjtrump.com/press-releases/donald-j.-trump-announces-a-plan-for-urban-renewal.

Ullman, S., Freedman-Schnapp, and Lander. (2013). *Inclusionary zoning in New York City: The performance of New York City's designated areas inclusionary housing program since its launch in 2005.* Office of Council Member Brad Lander. Retrieved from https://www.scribd.com/embeds/160544058/content?start_page=1&view_mode=book&access_key=key-2bgybm8sd271p68i13jw&show_recommendations=true.

United States Department of Justice. (2012, December 13). *U.S., Pennsylvania, and Scranton, Pa., sewer authority settle violations of sewage overflows.* Washington, DC: Office of Public Affairs.

United States Department of Labor. (2012). *The Latino labor force at a glance.* Retrieved from http://www.dol.gov/_sec/media/reports/HispanicLaborForce/HispanicLaborForce.pdf.

United States Environmental Protection Agency. (2011, August). *U.S. vs The Metropolitan St. Louis Sewer District—Consent decree—Clean Water Act.*

United States Environmental Protection Agency. (2012, November). Factsheet: Update on activities supporting the record of decision (ROD) amendment for the West Lake Landfill superfund site, Bridgeton, Missouri.

United States Environmental Protection Agency. (2014, 20 November). *West Lake update: EPA policy on temporary and permanent relocations at superfund sites.* EPA.

United States Environmental Protection Agency. (2014). *US EPA.* Retrieved from http://www3.epa.gov/.

United States Securities & Exchange Commission. (2014). Muni market then & now. Retrieved from https://www.sec.gov/spotlight/municipalsecurities.shtml.

Vakshin, A., & Nash, J. (2012, June 6). California pension victories could catch on nationwide. *Bloomberg News.*

Van Meek, S. (2012). Ilitch organization exploring development of new residential, retail office, and events center district in downtown Detroit. Olympia Development of Michigan. Retrieved from http://www.ilitchholdings.com/Portals/0/Olympia-Development-PR.pdf.

Varoufakis, Y. (2014). Being Greek and an economist while Greece is burning! An intimate account of a peculiar tragedy. *Journal of Modern Greek Studies, 32*(1), 1–23.

Wachter, S. (2015). Housing America: The unequal geography of risk and opportunity. *Housing Policy Debate, 25*(4), 813–816.

Wallison, P. (2015). *Hidden in plain sight: What really caused the world's worst financial crisis and why it could happen again.* New York, NY: Encounter Books.

Walliston, P. (2009). The true origins of this financial crisis: As opposed to a desperate liberal agenda. *The American Spectator.* Retrieved from http://spectator.org/articles/42211/true-origins-financial-crisis.

Walsh, M. W. (2011). Alabama governor fails to prevent county's record $4 billion bankruptcy filing, *The New York Times.* Retrieved from http://www.nytimes.com/2011/11/10/us/alabama-governor-fails-to-prevent-jefferson-countys-record-4-billion-bankruptcy-filing.html.

Walton, J. (1998). Urban conflict and social movements in poor countries: Theory and evidence of collective action. *International Journal of Urban and Regional Research, 22*(3), 460–481.

Wapshott, N. (2013). No, austerity did not work, *Reuters.* Retrieved from http://blogs.reuters.com/nicholas-wapshott/2013/11/07/no-austerity-did-not-work/.

Ward, K. (2006). "Policies in motion," urban management, and state restructuring: The trans-local expansion of business improvement districts. *International Journal of Urban and Regional Research, 30*(1), 54–75.

Warner, M., & Clifton, J. (2014). Marketisation, public services, and the city: The potential for Polanyian counter-movements. *Cambridge Journal of Regions, Economy, and Society, 7*(1), 45–61.

Waters, T., & Bach, V. (2013). *Good place to work, hard place to live.* New York: Community Service Society. Retrieved from http://b.3cdn.net/nycss/1c9817fd6343bf9c88_lkm6va7t8.pdf.

Weber, R. (2002). Extracting value from the city: Neoliberalism and urban redevelopment. *Antipode, 34*(3), 519–540.

Weber, R. (2010). Selling city futures: The financialization of urban redevelopment policy. *Economic Geography, 86*(3), 251–274.

While, A., Jonas, A. E. G., & Gibbs, D. (2004). The environment and the entrepreneurial city: Searching for the urban "sustainability fix" in Manchester and Leeds. *International Journal of Urban and Regional Research, 28*(3), 549–569.

Whitfield, D. (2013). *Unmasking austerity: Lessons for Australia.* Adelaide: University of Adelaide, Australian Workplace Innovation and Social Research Centre. Retrieved from https://www.adelaide.edu.au/wiser/docs/WISeR_unmasking-austerity.pdf.

Willett, M. (2014). New York hipsters are being encouraged to move to Detroit *Tech Insider.* Retrieved from http://www.techinsider.io/move-to-detroit-campaign-in-new-york-2015-4.

Williamson, V. (2013). *The Tea Party and the shift to "austerity by gridlock" in the United States.* Retrieved from http://scholar.harvard.edu/files/williamson/files/investment_or_austerity_in_the_united_states_williamson_apsa.pdf.

Wolff, R. (2013, 22 February). Taming capitalism run wild. Moyers & Company. Retrieved from http://billmoyers.com/episode/full-show-taming-capitalism-run-wild/.

Woolfolk, J. (2012a). Amid pension-cut fury, San Jose mayor sounds hopeful. *San Jose Mercury News.* Retrieved from http://www.mercurynews.com/ci_19933106.

Woolfolk, J. (2012b). San Jose Mayor Chuck Reed makes mark with pension reform. *San Jose Mercury News.* Retrieved from http://www.mercurynews.com/ci_20928833/san-jose-mayor-chuck-reed-makes-mark-pension.

Worth, O. (2013). *Resistance in the age of austerity: Nationalism, the failure of the Left, and the return of God.* London: Zed Books.

Wright, B. (2014, November 5). All Jefferson County residents can expect to pay more on their bills beginning this month, *Birmingham News.*

Wyly, E. K. (2009). *Good data, good deeds. Testimony prepared for Regulation C: The Home Mortgage Disclosure Act (HMDA) Public Hearing.* Retrieved from http://www.federalreserve.gov/communitydev/files/wyly.pdf.

Wyly, E. K., Atia, M., Foxcroft, H., Hammel, D. J., & Phillips-Watts, K. (2006). American home: Predatory mortgage capital and neighborhood spaces of race and class exploitation in the United States. *Geografiska Annaler, 88B*(1), 105–132.

Wyly, E. K., Atia, M., & Hammel, D. (2004). Has mortgage capital found an inner city spatial fix? *Housing Policy Debate, 15*(1), 623–685.

Wyly, E. K., & Hammel, D. (2004). Gentrification, segregation, and discrimination in the American urban system. *Environment and Planning A, 36*(1), 1215–1224.

Wyly, E. K., & Holloway, S. R. (2002). The disappearance of race in mortgage lending. *Economic Geography, 78*(2), 129–169.

Wyly, E. K., Moos, M., Hammel, D., & Kabahizi, E. (2009). Cartographies of race and class: mapping the class-monopoly rents of American subprime mortgage capital. *International Journal of Urban and Regional Research, 33*(2), 332–354.

Wyly, E. K. (2010). *Home Mortgage Disclosure Act public hearing, August 5, 2010.* Panel Two: Elvin Wyly. Retrieved from http://www.federalreserve.gov/communitydev/files/panel_two_wyly.pdf.

Wyly, E. K., & Hammel, D. (2000). Capital's metropolis: Chicago and the transformation of American housing policy. *Geografiska Annaler B, 82*(4), 181–206.

York, J. (2009). Vallejo closes another fire station. *Times Herald Online.* Retrieved from http://www.timesheraldonline.com/general-news/20090701/vallejo-closes-another-fire-station.

Yuan, B., Cordes, J., Brunori, D., & Bell, M. E. (2009). Tax and expenditure limitations and local public finances. In N. Y. Augustine, M. E. Bell, & D. Brunori (Eds.), *Erosion of the property tax base: Trends, causes, and consequences.* Cambridge, MA: Lincoln Institute of Land Policy.

Zukin, S. (1995). *The cultures of cities.* Oxford: Blackwell.

Contributors

Chalem Bolton is a PhD student in the sociology department at the University of Michigan. His research interests lie primarily in economic and political sociology, particularly on financial markets, taxation, and state formation. He has most recently examined investment and debt holdings of the City of Detroit over a period of several decades.

Xueying Chen is a PhD candidate at the Bloustein School of Planning and Public Policy at Rutgers University. She received her MA in geography from the University of Toledo. She has a particular interest in integrating Geographic Information Systems (GIS) technology with traditional urban and regional models. Her Master's work focused upon understanding the process and spatial patterns of home foreclosure in the Midwest. Her dissertation project concerns the economic effects of transport infrastructure investments, in particular those associated with agglomeration externalities.

Mark Davidson is an associate professor of geography at Clark University. He is an urban geographer whose research interests span gentrification, urban policy, society and community and metropolitan development, planning, and architecture. His current research is examining the impacts of municipal bankruptcies in the United States and includes an attempt to re-theorize critical urban theory. He has held fellowships at the Nelson A. Rockefeller Center for Public Policy and Social Science, Dartmouth College, and the Urban Research Centre, University of Western Sydney. He holds a BA (Hons) and PhD in geography from King's College London.

Dan Hammel is a professor of geography at the University of Toledo. His research has focused on the causes and consequences of gentrification in U.S. cities with an emphasis on the role of mortgage capital in the gentrification process.More recently, his focus has turned to the role of subprime lending in creating and maintaining America's racialized landscapes and on the relationship between mortgage foreclosures and mortgage lending.

Sara Hinkley is a lecturer in city and regional planning and the associate director of the Institute for Research on Labor and Employment at UC Berkeley. Her research focus includes public finance, urban politics, state fiscal policy, urban inequality, and public education. Her PhD examined the politics of recession, crisis, and austerity in four U.S. cities. Her professional background is in the politics of economic development in the U.S., low-wage labor organizing, and the restructuring of work.

L. Owen Kirkpatrick is an assistant professor of sociology at Southern Methodist University. His research has been published in *Politics & Society, International Journal of Urban and Regional Research*, and *Journal of Urban History*. His co-edited book *Reinventing Detroit: The Politics of Possibility* was published in 2015. He is currently working on a book manuscript entitled, *Sovereignty and the Fragmented City: The Many Citizenships of Detroit, Michigan*.

Kathe Newman is an associate professor in the urban planning and policy development program at the Edward J. Bloustein School of Planning and Public Policy and director of the Ralph W. Voorhees Center for Civic Engagement. Dr. Newman holds a PhD in political science from the Graduate School and University Center at the City University of New York. Her research explores urban change, what it is, why it happens, and what it means. Her research has explored gentrification, foreclosure, urban redevelopment, and community participation. Dr. Newman has published articles in *Urban Studies, International Journal of Urban and Regional Research, Urban Affairs Review, Shelterforce, Progress in Human Geography, Housing StudiesI GeoJournal, and Environment and Planning A*.

Aaron Niznik is a PhD candidate in sociology at Brown University and a graduate of the University of Wisconsin-Madison. His research is focused within community and urban sociology. Most recently, he completed a project on the effects of the Great Recession on family residential mobility in Providence, R.I. His current projects include a historical analysis of hurricane disasters and tourism in Rhode Island, and an ethnographic account of the quasi-public space of an urban shopping mall.

Jamie Peck is Canada Research Chair in Urban & Regional Political Economy and professor of geography at the University of British Columbia, Canada. His principal research interests are in urban restructuring, geographical political economy, labor studies, the politics of policy formation and mobility, and economic geography.

C. S. Ponder is a doctoral candidate with research interests in urban and economic geography. Her work focuses on those issues falling at the intersection of financialization, urban economic development, and social justice. She holds an MSc in economic history from Lund University, and her current research explores the political economy of U.S. urban water infrastructure under austerity.

Kevin Ward is professor of human geography, School of Education, Environment and Development and director of the Manchester Urban Institute (www.mui.manchester.ac.uk) at the University of Manchester, England. His research focuses on the geographies of urban policymaking, state reorganization, and the politics of urban and regional development. Author and editor of numerous books and journal articles, he is currently an editor of *Urban Geography*.

Index